Notes on Spiritual Discourses of Shrī Ātmānanda

Notes on Spiritual Discourses of Shrī Ātmānanda

TAKEN BY NITYA TṚIPTA

Volume 2 of 3

Notes 473 to 1121

NON-DUALITY PRESS
& STILLNESS SPEAKS

2nd edition published December 2009 by Non-Duality Press
& Stillness Speaks

Non-Duality Press | PO Box 2228 | Salisbury | SP2 2GZ
United Kingdom

www.non-dualitypress.com
www.stillnessspeaks.com

ISBN: 978-0-9563091-3-6

CONTENTS
(of all 3 volumes)

Notes on discourses

18th August 1952

473. WHY DID SHANKARA NOT EXPOUND ADVAITA IN THE DIRECT METHOD?

The shāstras, in the days of Shankara, had such a strong hold upon the people that no other method of approach, however direct, could attract or captivate their imagination. Therefore Shrī Shankara had, by force of circumstances, to adopt the laborious method of expounding the advaitic Truth through the shāstraic or traditional method.

But now, centuries after Shankara, people's blind faith in the shāstras has disappeared and they are obliged to rely upon their reason alone. The present conditions are best suited for the adoption of the direct perception method, and the best use is made of this opportunity here and now.

474. WHAT ARE THE PATHS TO REALIZATION?

According to the traditional method, they are mainly *bhakti*, *yōga* and *jnyāna*. Each of these paths, though dominated by one particular aspect and approach, happily has something of the other two also in it.

Take for example, the *rāja-yōga* path. Let us analyse its composition. Why does one take to this laborious practice? Evidently for the pleasure and powers one expects out of it. This desire for Happiness is the function of the heart, and is nothing but *bhakti* for your real nature of Happiness. The discriminative faculty and the reasoning aspect, much emphasized in the course of this path, is but the *jnyāna* aspect. And the active contemplation and other exercises form the preponderating *yōgic* element. Thus all the three paths have their proper place in rāja-yōga.

It is the same with the other two paths also. Therefore none of these paths is exclusive or watertight.

475. WHAT DOES 'FORMAL' (AUPACĀRIKA) MEAN?

Formal means not to be taken as literally correct. To be taken as a matter of concession only. Intended to serve a particular purpose alone, and that with the best of intentions.

For example, each path to the Truth is individually described as the most important in the particular shāstra which deals with it. This fallacy is perceived only when looked at from the phenomenal. But, on reaching the Ultimate, even the paths become illusions and the apparent fallacies also disappear.

19th August 1952

Every act, perception, thought, feeling, conduct etc. of yours proclaims to the world that you are the Reality itself.

476. HOW DO THE ACTIVITIES OF OUR ORGANS CONSTITUTE PŪJA TO THE REAL SELF?

Your organs in their functions seek Happiness alone. It has been clearly shown that your real nature is Happiness. So each organ is really seeking you.

How do its functions constitute a pūja? Each activity of the organs is independent in itself and different from every other activity. So also are the different actions in the pūja to the idol. But they derive their common relationship from the fact that they are all directed to the common goal, the idol.

Similarly, the activities of the organs are also all directed to you, the real Happiness; and thus their activities become pūja done to you.

After realizing the Truth, each sense organ appears to function, but really remains functionless. Thus each sense organ virtually becomes a jīvan-mukta.

477. A DISCIPLE ASKED: HOW TO ACQUIRE THE LOVE OF PADMAPĀDA FOR THE GURU?

Answer: 'By emptying your mind.'

Then how to empty the mind? Mind by itself does not want any thought. You can be said to have emptied the mind if you can so train your mind that only such thoughts as you require or permit come to you, or in other words when any thought or feeling comes to you only at your bidding. This can only be achieved by real *prēma* [love].

Reality alone has the right to come in unbidden; because that is the subject and the Reality. Thoughts and feelings sometimes come in unbidden, because you attribute reality to them. Know that they are unreal, and from that moment they will never be able to intrude upon you unbidden.

478. WHAT IS THE DIFFERENCE BETWEEN THE APPROACHES TO THE TRUTH, UPANIṢHADIC AND DIRECT?

All Upaniṣhadic methods try to eliminate you from the anātmā, and to establish you in the Ātmā.

But here, according to the direct method, you are shown that you can never get away either from your own shadow or from your reality. You are only asked to look deep into what you call anātmā, and see beyond the shadow of a doubt that it is nothing but Ātmā – the Reality.

479. CAN PHENOMENAL RELATIONSHIP BE AN OBSTACLE TO SPIRITUAL ENLIGHTENMENT?

Yes, sometimes. Shrī Shuka was the son of Shrī Veda-vyāsa, the Sage, and Shrī Janaka was the disciple of Shrī Vyāsa and a Sage himself. Shrī Shuka heard the whole Truth from Shrī Veda-vyāsa, but did not attain complete enlightenment. So Vyāsa one day sent Shuka to Shrī Janaka, the Sage king, for ultimate enlightenment, without disclosing the relationship between himself and Janaka. Shuka went to Janaka and after some trials and discussions attained ultimate enlightenment and satisfaction.

It was only then that he found that he had not yet known his father as he ought to have, because the phenomenal relationship of father and son prevented him from seeing Shrī Vyāsa as the Guru, the Absolute.

'The very same mistake is found repeated here, even now.'

480. An enlightening incident of the Gopīs at the bathing ghat, and its explanation

One day Shrī Shuka happened to pass by the ladies' bathing Ghat in the Yamuna (a tributary of the Ganges) where the Gopīs were bathing naked. The ladies saw Shrī Shuka, but ignored him completely – considering him only as a child – and continued to enjoy their bath. But another day, Shrī Veda-vyāsa himself happened to pass by the same way. Now, on seeing him even from a distance, the ladies rushed for their clothes and covered their bodies. How could this change in their conduct be explained?

Answer: The Absolute has two aspects – the dynamic and the static. All activities in life belong to the dynamic aspect, and all things passive belong to the static aspect. For example renunciation, relaxation etc. are passive.

Shrī Shuka was an embodiment of the static aspect of life, and there was nothing of life's activities visible in him. He was virtually dead to the world.

But Shrī Veda-vyāsa was a Sage who was the ultimate Reality itself, transcending both the static and the dynamic aspects. And in him, both these aspects were apparently alive.

The predominating aspects in the apparent life of these two great souls had their respective impact upon the ladies in the river, and at each different time they reacted accordingly. That is all.

481. How to produce the best results of action?

If you lose yourself in any action, that action will be most successful, in the sense that it produces the best results. How to attain this self-forgetfulness?

Direct the mind to its source, the Absolute, leaving a simple samskāra that certain actions are to be performed. When the actions are thus left to themselves with the sense organs, and the lower reason is not available to guide them, some principle from within – evidently the higher reason – automatically takes the full responsibility of guiding the actions.

Thus under the supreme guidance of the all knowing vidyā-vṛitti, the actions happen to be fulfilled to a wonderful degree of perfection.

But if ever the ego comes in, in any form anywhere in the course of the action, things go wrong lamentably.

The apparent life of every Sage, if closely observed, will provide numerous instances of the mysterious fulfilment of phenomenal activities in all perfection, without an effort on his own part and without his claiming the least credit for it.

20th August 1952

482. WHERE IS THE WORLD FROM THE STANDPOINT OF EXPERIENCE?

Experience alone is the proof of the existence of everything. Therefore, what is present in experience alone can be real.

Experience, which is apparently inside, has nothing in it but knowledge and Happiness. The world is nowhere in the experience and so the world is non-existent.

Therefore, the experience is neither *of* the world nor *as* the world, since the world is non-existent.

483. WHAT HAPPENS WHEN YOU SEE A THING?

When you say you see an object, you see only the dead part of the object. The Consciousness part, which alone is live, can never be seen.

If you say that the sense organ goes out of its centre to the object outside, in order to cognize it, the sense organ must necessarily get hurt if any injury occurs to the object, when the sense organ is contacting it. But it never happens. Therefore, seeing is all inside and it proves nothing outside.

484. SOME DEFINITIONS

Yōga-kṣhēma literally means the phenomenal as well as the spiritual needs of the individual.

Yōga (from another perspective) means directing your energies to acquire something which you are not already in possession of.

Kṣhēma means maintaining in the right manner that which you thus acquire.

Duty always depends upon your desires and upon what you want objectively. For example, a student and a teacher have different duties.

485. WHAT IS SVADHARMA AND WHY?

The life to which you have fitted yourself, by birth and inheritance, is the most natural and effortless one, so far as you are concerned. To continue in the same way of life, you require only a little extra energy. Therefore much energy is left to you which can be utilized for spiritual search, and you reach the goal sooner.

But if you change your own way of life, you will consume a lot of energy in establishing yourself in the new sphere, and your spiritual progress naturally suffers to that extent. Moreover, your activities in the phenomenal walk of life are of no avail in your spiritual progress, since the former is outward-going and the latter inward-going.

Therefore the Ācāryas of old have clearly warned you against any change of svadharma, since it entails a huge waste of precious energy and only increases the distance to your spiritual goal. Your station in life and way of life, whatever they be, are best suited for you to rise in life, worldly as well as spiritual.

Hence we see in vēdic lore occasional instances of great Sages continuing their svadharma even as butchers, priests etc. (e.g. Shrī Vyādha and Shrī Vasiṣhṭha).

21st August 1952

486. 'ONE IN THE ONE IS NOT ONE.' HOW?

The noumenon and the phenomenon, or the one and the many, are the two entities found in the apparent universe. The 'one' is not dependent upon the 'many', nor opposed to it. It is easy to prove that the one is in the many; but the many can never be in the one.

Therefore, if you succeed in taking anybody to the unique or the one, reaching there he finds that the oneness by itself does not exist there, but that it immediately becomes transformed into the Ultimate.

An individual who has reached the Ultimate no longer remains an individual.

487. WHAT IS ARUNDHATI-NYĀYA (POINTER)?

Arundhatī is a very dim and tiny star, not easily noticed, but important in the study of astronomy. Therefore it is the usual practice of teachers in astronomy to show the student first some visible object like a tree or a tower in the direction of that star, next some bright cluster of stars close to the Arundhatī and then the glimmering Arundhatī itself. Thus, the first two targets were only pointers to the actual goal.

Similarly, for those following the spiritual path, everything – from the witness down to the gross body – are all but upādhis or pointers to the Ultimate.

488. WHAT IS EXPANSION THROUGH LOVE?

This path usually starts with devotion to the personal God. In this path, the practices as well as the limited enjoyments of happiness all take place in the subtle sphere. But the life and activities of the devotee himself take place in the physical sphere. The latter appears more real and concrete from the point of view of the devotee at that level. His identification with anything else in the mental sphere can never be as strong as his identification with his gross body and senses.

But if the devotee persists strenuously, his love expands to the universal, and he himself becomes Īshvara, in that sense. As Īshvara, there is nothing outside him and thus he transcends bondage and pain. Thus it is possible to teach the Ultimate through the path of expansion of love.

But in practice, it is so full of pitfalls – and the chances of getting stranded at every little turn are so great – that very few who take to that path reach the right Ultimate. The devotee is very often carried away by the glamour of the expression of love, and he loses sight of the real background, the expressionless.

The exuberance of the expression of joy, in the course of this path, is more a hindrance than a help to the devotee's progress, unless he is being guided by a Kāraṇa-guru. This difficulty, in rising beyond the name and form, was clearly experienced at a stage in the spiritual lives of Shrī Caitanya, Shrī Rāmakṛiṣhṇa, etc.

God, as he is ordinarily conceived by man, is the highest manifestation of the human mind.

489. GOD IN HIS ESSENCE IS THE RIGHT ABSOLUTE

God is the most generic aspect of everything in this universe. There being nothing beside him, either gross or subtle, there is no duality in God. Just as his body is generic, his thoughts, feelings etc. are also generic. He is incapable of taking a particular thought or feeling. So the grossness and subtlety vanish altogether.

Thus reaching the most generic in all aspects, he stands as the right Absolute itself.

490. WHAT IS MY SĀDHANA AFTER TATTVŌPADĒSHA?

The only real sādhana for a jnyāna sādhaka is to try not to forget his real nature, whenever he is not occupied with activities which are necessary for his life in the world.

491. IS THE 'I'-THOUGHT THEORETICAL?

The thought of 'I' some say is theoretical. In that case, it will have to be admitted that you are yourself a theory, which I believe you can never admit.

Therefore, the 'I' thought is more practical than all apparently practical things.

23rd August 1952

492. WHAT IS THE WITNESS?

The witness is that which is changeless – the 'I' – amongst changes.

Changes cannot appear without the changeless. But the changeless exists independent of all changes.

Changes can take place only in the changeless. But changes when examined are found to be nothing but the changeless.

All changes are in the changeless. But the changeless itself never changes.

493. WHAT IS THE BEST TIME FOR MEDITATION?

It is at waking, but before becoming fully awake, so that the meditation might be the first activity on coming out of the Reality shining between the two states.

494. HOW TO TUNE MY SĀDHANA?

Nature works normally and regularly. Your sādhana should never be pitched against or contrary to the current of nature, but should always be in harmony with its course, and thus ultimately transcend nature. Otherwise, much energy will have to be wasted in counteracting the forces of nature.

495. WHAT IS LUNACY?

It is different according to the ignorant man and the vēdāntin.

An ignorant man calls a vēdāntin a lunatic and a vēdāntin takes the ignorant man to be the same. But the vēdāntin can see the position of the ignorant man and also know his own. So he rightly sympathizes with the plight of the ignorant man.

But the ignorant man knows only his own position and that with the basic error of which he is a helpless victim. He is incapable of even dreaming of the position of the vēdāntin, and therefore his thoughts about the vēdāntin are quite meaningless.

The vēdāntin's so called lunacy is the real Truth and the greatest boon to this world.

496. HOW IS THERE ONLY ONE THING?

One thing cannot prove anything other than that. This is an established fact and is true in all spheres.

Therefore, looking objectively, there is one thing and that is the Reality. Next, looking subjectively, we find that the 'I'-principle is the only thing that exists and that 'I' requires no proof either.

The objective cannot exist independent of this ‘I’, and therefore the ‘I’-principle is the only ultimate Reality.

497. HOW WAS ADVAITA DISCOVERED?

The following Upaniṣhadic verse describes it:

> parāñci khāni vyatṛṇat svayaṁ-bhūs
> tasmāt parāṅ paśyati nā ’ntarātman .
> kaścid dhīraḥ pratyag-ātmānam aikṣad
> āvṛtta-cakṣur amṛtatvam icchan ..

Kaṭha Upaniṣhad, 4.1

Dhīra means bold and he who dares to direct his mind inward to the Self. The meaning of the verse is as follows:

Line 1: The created sense organs are outward going.

Line 2: So your mind and senses become extroverted, and not directed to the inner Ātmā.

Lines 3 and 4: But one great soul directed his mind inward, desiring to reach immortality as a result thereof. Thus he visualized Ātmā, the inmost principle.

498. WHAT IS SAMSKĀRA?

It is the impress left in the mind by past thoughts, feelings, perceptions and doings, which are supposed to influence one’s subsequent activities.

499. WHAT IS MEANT BY ‘I AM I-ING’?

The ignorant man sees only changes in this world, and is ignorant of the changeless background behind all changes.

So the Ācārya first tries to show the changeless ‘I’ as distinct and separate from the changing body, senses and mind.

Then the disciple is asked to take his stand in that ‘I’-principle, and to look from there at the changing world. Immediately, the changes appear an illusion; and he understands that the changes are nothing but expressions of the changeless 'I'. And that is the changeless itself.

So, when I say the world is shining, it is nothing but myself expressing or shining. Or in other words, 'I am I-ing.' Because shining is not a function, but my real nature.

26th August 1952

500. HOW CAN OBSTACLES BE CONVERTED INTO HELPS TO REACH THE ULTIMATE?

Consciousness goes into the make of sense perceptions, and sense perception goes into the make of objects. Of these, Consciousness alone stands by itself. Therefore, an object is Consciousness alone. Consciousness is the essence of both perceptions and objects. It has already been proved that thoughts and feelings are nothing but Consciousness or Peace.

The only obstacles usually encountered on the spiritual path are thoughts, feelings, perceptions and objects. They become obstacles only when the emphasis is placed on the object side or material part of it and the subject ignored.

But when you begin to emphasize the subject part, which has been proved to be pure Consciousness, the objects thenceforward become means or helps to direct your attention to the Truth.

For example, if any of these so called obstacles were not there, how could you conceive of the witness and rise to the Ultimate? When there is an object, Consciousness is there to light it up. This most important part played by Consciousness is very often not noticed at all. Emphasize also that vital part of Consciousness in all your activities, and you will be surprised to find them all turned into means or helps pointing to your real Self, the 'I'-principle.

Thereafter, even the worst pain shows the real 'I'. When you tell a doctor that you have a particular pain anywhere in your body, it is not as the sufferer that you say so; because the sufferer can only suffer and cannot say. It is the knower alone that can say anything about the pain suffered. Thus the pain shows you that you are ultimately the knower, who is the real subject.

Therefore the world only helps you to know yourself. Evidently, the world was created in order to prove you.

30th August 1952

501. WHAT ARE THE KNOWN AND THE UNKNOWN?

By your merely knowing a thing, the thing does not undergo any change. You admit it was first unknown and that it was known only subsequently. By saying it is known, what you actually do is only this.

Your mind superimposes some attributes upon the original unknown. You know only the attributes thus superimposed. The unknown still remains as the background of the attributes, and remains still unknown. Thus looking objectively, we find that the thing which was the Reality was beyond both the known and the unknown, standing as the changeless background of both of them.

Now looking subjectively, you find that between two thoughts you remain alone in your own glory, and it is that Reality alone that expresses itself in your thoughts, feelings and perceptions.

So, subjectively as well as objectively, you know only the Reality. Or in other words, you can never say you have known it or that you have not known it. The real subject and object were both beyond the known and the unknown.

Thus the subjective and objective Reality is one. Before the object, there was only an indefinable 'it'. It is from that that the subject and object came into play. When it is seen that diversity springs from the indefinable one, no diversity remains.

Diversity springs from Me, and therefore it cannot affect Me.

502. HOW DOES GOD RESPOND?

From the level of the phenomenal, assuming that God is all powerful, it may be asked why did he not retaliate against the deliberate destruction by Tippu of the Hindu temples which were supposed to be the citadels of God.

Answer: It was only the citadel and not God himself that was destroyed. Moreover God was in the destroyer as well. So God must have chosen to raise the destroyer by love and forbearance, intending also that we should take that lesson from him, and not be carried away by the lower passion of the ordinary man.

503. OFFERINGS TO A PERSONAL GOD AS DIRECTED BY A KĀRYA-GURU

Every time you do it, you are really sacrificing a small part of your ego also along with the offering. But you should take care not to inflate the ego at the same time, by claiming that you have made such an offering or deed or self-sacrifice. Gradually, the ego gets much attenuated. At last your ego may disappear completely and you may become one with God, leaving nothing to be desired or offered.

But towards the later stages, the ego becomes so subtle and imperceptible that you will find it extremely difficult to deal with it. Your position with regard to the ego becomes quite vague and uncertain.

The *strange lady* who was attending upon the mother of Shrī Shankara was nothing but personified 'vidyā-vṛitti' itself. Vidyā-vṛitti also vanishes or is transformed into the Truth when the Ultimate shines. This was why the lady was in a desperate hurry to disappear before Shrī Shankara – the Sage, the ultimate Truth – appeared.

In the expression '*you remember*', there is a certain amount of effort involved. But when you say you are *remembering*, it means that you are in a state of remembering, and there is no effort at all in it.

31st August 1952

504. HOW TO TAKE A DEEP THOUGHT?

We are often asked to take a deep thought about certain spiritual ideas. For this, a one-pointed attention is the first requisite. To gain such attention, a deep craving of the heart is necessary towards that end. This craving is created by incessantly taking that very thought. When this craving thus created descends deep into the realm of the heart, your thought is said to have gone deep.

505. WHAT IS FUNCTION? (Its meaning and usages)

Function, according to the dictionary, means action plus an obligation. But in Vēdānta, function means only action.

When a participle is added to a verb of incomplete predication, it denotes a state as well as function. But so far as the verb in the present tense is concerned, only function is denoted.

1st September 1952

506. DOES ANY PATH LEAD ONE TO THE ULTIMATE?

Yes. Any path leads one to the Ultimate, provided the initiation is given by a Kārana-guru (a Sage).

According to the Sage, God is only another name given to the Ultimate, and denotes only that Reality through all the attributes heaped upon it. God is conceived as the Lord of all the universe and as such transcending the universe itself.

Devotion to God creates a spirit of self-surrender in the devotee. His ego is thus attenuated, little by little; until at last it is annihilated, leaving him alone. Transcending the ego, he becomes one with God. And being in God, he stands beyond the universe, as the ultimate Reality itself.

507. SIGNIFICANCE OF MARRIAGE

The Brahmin system of marriage is the ideal Hindu marriage. It is consummated with the marriage mantra being uttered by the couple. It means: 'You shall not part, even after death.' That principle which persists even after death can be nothing other than 'Ātmā', which is only one. The man and wife are only symbols or aspirants, and the marriage is conceived of as an initiation of the couple into that ultimate Truth, the Ātmā, as suggested by that marriage mantra.

In married life they cultivate the art of selfless love, each sacrificing the interest of the lower self for the sake of the partner. Ultimately, they come to understand that each of them does not love the other for the sake of the other, but for the sake of the self in the other – the self which is indivisible and one.

Thus they are enabled to reach the ultimate Truth by following the ideal married life, of course after initiation by a Kārana-guru, without the need of any other sādhana.

This is the secret of the invincible powers acquired and used with restraint by the celebrated pati-vratās of the vēdic age, like Anasūyā, Pāncālī and so on.

508. PERCEPTION NEVER PROVES AN OBJECT.

All objects point to 'you', the pure Consciousness.

Consciousness never proves the existence of any object.

The serpent is perceived in the rope, and the serpent alone is perceived. But the serpent is not there. Therefore perception does not prove an object.

509. STAGES OF PROGRESS OF BHAKTAS, ACCORDING TO THE *BHAGAVAD-GĪTĀ*

> catur-vidhā bhajantē māṁ janāḥ sukṛtinō 'rjuna .
> ārtō jijñāsur arthā-'rthī jñānī ca bharata-'rṣabha ..
>
> [Of those who rightly worship Me,
> there are four kinds: first those who aim
> for benefits to be obtained,
> then those who further wish to know,
> those who seek truth beyond all else,
> and those who truly come to know.]

Bhagavad-gītā, 7.16

Arthā-'rthi is the lowest type, desiring worldly pleasures and benefits alone.

Thus enjoying God's grace in the form of worldly pleasures for a considerable time, a bhakta begins to think of the almightiness, all-kindness and other supreme qualities of the Lord; and naturally a longing takes possession of him to come nearer to God and ultimately to know Him. In this manner, the bhakta becomes a *jijnyāsu* – an earnest aspirant.

This desire in him gradually becomes deeper and he begins to ignore and sacrifice the interests of his lower self more and more, until at last he becomes ready to sacrifice even his life for the attainment of his goal. Thus he becomes an *ārta*, crying from the depth of his heart for the attainment of the Reality.

Certainly at this stage, if not earlier, he gets the privilege of coming into contact with a Sage (Kāraṇa-guru) and is initiated into the ultimate Truth. Gradually, he becomes established in the Truth and becomes a *jnyānin.*

Thus the four stages are passed in regular order, in the above manner.

2nd September 1952

510. THE SAGE OR A JĪVAN-MUKTA

The Sage or a jīvan-mukta is nothing but the ultimate Reality itself, and can never be described by words.

Still, to enable the layman to get a glimpse of it, something could be said vaguely pointing to it. To the ordinary man, the Sage appears to be a *jīva* like himself. But from the standpoint of the Sage (assuming that there is such an imaginary standpoint), he is nothing but Ātmā, the Reality – and so a *mukta*. Thus the term '*jīvan-mukta*' is a misnomer, being the imaginary product of two opposing perspectives which can never be reconciled.

It can be further clarified. To the aspirant, who is a jīva, the world alone is real and all else, including even Ātmā, is unreal. But to the Sage, Ātmā alone is real and the world is unreal. Therefore, there is nothing in common between the two.

So left to himself the aspirant is helpless, since it is impossible for him to contact the Sage and thus rise to the Absolute. There is no bridge between the world and the Reality. Therefore, out of divine grace – if you may say so – the Sage comes down as the Guru, to bridge this gulf and to lift the disciple from the deep abyss.

Now let us examine the apparent activities of the ordinary man and the Sage. Both have three different perspectives, according to which they function in their lives.

1. The first and the lowest is the *perspective extroverted* (bāhya-dṛiṣhṭi), attributing reality to the world of objects. This is usually found in little children and in quite ignorant people.
2. The *inner perspective* (antar-dṛiṣhṭi), emphasizes the subtle activities of the mind. Here information is gained without the help of the sense organs. Everything gross becomes subtle here.

3. *Perspective introverted* (antar-mukha-dṛiṣhṭi): Here all that is gross and subtle cease to exist, ending in knowledge.

The Sage and the ignorant man have all these three perspectives. But the Sage has them all knowingly, and knows that the last one alone is real. The worldly man knows only the first two perspectives consciously. Occasionally, he is thrown unknowingly into the third perspective, but he neither notes it nor emphasizes it. The Sage, from his own standpoint, has only one perspective; and that is the third one.

In the case of the intelligent adult who has both the first and the second, he is able to function when he wants through the first perspective also, without giving up his emphasis in the second. For example, on meeting a stranger, though he first notes only the qualities and subtle attributes of the man such as his profession, qualifications, purpose of visit etc., he can also on second thought (if he wants) note his form, complexion and other physical details which form the object of the first perspective.

Similarly the Sage, though established in the third perspective, can (if he is so inclined) come down to any of the other two perspectives and function through them, without losing his stand in the third.

This is how a Guru works, apparently coming down to the level of the disciple in the gross plane; and lifting him slowly from there, through the subtle plane, to the Ultimate. But the Guru himself always remains in the Absolute, allowing his body and mind to come down and lift the disciple from the phenomenal.

511. THE INCENTIVE TO WORK

To the ordinary man, the fruit of action provides the incentive to work.

The fruit of action is desired simply because it is supposed to give you pleasure. And pleasure is liked for your own sake and not for the sake of pleasure. Your real nature has already been proved to be Peace and Happiness, which are the source of pleasure. Therefore, the ultimate incentive for any work is to touch your own nature of Happiness.

The ordinary man does not know this truth, and considers pleasure as something different from him. So he stands in need of some incentive to make the effort to reach it.

But the Sage knows well that this Peace or Happiness is his own nature and needs no incentive nor any effort to reach it, since it is already reached and established, so far as he is concerned.

For example, there is a saying about the life of mountaineers in Europe: 'Frugal by habit, temperance was no virtue for them.' It would seem a necessary virtue achieved after long practice, to those who were practising its opposite in their lives.

Similarly, an incentive for action is required only by those in the realm of duality. The Sage, having transcended duality, does not recognize actions to be real at all, much less the incentives for them. If ever he appears to do anything, those actions come up spontaneously, and he never takes a thought about it afterwards.

512. EGO

Every object is a pointer to the Ultimate. Even the much despised ego is a great help to the realization of the Truth. The presence of the ego in man, though in a distorted form, is infinitely better than the absence of it, as for example in a tree.

Through the ego, you perceive only objects at first. But the objects ultimately point to Consciousness. Therefore the first perception, though wrong, subsequently leads you on to the Reality; and the perception itself is made possible only by the presence of the ego.

Hence the ego is, in one sense, primarily responsible for the realization of the ultimate Truth.

513. THE GREAT WONDER

> ātmā 'ṁbu-rāśau nikhilō 'pi lōkō
> magnō 'pi nā 'cāmati nē 'kṣatē ca
> āścaryam ētan mṛga-tṛṣṇi-kāmē
> bhāvāṁbu-rāśau ramatē mṛṣai 'va

Ādishēṣha, Paramārtha-sāram

This verse means: Even though you always remain immersed in the sweet ocean of Ātmā, not only do you not taste a drop of it nor even turn to have a look at it, but you wander about running after the waters of the mirage to quench your ever-increasing thirst. No wonder you fail so miserably in your endeavour. What greater wonder can you expect in this world?

3rd September 1952

514. NOTHING CHANGES.

Change and changelessness both pertain to objects, and are perceived by me from beyond both. The one can never be perceived from the position of the other.

The most common mistake committed by an ordinary man is that, on the disappearance of something, he immediately substitutes an imaginary appearance of something else called its opposite or its absence.

Now let us examine what we mean by 'change'. An object is a mixture of the background and some qualities. The qualities come and go. When some qualities disappear, others appear, the background remaining the same. Then we say the object changes, and on the surface the statement appears to be true.

Let us look deeper. The qualities merely change their place and are not destroyed. Because some passengers have alighted from and some others have boarded a train at a particular station, can you say the train has changed? No. And because some passengers have alighted from the train and boarded a ship, can you say that they have changed? No. Neither the train nor the passenger has changed.

Similarly, in the object composed of the background and the qualities, the qualities change their place. That is the only activity that takes place. Neither the background nor the qualities undergo any change. Therefore, in fact, nothing changes.

4th September 1952

515. PŪJA, MEMORY AND URGE

Pūja: In the illustration of the pūja performed by the sense-organs, 'Happiness' is the image that receives the pūja.

It is the mind or avidyā that tells you to go into 'samādhi', because that is enjoyable. But don't listen to her. If you do so, you won't reach the ultimate Truth.

Memory is a false witness, because it was not present at the time of the activity reported as being remembered.

Urge: It is often said that a deeper urge is essential for realization of the Truth. But if you follow the urge to the last and attain realization, ultimately you find that the urge also was an illusion, and that you were never for a moment out of your own Self.

516. TALKING ABOUT A SAGE

Whenever anything is said about a Sage or a Jnyānin, it is the *personal* that is described, but with the accent always on the *impersonal.*

517. AM I STATIC OR DYNAMIC?

The static and the dynamic cannot co-exist as such. But they co-exist in the background, as the background. The static and the dynamic are both manifestations of the same background. Therefore, I am both simultaneously; or better still, I transcend the static as well as the dynamic.

> svakaṁ vapuś ca tēnai 'va buddhaṁ jagad iva kṣaṇāt
> kṣaṇāntarā 'nubuddhaṁ sad brahmai 'vā 'stē nirātmani

[Source of quotation uncertain]

He began to think himself the world. Immediately afterwards, it is all absorbed into him (in deep sleep). This is what you do every moment, by recording everything in knowledge and disposing of it for ever.

518. CONTROL OF THE MIND

Control of the mind is usually much talked of, and concentration of the mind is supposed to be the means of achieving it.

Concentration and distraction are both activities of the mind. Control of the mind is never possible from within the realm of the mind, but only from beyond both concentration and distraction. So one who has attained concentration cannot be said to have attained control over the mind.

Transcending the mind, there is only the 'I'-principle; and when you stand as that 'I'-principle, the vagaries of the mind disappear, not because the mind has been controlled, but because it has been destroyed.

Therefore, control of the mind – either from within the mind or from without – is a misnomer.

519. PROGRESS

A sādhaka progresses from activity to passivity (the witness); and reaching passivity, he transcends that also by other means.

520. HOW CONFUSION ARISES WITH REGARD TO THE WITNESS

Suppose you are the witness to a particular thought. A little later, you remember that thought and you say you had that thought some time ago – assuming thereby that you were the thinker when the first thought occurred, though you were then really the witness of that thought.

This unwarranted change in your relationship with a particular thought – from when the thought occurs to when you remember it – is alone responsible for the whole confusion with regard to the witness.

When you seem to remember a past thought, it is really a fresh thought by itself and it has no direct relationship with the old one. Even when you are remembering, you are the witness to that thought of remembrance. So you never change the role of your witnesshood, however much your activities may change.

521. INFERENCE AND PROOF

Inference depends upon the validity of past experiences of a similar nature. Inference is never finally correct.

Proof of anything. A thing can prove only itself. Seeing proves only seeing. Hearing proves only hearing. And so on.

Similarly, I prove only myself.

Nothing can be proved except oneself; and that needs no proof, being self-luminous.

Therefore, the statement 'I see a form' should correctly be put as 'I form a form.'

522. ABSORPTION AND GRACE

Absorption is the process by which the subject and the object become one in the 'I'-principle. Absorption of everything created by the mind back into the Self, the Absolute – with the help of 'vidyā-vṛitti' or the functioning consciousness – is the purpose of our lives.

The real *grace* of the Absolute is in having endowed us with the two simple instruments of Consciousness and Happiness, for the specific purpose of absorbing everything into ourselves by knowledge and love.

But often we do not recognize it in our ordinary activities, and yet we go through the whole process of such absorptions unknowingly.

523. NOTHING IS AN OBSTACLE TO REALIZATION.

> Adṛśyō dṛśyatē rāhur gṛhītēnē 'ndunā yathā,
> tathā 'nubhava-mātrā 'tmā dṛśyēnā 'tmā vilōkyatē

[Source of quotation uncertain]

> The invisible Rāhu is perceived through the eclipsed moon. In the same way the *Ātmā* who is mere experience is perceived through objects.

Translation by Shrī Ātmānanda, Ātma-darshan, *Preface*

1. The moon helps us to know Rāhu during an eclipse.
2. The phenomenon is necessary in order to know the noumenon.
3. The world helps us to know Ātmā.

524. WORLD A WITNESS

Since the world proves you, the world may well be said to be a witness.

525. WORLDLY TRAFFIC

Worldly traffic is as if you were first to draw a picture. The picture does no more than externalize the idea which was in you. But you stand before the finished picture as a stranger and begin to enjoy it. You are in fact enjoying yourself.

526. DEFINITIONS

Conviction comes in when what is said has been grasped.

Satisfaction comes in when what is desired has been gained.

Pleasure exists only in relation to its opposite, pain, and they are both enjoyed by the mind. But Happiness is beyond the mind.

Intuition comes in when your mind is expanded in time and you consequently become an expanded jīva. But you should remember that your misery also is equally expanded. Intuition is the highest expansion of the lower reason – still remaining within the realm of the mind.

Higher reason is the essence of the lower reason. It is connected always with the impersonal, and the lower reason is connected always with the personal alone.

Logic, *beauty* and *harmony* are all the 'svarūpa of Ātmā', viewed from different angles of vision.

Real renunciation is the employment of the Consciousness part in every perception knowingly. By this practice, the material part gradually gives way and the Consciousness part gains. This alone is real renunciation.

Causality comes in to establish relationship between objects. But it has been proved that every object is related only to its background Consciousness. Therefore two objects cannot exist simultaneously and so causality is not.

The hold of *time*, *space* and *causality* upon the ordinary man is so strong that he is not prepared to spare even the ultimate Reality from the dictates of time, space and causality.

The *phenomenal* means that which is changing. All change is in time, space and causality.

What do you *perceive*? You can perceive only the Reality. Unreality can never be perceived. Reality is in the senses and beyond the senses as well.

Life: You have three kinds of life, each distinct and separate from the rest. A *physical life*, confined to activities of body and perceptions of the senses. A *mental life*, confined to thoughts and feelings. A *self life* (or a life of the Self), being experience alone.

The first two lives are known to all. But you do not often know or note that you have a self life (or life of the Self).

527. EXPERIENCE OF BEAUTY IN AND THROUGH A PAINTING

Beauty is something by which you are attracted without a cause. You are most attracted to your own self. Or in other words, your own nature is the only thing that can attract you.

So beauty is only an experience of one's own nature, at the instance of an external object. It is then that you find beauty in that object.

The painter has had an experience of his own nature as beauty which he has attempted to express in the painting. It is only such a work of art that usually arouses the sense of beauty in you, by touching your own real nature; because the real nature of the painter and yourself, both being beyond the mind, can only be the one Reality – Ātmā. As soon as you see the picture, your attention is turned to your own real nature. Then you experience your own nature, and call it beauty.

When you enjoy the beauty, you do not perceive the painting. The painting is perceived only once and immediately discarded, yielding to beauty.

528. HOW TO FACE BEAUTY

Whenever you experience beauty, harmony, higher logic etc. beyond the realm of the mind, try always to merge into it. Do not try to stand as its witness. It is absurd. The witness stand is below the realm of experience.

529. 'A STATEMENT MADE BY THE GURU HELPS YOU NOT WHEN YOU TAKE IT, BUT WHEN YOU LEAVE IT.' HOW?

The statement, as it comes, consists of the gross form of words or sounds and the subtle form or idea meant to be conveyed by the words. If you cling to the gross form alone, you do not profit by it. On the contrary you must leave the gross far behind, and rise to its meaning or the idea behind the statement. Then alone will the statement help to raise you up spiritually.

What would happen if the food you swallow remains unchanged in your stomach? Not only would it not help to keep your body fit, but would soon make it sick. Similarly, spiritual statements if merely learnt and not assimilated will only inflate your ego and retard your spiritual progress.

12th September 1952

530. DEATH

Death is separation of the gross body from the subtle body, or of the mind from the body. Therefore 'you', as a jīva, are dying every moment.

531. ORDERS OF THE GURU

Orders of the Guru are generally of two kinds.

1. As originating from the ultimate Reality itself. It is an *imperative command and has to be obeyed literally.*
2. Originating from the Guru's love for the disciple. Sometimes this second kind of order might go against the spirit or tend to mitigate a past order of the first type. In such cases, there are instances of the disciple having respectfully chosen to go by the

first order, though a severe one, cheerfully evading the second one.

There is the example of the sannyāsin who was lying on the premises of Padma-tīrtha. Here the disciple's stand was that he had every right to consider himself unworthy of the Guru's love. This happens in the case of a disciple who is governed chiefly by the heart element.

But Shrī Tattvarayar, in whose sādhana both the yōga and jnyāna elements predominated, chose under exactly similar circumstances, to obey all the successive orders of the Guru to the very letter, without daring to interpret them in any manner.

Indeed, both were correct at their own different levels.

532. 'JĪVAN-MUKTA'

This is a misnomer, because *jīva* [personality] is perceptible to the external senses alone and *mukta* [that which is free] to the internal eye alone. The two are on entirely different planes, and as such can never meet. So if someone is a jīva [a person], he cannot at the same time be a mukta [one who is free]; and vice versa. Therefore, the term 'jīvan-mukta' ['free person'] is a misnomer.

533. THE PURPOSE AND RELEVANCY OF QUESTIONS

Questions often arise for those who have already heard the Truth from the Guru. The questions have a definite purpose and they have to be disposed of in the manner they deserve. Most of the questions are in the form of intrusion upon peace by uninvited thoughts. They come in only for quick destruction in the fire of knowledge. It can be done in three ways:

1. By yourself standing as the witness. Then the questions fail to reach you and return unheeded.
2. By understanding that every question points to Me (Consciousness), and on that account welcoming the questions as they come, only to be used as a help to reach my real nature.
3. By analysing the question itself and by finding that it is nothing but Consciousness – my own real nature.

534. QUESTIONS RELATING TO THE WORLD AS A WHOLE AND HOW TO DISPOSE OF THEM?

All such questions relate only to time, space and causality. These three form parts of the world itself, the solution of which the question is seeking. The world as a whole can never be explained in terms of its own parts. Therefore, every question concerning the whole world is illogical.

Time, space and causality, being parts of the phenomenal, can never affect the Ultimate. Therefore, with regard to the Ultimate also, the question does not stand.

535. YOU AND YOURS

You want your possessions also to be possessed of all your characteristics as qualities. You are free, permanent, happiness, and so on. Therefore you want what you possess also to have all those attributes in full. This is the secret of the embodied man's desire to be deathless, eternally free, and happy.

536. WHAT IS THE REAL GURU-DAKṢHIṆA (TO THE KĀRAṆA-GURU)?

The disciple's establishment in the ultimate Truth is the greatest and the only dakṣhiṇa (offering) one can humbly place at the feet of the Guru for the invaluable services rendered by him.

537. MIND AND CREATION

The creation of the world is not a fiat of the will, but is an unconscious creation. The will is only a function of the generic mind, functioning in the created world. If it were created by the fiat of the will, the many things which give you so much pain would never have been created at all.

The mind has that particular power of self-deception. Therefore, try to avoid all controversy confined to the realm of the mind alone. It is nothing but the ego's jugglery.

15th September 1952

538. SIGNIFICANCE OF THE ADVICE OF LORD KṚIṢHṆA TO ARJUNA, AND ITS APPLICATION IN PRACTICAL LIFE

The real object of the advice was to show Arjuna the path to the ultimate Truth. Human nature is composed of three distinct qualities: *tamas*, *rajas* and *sattva*, in ascending order. And progress consists in ascending from the lowest state of tamas to the next, rajas, thence to sattva, and ultimately to the beyond. There is no short-cut from the tamas to the sattva, except through rajas.

Tamas is dominated by sloth, dullness, despondency, inertia, etc. *Rajas* is dominated by the activity of the body and the mind; and *sattva* by knowledge or peace. Every virtue is supposed to lead one to the sāttvic.

In the lower shāstras, tamas is represented by deep sleep, rajas by active wakefulness and sattva by samādhi. Unfortunately, tamas and sattva appear alike on the surface; but are diametrically opposite in nature, like darkness and light. The highest state of sattva or samādhi is attainable only by well-disciplined activity of the mind. This is possible only in the wakeful state and belongs purely to the realm of rajas, but inclined more to the sāttvic.

Rajas, being the middle quality, is connected both with the preceding and the succeeding qualities; and one's progress to the sāttvic is made possible only by taking to activities which tend to the sāttvic.

The first requisite for this is the crippling of the ego which drags you down. The vital part of the ego is desire, usually for the fruits of action. For the ignorant man, this is the only incentive for action.

This incentive was taken away from Arjuna, when Lord Kṛiṣhṇa advised him to give up all desire for the fruits of his actions. Thus Arjuna was first made a free agent, by not being bound by the fruits of his actions. Then he was asked to engage himself in battle from a sense of untainted duty, merely because he was placed in a situation demanding it. Finally he was told also to give up that sense of duty or doership and thus he was shown the way to the right Absolute.

The three stages essential for progress, from the lowest to the highest [left to right]:

Passivity	Activity	Peace
Deep sleep or ignorance or tamas	Wakeful state or rajas	Transcendental state or sattva
Cowardice	Battle against forces of anātmā	Samādhi, pointing to ultimate Peace

Christ's advice in a similar situation was to assume complete passivity, by showing the left cheek if you are slapped on the right. This is not always an expression of the sāttvic element in you. If the aggressor is physically weaker and you know it and if you still keep silent and cheerful in the face of aggression, it might be an expression of the sāttvic in you.

But on the other hand, if you are physically weaker and the aggressor stronger and if you meekly submit to his assault, you are more likely to be thrown into that shameful passivity which is but the outcome of cowardice and a desire to escape without further hurt. This is not likely to lift you spiritually. Moreover, Christ did not enforce the positive substitute of the detachment from desire for the fruits of action, which alone could make the passivity at least lead to the sāttvic.

But to reach the sāttvic, one must wade through the rajas or activity, as advised by Lord Kṛiṣhṇa.

If, following Kṛiṣhṇa's advice, you fight and vanquish the adversary, it helps him by bringing him to his senses and to virtue, and helps you to transcend the doership by trying to forget the fight and help the vanquished. But if you follow Christ's advice and remain passive in all circumstances, the adversary always goes away with his ego highly inflated and sinks into ignorance, not having anything positive to hold on to. The result is injury to both.

539. THE SPIRITUAL VALUES OF THE ADVICES OF LORD CHRIST AND SHRĪ KṚIṢHṆA TO THE ORDINARY MAN

If you act according to Kṛiṣhṇa, you are faced with two possibilities and two alone – either to die in battle, or to win and not desire the fruits of the victory as already advised. In either case, the ego or body idea is considerably crippled and you rise to that extent in the spiritual ladder.

But Christ's advice, as it stands, is ambiguous. It is more likely to be misunderstood by an ordinary, ego-ridden man. He might easily pass into passivity either out of strength or out of fear; and nothing is suggested by which the ego can be crippled, without which spirituality is impossible.

540. Is there violence in Kṛiṣhṇa's advice to fight?

Kṛiṣhṇa's advice does not advocate raw violence, as the war maniacs of the present day do. He was advocating only activity or action.

An action can be condemned as violent only because of the motive behind it, and the motive is the expression of the ego. But Kṛiṣhṇa had already crippled the ego by removing the desire for the fruits of the action, which alone can act as the incentive to an ordinary man. Thus the spiritual ground was well prepared even before Arjuna was called to action, if necessary even violent action.

Courage was the one essential requisite for the performance of such an action. Courage is the offspring of the sāttvic or the selfless or the egoless.

541. Duty and incentive

For the ordinary man, every action needs an incentive, and the desire for the fruits of the action is the usual incentive. This inflates the ego and binds him to the phenomenal. He who desires to transcend the phenomenal must first transcend this incentive. It was for this that Arjuna was asked not to desire for the fruits of his action.

But being suddenly deprived of his usual incentive to action, he found it difficult to take to action without something to take its place. So Lord Kṛiṣhṇa shrewdly substituted duty as the incentive and asked Arjuna to fight as in duty bound.

Slowly, this duty also began to react as an object of attachment for Arjuna. Therefore later on, at a higher level, Arjuna was told in plain and unambiguous words not to be a slave to duty either, and thus to be completely free from all bondage.

Thus duty is also only a stepping-stone to the Ultimate.

> kartavyatai 'va saṁsārō na tāṁ paśyanti sūrayaḥ .
> śūnyākārā nirākārā nirvikārā nirāmayāḥ ..

[The world of change is always caught
in duty that is to be done.

Those who are wise don't see that duty
as their own; for they have realized
themselves as that which shines
where objects don't appear, as that
which has no form, which does not change,
untouched throughout by ill and harm.]

Aṣhṭāvakra samhitā, 18.57

542. WHY DID L-B [LORD BUDDHA] REFUSE TO ANSWER DIRECTLY, WHEN HE WAS QUESTIONED ABOUT ĀTMĀ?

Answer: Ātmā is the self-luminous principle that lights up the question. The master and disciple are also the same Ātmā. Therefore, to answer the question about Ātmā directly, Ātmā would have to be somehow objectified. This is impossible. Hence the question was answered only indirectly by him, and so the answer was unsatisfactory.

But the teacher did not then choose to take that disciple to the ultimate experience of Ātmā. We do not know why.

Ātmā is in the question and in the answer as well. Ātmā is not any of the expressions perceived. It is that which makes all expressions possible.

16th September 1952

543. HOW TO TACKLE QUESTIONS CORRECTLY?

All questions arise because you wrongly stress the objective part of your perceptions, instead of the subjective part which is Consciousness or Ātmā itself.

When you see an object, see what goes into the make of that object, and not merely its qualities which come and go.

The 'I', through the sense-organs, goes into the make of the object. The 'I', through thoughts, goes into the make of the sense organs. The 'I', through Consciousness, goes into the make of thoughts. And Consciousness is nothing but yourself, the 'I'.

In other words, the subject and the object are one.

544. WHEN YOU KNOW ANYTHING, YOU ARE IN THE REALITY ITSELF.

When you say you are beyond the central idea, who is it that says so? Is it the central idea itself?

No. It is that principle existing even beyond the central idea that enables you to say so. That is the 'I'-principle or Ātmā.

The bare statement of the Truth, 'I am the world', is often made. Is it true in every sense? No. I am the world not by my becoming the world; but only by the world, when dispassionately examined, becoming myself.

545. HIMSA (INJURY) AND AHIMSA (NON-INJURY)

An action becomes *himsa* only when there is the desire, however small, to enjoy the sensual pleasure as a result of that deed. It becomes *ahimsa* if nothing of that lower self comes in to prompt the action and to claim the fruit.

Even the law establishes guilt only if there is Mens Rea (motive or intention).

17th September 1952

546. HOW IS TRUTH TRANSMITTED (IF IT IS TRANSMITTED AT ALL)?

Some say it is through language, because the disciple understands the Truth only after listening to it from the lips of the Guru.

But it has been proved already that the talking and listening are incidents on the way; and that, when the disciple ultimately understands the Truth, there is neither talking nor listening, but only Truth and Truth alone – as experience without the experienced. Therefore language can, at the most, be said to have helped to point to that ultimate goal and nothing more. Hence its relationship, if any, to the realization is only indirect.

Others say that Truth is transmitted through silence or samādhi. Here, silence also is only a medium like language and serves the same purpose as language itself, only pointing to the Ultimate, and disappearing at the point of experience. Truth is far beyond even nirvikalpa samādhi (extreme silence).

547. How to read and understand the shāstras relating to Truth?

The mere cramming of the verses and their repetition as they are is everywhere condemned. The real method is pointed out by an illustration.

A cow in its shed gets loose at night, steals into an adjoining field, eats the green paddy there, and returns to its shed. There it chews, masticates and digests the whole food in the course of the night. Throwing out the refuse as dung and urine, it absorbs the essence of the food as blood into its system, eventually delivering it the next morning as ambrosial milk. The milk shows none of the superficial characteristics of the food taken the previous night.

Similarly, whenever we happen to read a shāstra, we should assimilate its essence by intense thought, till it becomes the blood of our blood and courses through our veins. The words of the shāstra, which form the material part, are forgotten or thrown out, as the cow threw out its excreta; and the substance, when it comes out of you should be as natural, sweet and refreshing as the delicious milk, with none of the characteristics of the hard shāstraic nuts.

Even the stealthy movement of the cow has its own significance in the analogy. It means that during your pursuit after Truth, you must first detach yourself in thought from the world, avoiding the notice of the ignorant public as far as possible, and avoiding all unnecessary contact with people. Controversies should be avoided at all cost. You should show no external signs of your spiritual activities, until all the food of learning is assimilated into the sweet milk of knowledge.

548. Tat tvam asi

'Tat tvam asi' is established by those who followed the cosmological path, by proving the identity between the changeless principles behind the apparent 'I' (*tvam*) and the objective world (*tat*). But they still have to transcend the sense of bigness of *tat* (as brahman), which is also relative, attached to that experience.

According to our method, the *tvam* is first examined dispassionately and reduced to its ultimate source, Ātmā. Thus you immediately transcend the basic error. Looking from the stand of Ātmā, which you have experienced to be the only Reality, you find that no world exists at all. Therefore, the question of any serious examination of the *tat* does not arise, so far as you are concerned.

According to Gurunāthan, the significance of the aphorism 'Tat tvam asi' is also different. The aspirant is seeking the Truth. So he is told: 'You are that Truth.' Here, you are shown the Reality in the apparent 'I'-principle itself, discarding all the appendages.

18th September 1952

549. PROBLEMS AND THE PRIORITY OF CONSIDERATION BETWEEN THEM

Problems are of two kinds, fundamental and auxiliary. The ignorant man never concerns himself with the fundamental problem, but is engrossed only with the auxiliary ones and gets lost amongst them.

The fundamental problem is the identity of the jīva with the body and mind. All other problems hang upon this central problem. None but the advaitin dares to analyse this jīva principle directly. He successfully eliminates the material part as unreal, from the crude mixture which is the jīva; and he stands identified with the self-luminous life principle in it, which is Ātmā itself.

Others who follow various other paths also progress to some extent, but do not reach the ultimate Truth. This is because their approach is purely objective.

Therefore, he who wants to solve his problems completely and for ever must face this fundamental problem first. When that is solved, you will find that all other problems vanish, like mist before the sun.

550. ACTIVITY AND INACTIVITY

The ignorant man conceives activity only as the opposite of inactivity. Therefore, when any activity ceases, he thinks that it has lapsed into inactivity and that inactivity has taken its place.

This is absurd. What we call activity is only a manifestation of the Absolute and even when so manifested it does not cease to be the Absolute, there being nothing other than the Absolute in it. Therefore when the activity ceases, it is the Absolute itself that remains over.

Similarly, what we call inactivity is also another manifestation of the Absolute, quite unconnected with any sense of activity. The inactivity also, when it vanishes, is transformed into the Absolute.

But seen from the position of the Absolute, there was no manifestation at all, because the Absolute did not undergo any change, even when supposed to be manifested or unmanifested.

20th September 1952

551. PROBLEM

Some people say, without thinking, that they have no problem. Just ask such a person if he has had any desires, and if so whether any of them had to be abandoned. If there was any such occasion he must then have been miserable. He might ignore it as being silly, or obstinately refuse to admit it. Still, that amounts to a problem, however small, so far as he is concerned.

552. TO THE ULTIMATE THROUGH QUALITIES AND THE QUALIFIED

The qualities and the qualified are dependent upon each other for their very existence. Therefore neither of them are real, but are only a seeming or an appearance.

Analysing the world cosmologically, it is reduced to the five elements and their qualities. The qualities and the qualified being mere appearances, the elementals and their qualities also disappear as unreal. And that principle (Consciousness), which thus examined the world, alone remains over as the Reality.

22nd September 1952

553. TRANSFORMATION OF A THING

A chair is a 'chair' by convention alone. It becomes an object when you perceive it. But when you *know* it, its objectivity vanishes and it becomes knowledge. Thus your role always is to destroy the world, whenever it appears.

The world consists only of perceptions, thoughts and feelings. As soon as any one of these appears, it is absorbed into yourself as knowledge, thereby destroying completely the objectivity of the world.

554. Form and formlessness

Form is of two kinds. Subjective as well as objective. Without the subjective form, the objective cannot exist. Both are one or of the same nature.

Similarly, subjective formlessness and objective formlessness both mean one and the same consciousness.

555. Significance of opposites

In ordinary life, one thing is supposed to depend upon its opposite or to be inseparably connected with it. Viewed from that stand, if one adopts the cosmological approach, one has to transcend both opposites (existence and non-existence of object) in order to reach the Truth.

But according to the direct approach, if you first understand that every object is directly connected only to the background, you easily reach the Absolute by transcending the objectivity of that one thing alone. Here, the opposite never comes in to trouble you. That opposite is only another object through which also you can reach the same background.

23rd September 1952

556. Time

> oťťattōnnalanēkamennu karutuṁ vyāmōhamē kālamāṁ .
>
> [Considering one thought as many:
> that's the delusion of time.]

Shrī Ātmānanda

'The one thought' ('oťťattōnnal') which is the permanent background of all thoughts is '*I am*.' Usually, this background thought is forgotten and immediately a plurality of thoughts come up. This illusion of plurality is what is called 'time'.

557. THE EFFECT IS THE CAUSE OF THE CAUSE.

Because it is the effect that suggests the existence of a cause and sets us in motion to seek that cause. Therefore the effect truly serves as the cause of the cause.

558. CORRECT EXAMINATION OF THE WORLD

The name 'world' denotes the gross as well as the subtle worlds. The subtle world is nothing but the mind or thought. The mind goes into the very make of the gross world, but is also quite independent of the world itself.

Even after the gross world has disappeared, the mind continues to exist, holding within itself the whole world deprived of its gross characteristics. Thus far, an ordinary man can well proceed, because life itself is composed distinctly of the physical and the mental aspects. So, standing on the mental plane, the physical can well be examined and reduced to the subtle.

This has again to be examined, taking your stand on a plane higher than the mind itself, but in substance not essentially different from the mind. That plane is the plane of knowledge, Consciousness or the 'I', which goes into the make of the mind. Taking your stand, at least in idea, in that plane of Consciousness and examining the mind, you will find that the subtle world loses its characteristics of being subtle and diverse; and it shines as pure Consciousness and one with you.

If you leave it anywhere else before taking it to this ultimate Truth, the examination is incomplete and the finding, to that extent, untrue.

559. THE CONCEPTION OF OPPOSITES

It does not come in, even in our ordinary statements. We bring in the idea of the opposite only subsequently, by way of interpretation or explanation to establish the first statement.

24th September 1952

560. THE CHIEF ADVAITIC APHORISMS

The chief advaitic aphorisms, according to the traditional path, are four in number. They are:

1. *'Ayam ātmā brahma.'* ['This self is all there is'], being a statement of the ultimate Truth.
2. *'Tat tvam asi.'* ['You are that.'] This is the instruction given by the Guru to the disciple, regarding the identity of the backgrounds of the jīva and the world.
3. *'Ahaṁ brahmā 'smi.'* ['I am all there is.'] This is the form in which the disciple contemplates the essence of the instruction imparted through the second aphorism. By contemplating this aphorism for a considerable period, the disciple transcends the littleness of the jīva and establishes his identity with the all-comprehensive brahman, which is the background of the universe. This conception of brahman is distinguished by its all-comprehensiveness or bigness. This is as much a limitation as the smallness of the jīva, and it has to be transcended to reach the Ultimate. For this purpose, another aphorism is given.
4. *'Prajñānaṁ brahma.'* ['Consciousness is all there is.'] With the help of this last aphorism, the disciple transcends also the sense of bigness and reaches pure Consciousness, the Ultimate.

'*I am conscious of something*', and '*I am consciousness*' are two significant statements.

The first statement is mental, fitful and personal. But it does the invaluable service of making you understand the nature of Consciousness.

The second statement is impersonal. There, Consciousness stands in its own right, as the only self-luminous principle.

Having understood the nature of Consciousness from the first statement, it is possible to direct attention to the impersonal nature of pure Consciousness, and thus to establish oneself in it.

561. JĪVA

When anything other than consciousness is added on to you, the real 'I'-principle, you become the personal or jīva.

The world should rightly be called the 'sense world'. See the world only as a 'percept' or 'object of perception'. The world is nothing but sense perceptions. So when you say you enjoy an object, it only means that you enjoy your own senses. Therefore, it is the senses that are always enjoying themselves.

This gives the clue to the manifold līlās of Lord Kṛishṇa. Lord Kṛishṇa, by his yōgic powers, split himself into innumerable Kṛishṇas; and each of the Gopīs enjoyed all kinds of līlā with the Kṛishṇa she took to be her own. How could anyone object to it, in a purely worldly sense? It was far beyond all conceivable worldliness.

562. THOUGHT AND ITS WORKING

A thought, when it is taken over and over again with increasing interest, goes deeper and deeper into one and becomes more and more intense, until at last its sense creates in us what is called a 'deep conviction'.

But if the thought is directed to the Reality which has already been visualized through the words of the Guru, it has no limited knowledge as its goal. Then, it is not a thought in the strict sense of the term, because it aspires to know nothing as a result thereof. What has to be known has already been known. Every time you repeat that thought you are brought into direct contact with the impersonal background and once again you visualize or experience the same Truth exactly as before.

Thought or remembrance are not what they are when directed to the Ultimate. Thought when it is directed outwards usually results in knowing. Thought is always taken with the object of coming to that knowledge.

Visualization by mere thought is possible only with regard to Ātmā, the Reality. With regard to nothing else is it possible. It is experiencing the same Truth in the same manner, again and again. Gradually, you get established in that Reality. Therefore, that thought takes you beyond all thoughts.

The so called thinking about the Ultimate is not a course of remembering either. What is remembering? Remembering consists in bringing before the mind's eye what is directly perceived by the sense organs. You admit that the correctness of the perception is lost in remembering. The direct seeing of the ignorant man becomes a mere thought form when remembered. Perception takes place in the gross realm, and memory in the subtle realm.

But the visualization of the Ultimate is made in the realm beyond the mind, after passing through several transformations on hearing the Truth from the lips of the Guru. Every time you think about the Truth afterwards, you actually pass through all the different transformations as before, until at last you actually visualize the Truth even more intensely than before in the very same higher plane. This is direct perception or direct knowing or direct being or Consciousness itself.

Memory is the gross giving place to the subtle.

25th September 1952

563. LOWER AND HIGHER REASONS

The lower reason differs in its interpretation and application according to individuals, since it relies only upon the personal experiences of each, which vary according to temperament and environment.

But the higher reason (vicāraṁ = viśēṣēṇa carikkuka [proceeding through discernment]), moving along a special path directed inward, relies only upon the being in the individual, which is unique. Therefore it can never be different in its application or finding.

564. THE CAUSAL BODY OF IGNORANCE

The causal body of ignorance [the unmanifested potentiality of the 'unconscious'] cannot exist. Ignorance is the absence of everything.

When you say there is the absence of a cow here, it only means that it is not present here to the fleshy organ, but is present only to the subtle organ of the mind. The absence of anything is dependent directly upon the presence of that thing.

Thus the negative of anything cannot exist by itself, without at least an unconscious reference to the positive. So the causal body of ignorance is a misnomer.

> suṣupty-ēka-siddhaḥ … śivaḥ kēvalō 'ham
>
> [I am that unmixed absolute,
> just that one perfect happiness,
> attained in depth of dreamless sleep.]
>
> *Shrī Shankara,* Dasha-shlokī, 1

565. IS LOVE DUALISTIC?

Some Jnyānins who had no experience of love or devotion say that love is dualistic since it stands in need of an object, and that jnyāna alone can take you to the Ultimate.

The same objection can be raised at that level against jnyāna also, that jnyāna always needs an object to express itself. But the Jnyānin knows from experience that jnyāna can stand independent of objects, as pure Consciousness beyond the realm of the mind. At that level, love also gets transformed into pure *ānanda* or Peace.

The first statement went wrong simply because jnyāna was taken at the absolute level of experience and love at the lower level of expression.

It is no wonder that the Jnyānin accustomed to the path of jnyāna alone should be so ignorant of the path of love. Because of his having reached the Ultimate through jnyāna, the world so far as he is concerned has disappeared altogether, including even the expressions of love. No necessity or occasion arises, in his case, to examine the world through any other perspective. Nor is any effort necessary for his establishment in the Ultimate. All such effort has already been made. Many persons had thus reached the Ultimate through the path of jnyāna alone, and were all jīvan-muktas.

But in order to take the role of a Guru or an Ācārya, one has to make oneself sufficiently acquainted with the experiences in each of the different paths of jnyāna, bhakti, and yōga. This is necessary in order that the aspirants coming with partial and preliminary experiences, helpful or perverted, in any of these paths might be safely directed along the paths of their own taste and choice, and their difficulties in their own paths explained to their satisfaction. Such Ācāryas are of course extremely rare, not to be found even in the course of several centuries.

566. UPON WHAT CAN ONE SUPERIMPOSE SOMETHING?

Only upon something changeless.

We usually say that the serpent is superimposed upon the rope or that the thief is superimposed upon the stump of a tree. Neither of these statements is literally true. If the statement that you have superimposed something is to stand, it is essential that the thing superimposed and the thing upon which the superimposition was made should both be present in the resultant. But neither the rope nor the stump of a tree are to be found in the resultant.

Therefore it is clear that the superimposition was made not upon the rope nor upon the stump of a tree, but on that conscious principle upon which the rope and the stump of a tree themselves were both similarly superimposed.

So you can never superimpose one object upon another object, nor one thought upon another object, nor one thought upon another thought.

567. EXISTENCE

> 'The non-existence of the non-existent is existence itself.'
>
> 'Existence of the non-existent disproves non-existence.'

26th September 1952

568. PRATYAKṢHA AND PARŌKṢHA

Pratyakṣha literally means 'perceivable by the sense organs'. It is opposed to *parōkṣha* meaning 'indirect' or *aupacārika* meaning 'formal'.

According to Gurunāthan, there is only one pratyakṣha. It can be experienced only in the 'I', without being connected with anything else. All else is indirect or formal. According to this, an object perceived is parōkṣha. When that is subsequently known, it merges into the 'I' and becomes pratyakṣha and the object vanishes.

Every one has a deep sense of the Self in him which stands clearly transcending the body, senses and mind. Its form is 'I know I am.' This is direct knowledge that is known without the help of any instrument.

569. CREATION AND DESTRUCTION OF THE WORLD

Self-forgetfulness is the cause of the creation of the world, and self-remembrance or withdrawal to the Self is the destruction of the world.

570. ACT KNOWINGLY.

This is the practical instruction by which the 'I' is visualized.

In all human activities, there is a fundamental difference between the words expressed and the actual activity. The words 'I see him', 'I hear it' etc. are quite in order. But in the activity proper, the first and the most important part 'I' is lamentably ignored and the activity or objectivity part alone emphasized. This is responsible for all bondage. The only means to liberation is to fill the omission you have so ignorantly made.

In all your daily activities, try to bring in the 'I' to the forefront. If you succeed in doing this, you have gone a long way towards visualizing the 'I'. When you do this exercise for some time, you will find that you are that changeless principle in all activity and that the activities themselves change every moment. This clearly proves that action, perception, thought and feeling do not go into your nature at all.

The activities of the ignorant man or the objective part of them usually cloud the 'I'-principle in him. But this exercise removes all possibility of such clouding of the 'I'-principle, since the 'I' is emphasized every moment.

My role is to remain changeless in the midst of incessant change, or to be unaffected by all opposites, like happiness and misery. To make this possible, one has to understand that one is beyond all opposites and that one is neither the doer nor the enjoyer.

When you say every activity belongs to you, it means that nothing belongs to you in fact, or that I am the 'svarūpa' without their touching my svarūpa.

571. Perception and the 'I'

Perception is composed of the lighting up by the 'I'-principle plus the objective part of the perception. Take for example 'seeing'. The seeing cannot exist in an unmanifested form, either before or after the activity of seeing. But the 'I'-principle does exist as unmanifested both before and after the activity, and the very same 'I' is manifested in the seeing as well. Therefore, the object is the manifestation of the 'I' alone, and not of the senses.

This shows that when the world appears, the world is '*I-ing*'; or in other words, when anything appears I am the 'shining' in it.

All paradoxes are dissolved in the Sage.

572. When I say I walk, it really means I am not walking.

An activity is a deviation from the normal state. When I say I walk, I mean it as an activity opposed to my normal state of non-walking. Walking is only something which comes and goes, while I am by nature non-walking or changeless. You admit you have not changed by merely walking. Walking refers to my nature which is non-walking. Thus every activity shows I am not that.

Every activity appears and disappears in me. I am changeless, and activity is incessant change. So I cannot be an activity as it is.

This 'I' has to be emphasized in the present tense just before every activity. The 'I' has to be in every activity but it is there only as the silent witness. If I am in everything which is diversity, it can only be by my being that unity itself.

573. THE BEST FORM OF MEDITATION (IF YOU MUST HAVE ONE)

If you obstinately want to practice meditation, the best form for your purpose is 'I am.' It will give the mind nothing objective to cling on to, and in the very effort the mind will cease or die.

This contemplation drives away all intruding thoughts, and you are established in the 'I'. Slowly, it becomes deeper and deeper and the nature of Consciousness and Happiness begins to be experienced, since these are intrinsic in the 'I'.

During chanting or contemplation, though we begin with the word or sound, we never stop there. We begin to dive slowly into its meaning or goal of the idea; and then the chanting gradually stops, leaving you at the very goal.

Thus when you contemplate 'I am', you stand established in the real 'I'-principle. But this 'I am' can never be replaced by the term 'Guru'. Because the Guru is never an experience to anybody, while 'I am' is a clear experience for all. Therefore, to lead you to the ultimate experience, 'I am' is essential. It is true that after experience the 'I am' also merges into the Guru, who is transcendental, beyond even the background of all this world.

Shrī Shankara describes the state of nirvikalpa samādhi as the *witness of everything* (sarva-sākṣhi) but the *Absolute am I* (shivō-ham)

> nityānandēturīyēvigatamatigatissarvasākṣīśivōham

Shrī Shankara

Truth is experienced in three distinct stages.

In the first stage, in which you just touch the ultimate background, you reach the witness.

In the second, as you stand as the witness, the witnesshood disappears and you find yourself the Ultimate, without a second to make you miserable.

Lastly, the sense of absoluteness also vanishes and you stand established in the ultimate 'I'-principle, the only Reality.

The same idea is expressed in *Ātma-darshanam, 16.3.*

> dṛṣṭāvāṁ bōdhamātraṁ ñān
> ennayāṁ dṛśyameppoṟuṁ

kāṇippatennu sarvvatra
kaṇṭu ñān viharikkayāṁ

I am pure Consciousness. Realizing that every object wherever placed is asserting Me, I enjoy Myself everywhere and in everything.

Shrī Ātmānanda

30th September 1952

574. WHAT IS KARMA?

The direct answer to the question is that there is no karma. It is the responsibility of the questioner to prove that karma exists. Let us examine 'karma' in detail. What is that principle which makes every karma possible?

It is evident at the outset that karma cannot exist without a doer or an agent. The proof of the existence of the doer is that you know it, or that you are the perceiver of the karma as the doer, doing and the deed.

Now take note of the fact that such a witnessing agent is indispensable for the existence of karma. Then turn your attention more closely to that agent and see if he is really an agent. Immediately you see that the so called agent is no agent, but only the perceiver of karma. As perceiver one cannot be bound by the karma.

Thus karma is no karma in the ordinary sense of the word, and all samskāras die with it.

Karma consists of three parts, namely:

1. The incentive (being samskāras),
2. The activity (of body or mind), and
3. The results or fruits thereof.

When you reach the perceivership, both the incentive as well as the desire for the fruits of action vanish. Thus divorced from the perceived and the perception, the perceiver also ceases to be a perceiver and becomes the Ultimate.

Therefore, karma is nothing but the ultimate Reality itself, and as such can never bind you.

575. KARMA AND SAMSKĀRAS

Samskāra is the deep impression left behind by that which was done. Karma gives rise to samskāras and samskāras induce karma. Thus karma and samskāras depend upon each other for their very existence. This is impossible. Therefore, karma and samskāras are both a misnomer, and the perceiver or 'I' alone is the Reality.

This is what Lord Kṛishṇa has said about karma in general.

> ... gahanā karmaṇō gatiḥ
>
> [Unfathomable is the way of karma.]

Bhagavad-gītā, 4.17

The significant story of the non-existent (kathayillātta katha) in the *Yōga-vāsishṭha* also shows the unreality of all karma. It has a sublime moral for each one of us. It is this: 'We, the children of the unborn barren woman, are enjoying the unborn world, just as the child in the story listened to and enjoyed the whole story of the non-existent.'

1st October 1952

576. A TEST OF THE NATURAL STATE

When you are asked what you are, if the answer comes to your mind spontaneously 'I am pure Consciousness', you may be said to have reached the natural state.

577. LOVE AS VIEWED BY RELIGIONS AND BY VĒDĀNTA

Religions teach you to love others at the physical and mental levels. But Vēdānta teaches you to become that love, pure and impersonal, beyond the mind's level.

578. BHĀRATA'S RENUNCIATION

An act becomes true renunciation only if you renounce thereby something nearest and dearest to your heart. The greatest desire of Bhārata, when he started in search of Rāma, was that he himself should take the place of Shrī Rāma in the forest and send Rāma back to Ayōdhya to rule the kingdom.

But somehow Bhārata was persuaded by Shrī Vasiṣhṭha their Guru to return to Ayōdhya to rule the kingdom himself till Rāma came back. This was indeed an act of supreme sacrifice and renunciation on the part of Bhārata, since he was forced by circumstances to give up his heart's greatest desire to renounce the kingdom and take upon himself Shrī Rāma's exile in the forest.

579. SOME IMPORTANT STATEMENTS MADE BY JESUS CHRIST

Their levels and relative significance:

1. 'I am the son of God.' (Often repeated in the New Testament.) This is purely a preparation of the ground for spiritual progress and is in the *dvaitic* [dualistic] plane.
2. 'I am the vine and ye are the branches.' (St. John, 15.5) This is in the level of *vishiṣhṭādvaita* [qualified dualism].
3. 'I and my Father are one.' (St. John, 10.30) This is from the pure *advaitic* level.

Evidently, these are different statements addressed to different persons, at different levels of understanding.

2nd October 1952

580. IF THERE IS ANY COMPLAINT, WHO MAKES IT?

Never the Ātmā. In that case, what have 'you' to worry about?

It is only that which has no form that can assume any or many forms.

If you want to know anything subjective, you must never refer to anything in the objective world.

581. WHAT HAPPENS WHEN I SAY 'I AM ANGRY'?

1. Since you perceive all the three states and all your activities from birth till death, you are evidently a changeless being. But when you say you are angry, you actually become anger itself. This is,

of course, a clear change from your centre and that cannot be. Therefore anger, or any other feeling, is only an appearance.

2. You can remember your anger afterwards. So you must have perceived the anger yourself. As perceiver, you can never be affected by the anger. So you were never angry.

3rd October 1952

582. THE GIST OF THE GURU'S TEACHING

You had been enamoured of the pot. The Guru has been showing you that it is nothing but earth, without doing the least violence to the pot.

583. HEAD AND HEART – ARE THEY DIFFERENT?

When you reach the Ultimate by following the path of pure jnyāna, you experience deep Peace or Happiness expressing itself sometimes in the form of gushing tears and choking voice. This is not an expression of the head, but of the heart in you.

On the other hand, there are many instances of Sages like Shrī Padmapāda and Vaṭivīshvarattamma who have reached the Ultimate through the heart and heart alone, directed to their Guru – the Absolute – with deep devotion. They have subsequently guided aspirants to the Truth, even on the Jnyāna path, most successfully.

Thus it is clear that what one experiences through either path is the same Reality; and that jnyāna and devotion are but the expressions of that one Reality, the one through the head and the other through the heart.

A jīvan-mukta who is established in the Absolute does not seek to be conspicuous in any phase of his apparent life.

5th October 1952

584. WHERE IS HARMONY?

We see harmony in this world only on rare occasions. But the Sage sees the same harmony always and everywhere, nay even in apparent misery and discord.

585. The mind and the world

The mind is the most essential part of the world and it goes into the make of the world itself.

586. Fear

> … dvitīyād vai bhayaṁ bhavati .
>
> [It's only from a second thing that fear arises.]
>
> *Bṛihadāraṇyaka Upaniṣhad, 1.4.2*

Fear arises out of the consciousness of the existence of one other than yourself.

587. Remembrance

When you say you remember a dream, you superimpose the dream subject upon the witness. The same process repeats itself when you remember a past incident in the waking state.

The seeming continuity of any state by itself is no proof of the reality of that state. It appears so both in the waking and in the dream states.

588. Why do we attach more Reality to the waking state?

No, we do not do so. Both the active states [waking and dream] are waking states when actually experienced. That state in which you remain at any particular moment is then considered to be the waking state and more real than any other.

589. How do I visualize a past incident in the waking state?

Certainly, you cannot visualize it before the waking, fleshy sense organs. So you have to create a set of suitable sense organs for the purpose, as you do in the dream state, and visualize the incident before them. So everything in the past is equal to a dream.

590. MEMORY

Memory merges the past into the present; and the present, when examined minutely, disappears altogether. Thus time is really destroyed and you are brought nearer the Reality.

So memory helps you to a certain extent to approach the Reality, though memory itself is part of the unreality.

591. EVEN AFTER UNDERSTANDING THE TRUTH, I SEE THE WORLD AGAIN. WHY?

It is not you who see the world again. It is the illusion of the apparent 'I' seeing the illusion of the world. What does it matter to You?

6th October 1952

592. HOW TO APPLY THE USUAL ILLUSTRATIONS FROM THE PHENOMENAL TO THE ABSOLUTE?

The usual illustrations are the snake in the rope, the water in the mirage, etc. Here the snake or the water stands for the whole world – gross or subtle, including the individual perceiver – or in other words the world of objects, senses, thoughts and feelings. Even the error of seeing the snake or the mirage forms part of the perceived world. This includes the entire realm of body and mind. This could be seen only from some position beyond them – that is, from the Truth or the 'I'-principle. But then there is no world to be seen.

Still you might say you see the world again. Will you please tell me who sees it? Do *You* see it? No. Then why do you worry? Seeing, see-er and the seen all form part of the unreality. Don't forget that. Let objects of unreality play between them. What does it matter to you – the Reality?

In an enquiry of the Truth, usually the activities of the sense organs and the mind alone are taken into consideration. But the activities of the organs of action by themselves are almost mechanical or unconscious. There, awareness does not necessarily come in. But, for the activities of the senses and mind, the presence of awareness is essential.

7th October 1952

593. HAPPINESS, MISERY AND THE 'I'-PRINCIPLE

Misery depends upon diversity or objects for its very existence, and very often it bursts out into vociferous violence.

Happiness depends only upon the one Reality, the 'I'-principle. When the jīva is in a state of Happiness (not pleasure) he is touching the background unawares. And when he is in misery, he is in unmistakable duality.

When you say 'I am miserable', it means I am misery, or that misery has come upon me or merged into me, or that I am the svarūpa of misery. But misery cannot be my svarūpa.

When you say 'I am happy', it means I am Happiness or that I am the svarūpa of Happiness. But in this case the opposite is also true, that is to say Happiness is my svarūpa.

Since I am the svarūpa of misery, it can very well merge into me. But I can never merge into the misery. Thus I am the svarūpa of all.

The pot is able to merge into the earth because even when it appears as pot, it is earth and earth alone.

594. THE REAL 'I', THROUGH DIFFERENT STATES AND ACTIVITIES

It has been proved that the 'I'-principle is persistently present in all the three states and that none of the changing states can be superimposed upon the 'I'-principle.

Similarly, the 'I'-principle is present in all the activities of the waking state and so none of these activities can be superimposed upon that 'I'. None of these go into the make of that 'I'-principle.

Therefore, you as that 'I' is the one, untainted Reality.

595. AN ENQUIRY ABOUT THE TRUTH OF THE WORLD, GROSS AS WELL AS SUBTLE

The world has been taken up for examination from time immemorial by scientists and philosophers. Both of them rely upon the generic mind, with its varied aspects, as the only instrument for the purpose. The scientists have tried to solve the objective diversity by reducing everything to atoms or electrons, but cannot find the way beyond. Philosophers, ignoring the gross, have taken up the subtle world of thoughts and feelings (the apparently subjective diversity) for analysis, and cannot go beyond nothingness. Thus both of them are entangled in the same vicious circle.

In every perception, thought or feeling, two aspects come into operation. The view part and the material part. The view part is the result of one's own individual experience and samskāras and therefore differs with different individuals. This part, the more important of the two, is lamentably ignored by scientists and philosophers alike. They analyse only the material part of their so called experiences, taking their stand in the changing mind alone.

Their fundamental mistake is their inability to take note of a changeless principle, the 'I' standing behind, lighting up all their so called experiences. Without this stand in the changeless 'I', the changes can never be correctly examined, whether in the gross or in the subtle realm. This irrefutable stand is shown only by the vēdāntic or advaitic approach.

For diversity to be, unity must stand behind, supporting it. You are merging diversity into unity every time a perception, thought or feeling merges into Consciousness, the 'I'.

8th October 1952

596. THE PROCESS OF REALIZATION

1. You identify yourself with objects (body, senses and mind).
2. Next, you eliminate yourself from the object.
3. Lastly, the object is made to merge in you.

9th October 1952

597. REAL SLEEP

yadi dēhaṁ pṛthak-kṛtya citi viśrāmya tiṣṭhasi ...

Aṣhṭāvakra-samhitā, 1.4

This means: '*Sleep in Consciousness.*' This is the royal road to the natural state.

The thought, '*I am Consciousness*', consists of two parts: the 'I' and 'Consciousness'. Of these two, Consciousness can apparently be objectified when attached to objects. But the 'I' can never be so objectified. In this thought, Consciousness, being linked on to the 'I', cannot also be objectified. Therefore, this particular thought can never draw you outward, but will only allow itself to be drawn inward, ultimately merging in the 'I' or 'Consciousness'.

598. THE SAGE AND LOVE

The Sage is impersonal, and as such can never act, think or feel as a person. As he really transcends the limits of love, he cannot limit it to an individual, society or country. His love can never be mutilated in that manner.

599. HOW TO SLEEP KNOWINGLY?

Know that you are going to sleep. Let that thought be as vague as possible. Then empty your mind of all intruding thoughts, taking care not to strain the mind in the least. Having understood from the Guru that your real nature alone shines in its own glory in deep sleep, if you relax into deep sleep as already suggested, the deep sleep shall no longer be a state, but your real nature, even beyond 'nirvikalpa samādhi'.

11th October 1952

600. TRANSMIGRATION OF SOULS

A paragraph in which transmigration of souls is discussed by Socrates was brought to the notice of Gurunāthan. He remarked: 'So you take it for granted that you have a soul and that you are its possessor. The possessor is decidedly different from, and superior to, the thing possessed. If so, how does transmigration of your soul affect you more than the transformation of your hairs? But I question your fundamental assumption itself that you have a soul. Your knowledge and your experience are the evidence you put forward to prove it. But I have already proved to you that no one can know or experience anything other than one's own Self, the 'I'-principle. So the existence of the soul itself cannot be proved. Therefore, the question of transmigration of souls does not arise at all.'

The only experience is 'I', and 'I' is the only word which denotes experience. ('*Anubhava-mātram ātmā.*')

601. The path of the 'I'-thought

The ordinary man has the deep samskāra ingrained in him that he is the body and that it is very, very insignificant, compared to the vast universe. Therefore the only possible mistake you are likely to be led into, while taking to the 'I'-thought, is the habitual samskāra of the smallness attached to the 'I'.

This mistake is transcended by the contemplation of the aphorism '*Aham brahmāsmi.*' Brahman is the biggest imaginable conception of the human mind. The conception of bigness no doubt removes the idea of smallness. But the idea of bigness, which is also a limitation, remains over.

Ultimately, this idea of bigness has also to be removed by contemplating another aphorism: '*Prajnyānam asmi.*' ('I am Consciousness.') Consciousness can never be considered to be either big or small. So you are automatically lifted beyond all opposites.

602. Bondage and liberation

Bondage is the wrong groove of thinking.

Liberation is effected only by the right groove of thinking, as directed by the Kāraṇa-guru.

603. Objects, perception and Reality

The reality of every object perceived by you is only your own reality; and that object has no independent existence other than yourself.

No perception ceases until the object has been reduced to knowledge or recorded in knowledge. Then the object no longer exists as such.

But the ego wants to continue the illusion; and so says 'I know it' – even when the 'it' (meaning the object) is nowhere in the knowledge to which every perception is reduced.

13th October 1952

604. Be unqualified and you are free.

What we call an object is the real background, which is unknown, and a heap of qualities superimposed upon that background, those qualities alone being known. The qualities themselves come and go, and do not go into the make of the object. So the object is in fact only that unknown and unqualified background. Thus every object is only that unknown background.

There cannot be two unknowns either. Because, even in order to distinguish between the 'two', we must know them. So there is only one unknown, and that is yourself, and it is the background of yourself as well.

That is the only Reality, the Ātmā, the ever free. Know that and be free.

605. Reality

What is not conceivable, not knowable and about which you are deeply convinced, that is the Reality. That you are.

606. The world and what it shows (proves)

The world is nothing but perceptions, thoughts and feelings. Now let us examine what these are. Many 'presents' (experiences of the present) made into one 'present' constitute a concept or a thought. Similarly, many spatial points made into one constitute a percept.

Admitting that you cannot have more than one simultaneous experience, many 'presents' or many spatial points become impossible. So there are no percepts, thoughts or perceptions.

As ordinarily accepted, a thought is made up of many time points or 'presents' at one point of time. But there can never be more than one present at one point of time. Therefore, thought is a misnomer. And so is the world.

But still you see the world. Yes, let us for the time being concede that seeing exists. Yes, I see. But then what does this prove? It proves only 'Me' and not anything else. You say: 'The world appears.' When you say it 'appears', you mean that it is lit up by Consciousness, on your side. In the statement, the 'world' is objective and 'appears' is subjective. To whom does it appear is the next relevant question. Of course to you. You light it up by your Consciousness. So every object points to Consciousness and proves nothing else.

607. DEEP CONVICTION

Deep conviction is direct knowing. Conviction is the last word of the worldly man or the mind regarding any search. If you are convinced you have attained the object of your search, it is a signal to stop all further enquiries regarding it.

Gurunāthan only uses the same word for want of a better one, to denote spiritual understanding also. But he improves upon that word by qualifying it as deep conviction. Your spiritual understanding becomes deep when you become established in it, by experiencing it again and again. And then it becomes experience pure.

608. THE MEASURE OR INSTRUMENT AND THE MEASURED

Every measure or instrument is only a miniature of the measured. You measure length with an artificial unit of length. You do the same with weight, volume, etc. Thus every instrument used to measure variety is only variety in miniature; and everything measured with that instrument will be expressed only in terms of variety which is the nature of that instrument itself.

Therefore, if you use such an instrument to measure unity, it is no wonder that the unity is also expressed as variety. This is what happens when the mind is utilized to examine the 'I'-principle – which is unity itself. Thus the attempt fails miserably.

609. VARIETY

'When', 'where' and 'why' are the expressions of time, space and causality in the realm of the mind, or each of them constitutes the mind itself. These three questions have *created variety* and have regular traffic with that variety, as though they have nothing to do with it. They also proceed to measure that variety.

The story of the pseudo-sannyāsin explains this beautifully. Once there lived in a village a strange sannyāsin who knew nothing of the Truth or of sannyāsa, but had only the rough externals of a sannyāsin – the ochre coloured robes, tuft and beard. However he was shrewd enough to deceive the simple villagers and command their love and veneration.

Once a real sannyāsin happened to pass through that village. The simple villagers wanted to bring about a meeting between the two sannyāsins. But the village sannyāsin was very reluctant, for fear that he might be exposed. At last he discovered a way out. He told the organizers of the meeting that he would first ask the visitor three questions. If the visitor yielded to all the three questions and had nothing to say about any of them, then it should be taken that the new sannyāsin is defeated and should be sent away immediately. The villagers agreed. The new sannyāsin, not suspecting any foul play at the meeting, also agreed to come. At last they met and the village pseudo-sannyāsin asked his three questions, one after the other, in great haste.

1. 'Have you not had a father?' 'Yes.'
2. 'Are you not a sannyāsin?' 'Yes.'
3. 'Are you not on your way to somewhere?' 'Yes.'

Alas! the three questions were answered all in the affirmative. The innocent villagers believed that the new sannyāsin was really defeated and, according to the agreement with their own sannyāsin, they drove the visitor away without a word.

This is exactly how the pseudo-sannyāsin of the ego has invented the three crucial questions of 'when', 'where' and 'why'; and flings them at every expression of the Reality.

The Reality stands illuminating even those questions and never stoops to argue. The satellites of the ego interpret this silence in favour of their own master, and altogether ignore the Reality.

610. IS NOT THAT ITSELF A THOUGHT WHICH ARGUES AND ESTABLISHES THAT THOUGHT IS NON-EXISTENT?

No. Thought is that which is concerned with the outside world alone. That faculty which takes even that thought as an object of discussion can never be called a thought in the same sense, though both might superficially appear alike.

The first, thought directed outwards, creates; and the second, called vidyā-vṛitti, destroys all that the first has created. That is its only function. When nothing is left to be destroyed, it vanishes and stands as the Reality itself.

611. FEELING A DREAM A DREAM

If during the experience of a dream you ever feel that it is only a dream, many seconds have not to elapse before you wake up from the dream.

Similarly, if you feel that this waking state is only like a dream, you are sure to wake up to the Reality soon.

14th October 1952

612. THE SHIFTING OF EMPHASIS

The shifting of emphasis, from the objective to the subjective part of your activities, is alone necessary to establish you in the Reality.

613. EXPRESSIONS LIKE ANGER AND THE SAGE

Anger can exist only where there is love behind it, supporting even that anger, or in other words anger is only distorted love. Look through the expression and see the background, or look through the anger and see the love behind it.

Love, as it is, is imperceptible. But anger has more visible symptoms. Therefore, if ever a Sage appears angry, take it only as a blessing in disguise; and try to see the love behind, through the visible anger.

614. HATE AND HOW TO DESTROY IT

It is a usual occurrence in worldly life that you love someone when he loves you and that you hate him when he hates you.

Looking at it more closely, you see that your response was dictated purely by the other's feelings alone. Therefore, you should also direct your feelings not to him, but only to his feelings. So you should hate the hate in him; or hate hating, wherever it be. Therefore naturally, you should hate the hate in you first. When that is done you will cease to hate anybody.

You can deal effectively with all feelings in this way.

615. THOUGHT A MISNOMER

Thought rises up in pure Consciousness beyond time; so thought cannot be anything other than Consciousness. Therefore, the usual conception of thought is wrong, or 'thought' is a misnomer.

616. WHO SEES?

Not you, but the see-er or perceiver. The perceiver alone perceives. Each perceiver that perceives is different from every other perceiver, as a perceiver.

But you say you saw the same form as you did yesterday. Both the perceiver of yesterday and the perceiver of today saw only the particular form before each of them. They were both ignorant of what the other perceived.

But there was some other principle that perceived the sameness of the two forms. It was not either of the former perceivers of form. And that principle that perceived the sameness did not perceive the form.

Question: How to transcend the wrong groove of thought?

Answer: When the 'How' disappears.

Question: Why am I not able to experience the Truth when I am away from Gurunāthan as deeply as when I am in his presence?

Answer: Because you give room to that unwarranted sense of awayness. You mistake the Guru to be the body and think him away or near. But he is never the body but Ātmā itself, and as such knows no nearness or away-ness. Be convinced of this Truth and your sense of away-ness will disappear, and your experience will become steady.

617. AN OBJECT POINTS TO CONSCIOUSNESS.

You generally say 'The form appears.' This statement has two parts: 'form' and 'appears'.

'Form' is objective and 'appears' is something subjective. To whom does it appear? Certainly to you. Therefore you light it up by your Consciousness. So every object points to Consciousness.

618. HOW TO INTENSIFY THE THOUGHT OF THE ULTIMATE?

Not like a yōgin, by applying your mind intensely to that thought.

But like a Jnyānin, relaxing all activity of the mind and merging even that last thought in the Truth itself. You have visualized the Truth in a particular state transcending the three usual states. To think of that Truth means to repeat that visualization once again, by going back to that same transcendental state. By going into that state again and again, you gradually become convinced of the Truth that that transcendental state really extends through all the usual states. Thus you become established in the Reality.

15th October 1952

619. POINTERS TO THE TRUTH

Everything is a pointer to the 'I'-principle or Truth. But Consciousness and Happiness are the ultimate pointers to the same.

620. KNOWING AND ITS ORGAN

If we consider knowing as a function, just like any of the senses, it should also have a corresponding organ and that is the 'I'-principle.

'I am seeing form.' Here 'form' is only another word for 'seeing'.

Similarly, when I say, 'I am knowing Consciousness', Consciousness is used only as another word for knowing.

621. CONSCIOUSNESS RECOMMENDED AS THE BEST OF THE THREE MEDIUMS FOR VISUALIZING THE ULTIMATE. WHY?

Consciousness alone tells you that Existence and Happiness are both implied in Consciousness and so the Truth, visualized through Consciousness, comprehends the Existence and Happiness aspects as well.

But it might be said that Existence and Happiness also might say the same about the other two. In that case, Existence and Happiness are indenting upon the services of Consciousness even to say so. They themselves are established only by the help of Consciousness. Otherwise Existence and Happiness would never have been noted at all.

622. TEARS OF SOFT DIVINE EMOTION ARE THE PANACEA FOR ALL YŌGIC ILLS.

623. ALL MENTATIONS TAKE ONE TO THE TRUTH

You can reach the background, the Ultimate, through any feeling provided you are sincere and consistent to the last.

Take, for example, hate. Here, you must continue to hate the creator as well as the created, including all the objects of your perceptions, thoughts and feelings – particularly your own body and mind and everything you call yours. Ultimately, when everything other than yourself is thus separated from you, you remain alone in your own glory as pure Consciousness and Happiness.

Looking back from that position, you find that all that you hated once was nothing but Consciousness and so you absorb it all into you as Consciousness. Thus hate is ultimately transformed into Love.

624. YOU DO NOT KNOW ANY SENSE OBJECT.

When you say you know a sense object, the word 'know' is grossly misplaced.

Form can be perceived by seeing alone. To see a form, seeing is essential, and to know a form seeing and Consciousness are both essential. But seeing is not in Consciousness. On the other hand, Consciousness is in seeing.

Therefore, it is wrong to say you know form.

16th October 1952

625. 'I AM WALKING.' WHAT DOES IT MEAN?

1. The statement implies that I was not walking, before starting to walk. Walking by itself was only something that temporarily came over me for a short period. Therefore it was distinct and separate from me, and so unreal.
2. From another standpoint, it may be said that I am 'walking' itself. I stand as 'walking' for the time being and there is nothing other than walking then.

> draṣṭra-darśana-dṛśyēṣu pratyēkaṁ bōdha-mātratā
> sāras tēna, tad anyatvaṁ nāsti kiñ cit kha-puṣpavat
>
> *Shrī Shankara*

Each of the triad [of see-er, seeing and seen, or doer, doing and deed] is nothing but Consciousness. That is the Truth about it. Everything other than that is like a flower in the sky – mere illusion or imagination.

626. PERSONAL AND IMPERSONAL

> You are the *personal*, when you are conscious of anything.
> You are the *impersonal*, when you are Consciousness itself.

627. ALL BODIES ARE MINE, OR NO BODY IS MINE.

When I am identifying myself with a body I call mine, all other bodies become alien to me as objects, the two together – my body and all other bodies – comprising the world.

But when what I call 'my body' is seen as my object, distinct and separate from me, naturally I have no other option left except to extend the same perspective to the whole world and group my body also along with the world of objects.

Then all bodies become mine, or no body is mine at all. In either case, I stand as the real background of the whole world.

628. Bliss seems to appear and disappear. Why?

It is not the bliss that comes and goes, but it is you, the ego, that often goes into the bliss which is your very nature, and comes out into the mind. Your ego alone is responsible for it.

17th October 1952

629. Is reading of the shāstras essential for realizing the Truth?

To this question Gurunāthan asked a counter question. Did the shāstras come from jnyāna or jnyāna from shāstras? Of course, the shāstras came from jnyāna. Then certainly, jnyāna can well be attained without the help of the shāstras, if one is guided by a Kāraṇa-guru.

(But before obtaining a Kāraṇa-guru, shāstras may sometimes be helpful to an aspirant and sometimes may be harmful as well. Because all shāstras may or may not point to the spiritual, and the aspirant may not have the right discrimination to choose or interpret.)

630. Nirvikalpa state

Some yōgins hold that you can experience the Absolute only by going into the nirvikalpa state. If this is so, it is not the highest; since it limits the Absolute to a state, however broad.

Therefore, in order to reach the natural state, which is the highest, you have also to transcend this last taint, namely the misunderstanding that you can experience the Absolute only through nirvikalpa samādhi.

631. Name and form

Name and form as such are not the Reality.

Name is non-existent without your being present. Form is also non-existent without your being present.

Therefore it is your presence alone that makes name and form real. So name and form are yourself, the Reality.

18th October 1952

632. SINCERITY AND EARNESTNESS

1. Suppose you were to be sentenced to jail if you fail to pay up a huge debt before 11 a.m. tomorrow. How you would strain and apply every nerve to make good that amount in the time given! Similarly, you should also feel that life is not worth living until you have visualized the ultimate Truth.
2. Complete dissatisfaction with your present state of life and a longing for something better still also show sincerity and earnestness.

633. VICĀRA-MĀRGA OR THE DIRECT PERCEPTION METHOD

This is the rationalistic exposition and establishment of Truth, put through the higher reason alone.

Spiritual 'vicāra' also creates sāttvic samskāras which are doubly strong. They destroy the worldly samskāras and at the same time themselves become stronger and stronger. When the worldly samskāras are thus obliterated, the spiritual samskāras also disappear and stand transformed as the background Consciousness.

Examining deep sleep more closely, it is found to be no state at all. The dream and waking states are only appearances on deep sleep.

It is in and through Me that all activities take place. But all the mischief is created by the attempt to objectify that non-doer Self and its experiences, exactly as we do with the activities of the ego.

634. SAMĀDHIS

The cosmological jnyāna sādhaka's samādhis are generally of six types:

1. bahir-dṛishyānuviddha [with sight outside]
2. antar-dṛishyānuviddha [with sight inside]
3. bahir-shabdānuviddha [with sound outside]

4. antar-shabdānuviddha [with sound inside]
5. bahir-nirvikalpa [with no diversity outside]
6. antar-nirvikalpa [with no diversity inside]

[See note 171 for explanation.]

26th October 1952

635. WHAT IS THE REALITY?

Whatever you feel 'is' and 'is not', in the realm of the mind and the sense organs, is the Reality. Existence, Consciousness and Happiness when limited by the mind become life, thought and feeling. So it can even be said that there is only one thing and only one name – thing and name being only synonyms.

You suppose that world exists there. But the 'there' exists in Consciousness, i.e. your Real nature. So the world appears and disappears in Consciousness, in You.

You need only to live as a man *in* this world, and not as a man *of* this world.

636. 'FEELING WITHOUT FEELING'

You say it was all Peace or Happiness in deep sleep. But neither the heart nor the mind was there to enjoy it. That experience is a typical instance of 'Feeling without feeling'.

Happiness or Peace alone is the subject, and all feelings or emotions are objects.

637. PURIFICATION OF THE MIND

The purification of the mind is sought only as a help to reach the Truth.

The best way to purify the mind is to think of the Truth which you are and which is purity itself. When you know you are the purest of the pure, all thought of purifying the mind drops away. Your earnestness and sincerity to reach the ultimate Truth is the best means of purifying your mind before realizing the Truth.

638. HOW TO KNOW THE GURU?

Answer: You need not and cannot know the Guru. If you know the Guru or if you do not know the Guru, in either case you cannot become a disciple. So you had better accept him when you feel you must.

639. DOES THE GURU ACCEPT ANYONE?

Answer: It is not the Guru personally who accepts anyone. The Guru accepts everyone who is sincere and earnest about knowing the Truth.

Therefore, if the aspirant has accepted the Ultimate Truth as his goal, certainly the Guru's acceptance of him is a foregone conclusion. It is the spontaneous corollary to the decision of the aspirant. If the aspirant is only prepared to open the mouth of spiritual earnestness, the nectar of advaita will come in from the Guru, uninvited.

640. THE REAL BONDAGE

Sense objects tie you down to the world. But when you come into contact with a Sage you get tied down to the Ultimate.

You can be relieved from the former bondage no doubt. But there is no escape from the latter.

641. WHO LIVES AND WHO DIES?

It is said that an ignorant man never dies, because he is immediately born again; and the Sage alone is dead, since he is never born again.

But from another point of view, the opposite is also true, that the ignorant man always dies and the Sage alone really lives.

Seeing the Guru's body is like trying to catch the figure on a silver screen.

27th October 1952

642. THE DREAM STATE

If the percept is proved to be non-existent as percept, the perceiver and perception both die at once. This is true equally of both the dream and waking states. Remove any one of the triad, and the other two also disappear immediately.

From the apparent perceiver, remove all that is perceivable or see-able and what remains is pure Consciousness.

643. MEMORY

Memory is the last link in the life of an individual, binding him to the world. What has never been perceived before is supposed to have been perceived by you in a dream, by a mere statement of the memory. But memory itself was not present in the dream. Therefore memory is no proof of any former perception.

If you have seen, you cannot remember, because the rememberer is different from the see-er. When memory – which is a mere appearance – is removed, the Reality alone remains over.

30th October 1952

644. FALLACY OF SUB-CONSCIOUS AND SUPER-CONSCIOUS STATES

The sub-conscious state: When the mind involuntarily and without any effort goes into a state where the mind dies, it is called a sub-conscious state – e.g. deep sleep.

Super-conscious state: When, as a result of an active effort of the mind, the objects gross as well as subtle vanish and you are thrown into a state where the mind becomes still, it is called the super-conscious state or samādhi.

But when you direct your attention to the Consciousness aspect of any activity, in any state, you transcend the mind and reach the Ultimate.

The taint of the 'sub-' and 'super-' consciousnesses lies in the samskāra that they are the cause of some other results, as ignorance is supposed to be the cause of the world.

Even when Consciousness appears limited to any object, know for certain that it is not limited. This knowledge takes you to the natural state.

Consciousness can never be 'sub' or 'super'. It is always Absolute.

645. WHAT ARE BONDAGE AND LIBERATION?

> When personality comes into the impersonal, it is *bondage*.
> When personality merges in the impersonal, it is *liberation.*

But when it is established – so far as you are concerned – that there can be nothing other than the impersonal, it is immaterial whether you stand as the personal or as the impersonal.

646. WHAT ARE THE RELATIVE ADVANTAGES OF THE TWO APPROACHES, NAMELY OF THE WITNESS AND OF PURE CONSCIOUSNESS?

The witness is intended only to help you to transcend or dispose of any objective appearance as object, perception or thought, if such comes in from the outside.

But sometimes the Consciousness aspect is considered better to contemplate the Absolute, because no activity of body, senses or mind is possible without the help of Consciousness. So the Consciousness aspect comes in without any strain on your part.

Consciousness is Happiness. We should always look upon it as conscious Happiness or happy Consciousness.

647. HAS THE SENSE OF POSSESSORSHIP ANY ADVANTAGE?

Yes it has. The personal God is first conceived as great on account of his possessing qualities of greatness. Thus the possessor is really the great one. But Ātmā, the ultimate background of all qualities, is the ultimate possessor.

As you begin to contemplate the qualities of greatness, you first begin to possess some of those qualities yourself and then gradually to transcend them. At last, when you begin to conceive of the iṣhṭa-dēva as the background of all qualities, you too rise to the same background and you stand as one with the Reality.

648. What is the fourth dimension? 'Time.'

Length, breadth and thickness are the three usual standards adopted to measure space. If this space is supposed to move in any direction other than length, breadth and thickness, it is called the 'fourth dimension'.

For the vēdāntin, this is 'time'.

31st October 1952

649. Your real faculties and their functions

Your real nature has two distinct aspects, namely Consciousness and Peace; and they seem to function as though they are two distinct faculties of knowledge and love. They absorb everything into you. When an object comes into direct contact with knowledge or love, the object is spontaneously transformed into knowledge or love and it loses its identity as an object.

So knowledge and love really destroy everything external. They make the name 'destroyer', given to Lord Shiva, significant and meaningful.

650. The origin and solution of questions

The ordinary man thinks that the objects of the world – gross as well as subtle, including body, senses and mind – are the legitimate outcome of the ultimate Truth. It is this erroneous conviction that gives rise to all manner of questions relating the objects to the Ultimate.

Whenever any question is asked touching the impersonal, what we have to do immediately is to refer to our own experience in the deep sleep state, which is purely impersonal. See if your question arises in the deep sleep state. If not, dismiss it summarily from your mind. In the world, each such question only multiplies diversity.

651. PLANES, CREATION AND THE TRUTH

The gross and subtle planes are distinct and separate, the one from the other. The gross cannot be perceived from the plane of the subtle, nor the subtle from the plane of the gross. We see both from beyond both. Both of them are the expressions of their real background.

There is a lot of confusion about creation itself. The subject and objects of a state are not created individually. They come to light simultaneously and also vanish simultaneously. Look at the dreamer and the dream. When the dreamer disappears, nothing of the dream remains over. Similarly, the mind and the world are also simultaneous creations, if creation is conceded in any sense.

There are some sets of people who try to cover their ignorance and white-wash the confusion by saying that the whole is a play of the Absolute. Play can have no other purpose than innocent pleasure, or in other words, enjoyment. So the Absolute will have to be admitted to be imperfect. So they make a sorry figure of the Absolute itself.

The real solution lies ahead, in adopting the right perspective, in examining the content of any one activity as representative of the whole universe. Such an examination proves that the content of every activity and therefore of the world is nothing but pure Consciousness. But this is possible only when one has visualized one's own real nature to be that pure Consciousness and Peace (under instructions from a Kāraṇa-guru). When one's own centre is thus established in the 'I', the illusion of the world appears simply frivolous. You continue to see the mirage, knowing that it is a mirage.

Consciousness appears limited only because we look through the mind which is itself limited.

652. THE EGO'S DUPLICITY

1. The ego is like a bastard born out of the illicit connection between the Absolute and the unreal. He does not appear any-

where during an activity, perception, thought or feeling. He appears only after the event, saying 'I have done it.'

2. The ego is like the bachelor who dreamt that he was married and brought forth children, and woke up a bachelor again. The bachelor represents the Consciousness part of the ego, and married life in the dream represents the illusion or the ego proper.

1st November 1952

653. WHAT IS THE PURPOSE OF TIME?

Time strives hard in this world not to connect events, but to disintegrate them and to establish diversity.

654. WHAT IS MEANT BY 'I KNOW I AM'?

'I know I am' is a single experience, recognized by all persons. It consists of two parts: 'I know' and 'I am'. The 'I am' can never be an object of 'I know'. Therefore both mean the same thing, and together are an experience in identity. When knowledge is objectless, it is not the subject either. These are the only two statements that require no proof.

Knowledge uninterrupted is Consciousness; happiness uninterrupted is Peace. Happiness is the first ebullition or sensation of Peace.

655. WHAT IS THE GUARANTEE THAT REALIZATION WILL NOT LAPSE?

If it is something you get at this moment you may very well lose it later. However, your liberation is not an escape from bondage but an expression of real freedom behind that apparent bondage, knowing that bondage also is but an expression of freedom.

Bondage is ego, and the essence of ego is my real self – Consciousness.

656. HOW A QUESTION OFTEN MISFIRES?

If you ask a question regarding a particular state, you throw the listener immediately into that state. If the question does not legitimately arise in that state, you cannot expect a regular answer to it.

If the questioner was not in the realm questioned, he has no authority to put that question; and even if answered, the questioner will never be able to understand it.

657. WHAT IS THE PRAKṚIYĀ OF QUALITIES AND THE QUALIFIED?

Qualities and the qualified are distinct and separate. Experience is the only proof of the reality of a thing. The qualities alone are experienced everywhere and the qualified is never experienced by anyone. Therefore the qualified as such is non-existent.

The qualities cannot exist by themselves without the presence of the qualified. Therefore the qualities are only mere appearances.

The qualities of the object alone being perceived and those qualities being proved to be unreal, the object as such is also unreal. The background of the changeless Reality (Consciousness) on which the changes, namely qualities, appear and disappear is alone what *is*.

It is only the expressed in the expression that makes you covet the expression.

658. ASKING QUESTIONS ABOUT REALIZATION OR THE ULTIMATE

In every question or comparison involving the Absolute, an attempt is made to objectify the Ultimate in however pure and sāttvic a manner. Just think where you were just at the point of putting that question. You were certainly beyond the phenomenal, and you were also beyond the ideas of the Absolute or of the experience implied in the question. That is certainly the stand of Truth. *Be there and you shall be free.*

Neither the question nor the answer really enriches you. The level at which you ask that question is beyond the relative. *Be that and you are free.*

This is true only of those who have heard the Truth from the Guru. But a real Sage and a Guru may answer such questions in such a way as to take you immediately, beyond the question and beyond the usual answer, to the right Absolute afresh, without allowing such a question to arise a second time.

659. HOW A BOY OF FIVE WAS ENLIGHTENED ABOUT DEATH. AND ABOUT GOD.

Ānanda, a boy of five, was incessantly tormented by thoughts and nightmares about death, which is supposed to be inevitable.

Gurunāthan: Were you not a small baby some years ago?

Boy: Yes. Yes.

G: Where is it now?

B: It is gone.

G: Where? Can you bring it back?

B: No. No. It is impossible.

G: So it is dead. Is it not?

B: No. But I am here.

G: I mean the baby you were once. It is gone for ever and will never be able to come back. That is what I mean by death. Did you cry when the baby was gone?

B: No. But till now I did not know it.

G: Similarly this boy will also die and you will be a youth. Then the youth also will die and you will become an old man. All these deaths one after the other you take pleasantly, don't you?

B: Yes, of course.

G: Then why do you cry and make noise when the old man dies? Is it also not like the many deaths you already had?

B: Yes. If this is the meaning of death, I shall not cry or be afraid of it any longer.

G: Why were you not sorry when the baby in you died? Because you knew that the baby alone dies and that you do not die. Similarly, it is only the old man in you that will die. You know that you will never die. You know your many deaths from your babyhood onwards. Similarly, you are the knower of the death of your old age also.

B: Yes! Yes! (With a luminous face.) Now I understand. I shall never more be afraid of death.

G: Now you are deathless, the Eternal. That is God. Do you follow me?

B: Yes, Gurunāthan. And the boy prostrated with tears dripping down on Gurunāthan's feet.

4th November 1952

660. WHAT IS PURITY?

Only the Truth or Ātmā is pure. Everything else is *anātmā* or impure. The body, senses and mind are all impure, each in its own way. Mind may be purified by effort to the extent of even getting merged in nirvikalpa samādhi. Still, it is mind and may be highly pure in the relative sense, but it is impure in the sense that it is *anātmā* still, and limited by time.

Doing good to others is no criterion of purity. It is the pleasure you derive from doing good that prompts you to do it. Suppose you are prohibited by law from doing good. Certainly you feel sad. So you have to transcend both pleasure and pain, evil and good.

So you can become ultimately pure only by visualizing the Reality and establishing yourself in it.

6th November 1952

661. RELIGIONS AND THEIR MISSION

Religion = Re + Lega
Re = Background; Lega = Binds

That which binds you to the background. But unfortunately no religion interprets it in this ultimate sense. All religions have the common goal to help man to lead a relatively moral, happy and contented life. Religion has been the greatest force and sanction in the world to keep man wedded to relative morality and goodness in life. It caters only to the satisfaction value, in response to the desires of man, varied as they are, according to countries, customs, manners and temperaments of people. Religion helps its adherents to prepare the ground by considerably attenuating their ego. When the ego is thus sufficiently attenuated so as to enable them to imbibe the ultimate Truth, the exceptional few get a *Kāraṇa-guru* who initiates them into the ultimate Truth.

So far as every religion goes, it is quite good and helpful to the followers. But Vēdānta comes in to supplement what religion had not been able to do. Thus Vēdānta is, strictly speaking, the fulfilment of all religions. It has no quarrel with any religion. It says to every religion: 'Please do not stop where you do. Come up higher still.'

Religious teachers and their instructions as a rule do not help one to go beyond the relative. Their goal itself is only the maximum of enjoyable happiness in duality. Some of the ancient devotees of Hindu personal Gods had the good fortune to get at the ultimate Truth in spite of the retarding influences of religion. After establishing themselves in the Truth, they looked back and analysed the stand they had formerly taken in religion. Now they could easily discover the slip they had made in religion. But they could not deny the immense purity of mind obtained through religion. This, of course, gave the devotee a good chance of imbibing the ultimate Truth, if only his attention was earnestly drawn towards Truth.

Therefore the ancient devotee-Sages codified and arranged the experiences they had had along the path of ultimate Truth, and added it on to Hindu religion in the name of '*darshana*', even though in fact the *darshana* was a complete negation of religion. *Darshana* is pure Advaita Vēdānta. The mere fact that it is added on to certain Hindu religious texts does not make it part of Hindu religion. It is the fulfilment of all religions, including the Hindu religion.

662. WITNESS

Question: Why am I asked not to contemplate the witness, nor deliberately take the role of the witness?

Answer: Because both are impossible.

Witnessing is done by the real 'I'-principle in the plane beyond the mind; and activities like contemplation, remembrance etc. take place in the mental realm. When you try to contemplate the witness, you have to drag down the witness from the Ātmic plane to the mental. Then the witness ceases to be the silent witness, and what you conceive of the witness is only a thought form.

Remembrance in the realm of the mind is made possible by the presence of the witness alone. But the witness, as it is, is never capable of being remembered. Just examine – to whom does an activity appear? Certainly to Me. Or, in other words, I light it up. So I am the *witness* of the whole triad (tripuṭi). 'The witness is an antidote to the poison of illusion.'

663. HOW DOES THE SAMSKĀRA OF UNHAPPY EVENTS BIND ONE?

In the phenomenal world of duality, unhappiness has its counterpart happiness, inseparably linked with it. It is this happiness aspect, though latent, that binds one.

Looking from a slightly different standpoint, unhappiness is unfulfilled desire or obstructed happiness. As such, the essence of unhappiness is nothing but happiness itself, and it is this happiness that binds one.

664. WHY IS SUICIDE UNIVERSALLY DECRIED?

Suicide is prompted by misery and desperation, and your want of boldness to face and overcome them. *Pauruṣha* does not come into play there.

665. IS THERE ANY SPIRITUAL VALUE IN FACING A PHENOMENAL PROBLEM?

The world is a bundle of knotty problems and life is an incessant fight to overcome them. The fight against each problem has two distinct aspects.

1. The effort to solve the problem, and
2. The solution itself.

It has to be understood that a sincere and consistent effort at solving the problem helps one much more than the solution itself. This effort successfully develops in one a genuine spirit of self-reliance, which alone helps one to reach the ultimate Truth.

For example, look at the famous 'Cārvāka' who is honoured as a *ṛiṣhi* in Hindu shāstras. He denied God and religion outright. He was sincere and earnest all through his striving, though he erred in his conclusions for other reasons. It was purely out of honest respect for his sincerity that he was honoured as a *ṛiṣhi*.

It is rightly said: 'A sincere atheist is much nearer the Truth than a superstitious bhakta.'

7th November 1952

666. WHEN AM I REALLY AND COMPLETELY LIBERATED?

On listening to the Truth expounded by the Guru, you visualize the Truth and you know that you are the Truth always.

The ignorant one does not know it and cannot know it. But if you claim you have become liberated, a taint clings to your claim. You have to remove that taint also, by knowing that you have only become aware of the fact that you were never bound, and so never liberated either. Then liberation is beyond time.

667. WHAT IS THE POSITION OF THE WITNESS, AND HOW AM I TO DO THE WITNESS EXERCISE?

The mind perceives objects – gross or subtle. The witness perceives the mind perceiving objects. The witness is the intermediary between the real 'I'-principle and the apparent 'I'-principle.

The witness has no body and so it has no outside. It has no mind and so it has no inside either. So the witness is always subjective, and the witnessed are all inside (meaning inside the mind) and not outside.

Everything past remains only as thought-forms, and thought-forms are cognized only by the witness. Therefore whenever any statement is made relating to the past, it means you were the witness; and if you say you had no mental activity, you were the witness to that absence also.

In the exercise of the witness aspect, you are not examining the witnessed at all. You are only eliminating – by the use of discriminatory logic – the known (witnessed) including body, senses and mind from the knower or witness. The knower is further proved to be nothing but knowingness or pure Consciousness, the real Self. Thus you rise gradually from the ego to the witness, and then you find that you are the right Absolute.

After visualization of Truth, conceding the existence of the world, the same exercise can be done in an improved form for the purpose of getting established in the Truth. You may begin by thinking that you are the witness as already known. But this thought does not continue as a thought. Because the witnessed being absent, the witness refuses to be objectified. Thus you stand as the disinterested witness, which you know to be nothing other than the Absolute. This perspective enables one to continue worldly activities effectively and disinterestedly.

668. WHAT IS THE SIGNIFICANCE OF THE OCHRE COLOUR OF THE SANNYĀSIN'S ROBE?

Ochre is the colour of fire; and it is supposed to represent the fire of pure knowledge, which destroys the stains of the mind – namely *tamas*, *rajas* and *sattva*. The external colour of the robe is expected to remind the *sādhaka sannyāsin* about his ultimate goal of Truth.

But to the householder on the direct path to the Truth, every object, thought, feeling or perception is an ochre coloured robe in effect, all pointing to his real nature.

For the sannyāsin who has reached the goal already, the robe is of no more personal service. Still, it continues to proclaim to the world the spiritual goal of his life and activities.

669. Real sleep

Strict inactivity is sleep.

In relaxation one should have something to hold on to. If you hold on to the 'I' and relax the senses and mind, you get to real sleep.

Let the mind be asleep to the whole world, and wakeful to the 'I'.

670. Psychic rheumatism and its remedy

There is a vicious habit of locating in the world outside the cause of one's own experiences of misery, and naturally attempting to apply the remedy also to the outside. This is just like applying a local remedy to the particular part of the body which suffers rheumatic pains. Of course the ailment responds favourably for the moment and disappears, but only to appear elsewhere soon after. This play of hide and seek is no permanent remedy at all. The only true remedy is to see that even that evil is itself lit up by Truth and is Truth in essence.

You have only to correct yourself. Then your thoughts, feelings, perceptions, body – in fact everything – will undergo a simultaneous change. In this perspective, misery loses all its sting, because you see Truth or Peace as the background even of the misery.

671. Spiritual larceny

The personal in man usurping what really belongs to the impersonal is called 'spiritual larceny'.

672. Is there any type of love in this world which may be considered ideal and accepted?

Yes. The love of the Guru for the disciple is the solitary example.

Even the love of a mother for her child is not disinterested, as long as she does not love any other child in the same way. No credit is really due to her on that score. She loves only her own flesh indirectly.

673. DOES NOT VIRTUE HELP ONE SPIRITUALLY?

Yes. But not always. Even virtue by habit is no virtue. Conscious virtue alone becomes a virtue, and it is the motive or sympathy of heart that really elevates one. Frugality for any purpose is no virtue. But frugality for frugality's sake alone is good, because it inculcates selflessness which attenuates the ego.

674. WHAT SHALL WE DO WHEN YOU ARE NO LONGER WITH US?

Answer: That which spoke to you will always be there to help you, and that which spoke to you should always be loved.

9th November 1952

675. PHYSICAL STRENGTH AND THE GOAL OF LIFE

Question: Some say India has degenerated by losing physical strength as a result of her giving up meat eating. Is this statement justifiable?

Answer: No. What do you mean by degeneration? Is sturdy health the goal of life? *No.* It is only a means to one's own perfection. And perfection is not in the planes of body, senses or mind, but beyond. Developing sturdy health at the sacrifice of the ultimate goal of life, is nothing short of foolishness.

The thought waves of one who has attained such perfection (a Sage), permeate the whole world and sustain it in Truth and justice. Thus a spiritual aspirant is preparing to save the whole of humanity, while the aspirant to physical health is preparing for a physical war of defence or offence, in the name of self-preservation, without caring even for a moment to know what the 'Self' is. The Sage who knows the 'Self' finds nothing else to be preserved.

676. FOOD AND ITS REACTIONS

The gross part of the food goes to the body and the subtle part goes to the mind. Foods like flesh and fish are purely *tāmasic*. They make the mind also *tāmasic*: incapable of rising to *sāttvic* heights and to higher logic.

We are also responsible morally for the *himsa* (injury) we cause in that connection. The butcher, the seller and the eater all partake of the *himsa* caused by meat-eating.

You might ask if this is not also true of consuming vegetables. No, the rudiments of mind and feeling begin only with animals. Vegetables have no such active thought or feeling which can react upon us and cause us misery.

11th November 1952

677. HOW TO DISTINGUISH BETWEEN THE DEEP SLEEP STATE AND THE SAHAJA (NATURAL) STATE?

Before explaining this, the terms Ātmā and non-ātmā (anātmā) have to be defined.

Ātmā is the real 'I'-principle beyond the mind and so beyond time also.

Non-ātmā (also called anātmā) comprehends everything objective, including thoughts, feelings, perceptions and actions.

1. tannēyuṁ tānallennukāṇunnavayēyuṁ
   maṙannirikkunnatŭ "nidra"

Forgetting oneself and forgetting the non-ātmā is *sleep.*

2. tānallennukāṇunnavayēyuṁ tannēyuṁ
   maṙannirikkunnu ennuḷḷatŭ tānallātta-
   vayetannilākki, tannēyuṁ maṙannirikkuka-
   yākunnu, ennaṙiyunnatŭ "vastusthiti"

He who knows that the forgetting of non-ātmā is merging the non-ātmā in the Ātmā, is in the reality.

3. tannēyuṁ tānallennukāṇunnavayēyuṁ
   maṙannirikkunnatŭ tannilāṇennukāṇu-
   nnatŭ "vastusthiti"

He who sees that the forgetting of non-ātmā and the apparent 'I' (wrongly called Ātmā) takes place in the Ātmā itself, is in the Reality.

4. tānallennu kāṇunnavaye tannilākki
   tannēyuṁ maṙannirikkunnatŭ "vastusthiti"

He who deliberately merges the non-ātmā in Ātmā and remains forgetting himself, is in the Reality.

These four approaches are only slightly different from each other.

678. WHAT IS DISINTERESTED ACTION? HAS IT ANY TEST?

Disinterested action is not possible to the ego. An action becomes disinterested only when you stand as the witness beyond the doership and enjoyership. The renunciation of enjoyership (the fruits of action) takes you only half way to the Truth. The other half, namely doership, has next to be renounced, if the action is to be made strictly disinterested.

There is no definite standard or test by which the disinterestedness of an action can be ascertained; because all standards and tests are mental, and disinterestedness concerns only the witness which is beyond the mind. The activity of a jīvan-mukta, which is disinterested action, cannot on the surface be distinguished from that of an ignorant man. Something vague can be said about disinterested action, but all that will only be a mere caricature of the Truth. There are, however, several tests and characteristics by which actions that are not disinterested can be distinguished.

Disinterested actions do not create a habit. At the same time they are performed with the greatest care and attention to detail. If you cannot exploit a particular action for subsequent pleasure or pain, that action may also be considered disinterested. The mere memory of such actions does not awaken any spirit of interest in you.

Interested actions have exactly the opposite effect. They bring in other thoughts or feelings in their train, and they create all sorts of habits. If an action lacks in perfection in any manner, or if its memory tends to create any kind of interest in you, you may be sure that such actions are also interested. If the action was prompted by the ego in the form of saṁskāras or the like, or if the action was done to the satisfaction of the ego, such action is also interested.

679. SHAKESPEARE'S SPIRITUAL POSITION IN THE LIGHT OF VĒDĀNTA

Shrī Ātmānanda: In my opinion, Shakespeare was a realized soul (in the language of the west) or a jīvan-mukta (in the language of India). Spirituality is not the monopoly of any nation or country. Conditions might be favourable or partially favourable to the development of spirituality in one part of the world, and the means adopted might not be perfect in all places. But that does not preclude the possibility of rare individuals coming to perfection.

It is the law of nature, without exception, to provide the environment necessary for the fulfilment of the spiritual thirst for perfection in an individual in any part of the world, if the aspirant is sincere and earnest enough. Therefore the Sages have said: 'If you really want to know the Truth, you shall have it.'

Shakespeare was one such. No intellectual standards can ever test the spiritual greatness of a jīvan-mukta. Shakespeare, in his dramas, has created diverse characters of conflicting types, each with a perfection possible to perfection alone. A writer who has an individuality and character of his own can successfully depict only characters of a nature akin to his own. It is only one who stands beyond all characters, or in other words as *witness*, that can be capable of such a wonderful performance as Shakespeare has done. Therefore I say Shakespeare must have been a jīvan-mukta.

14th November 1952

680. IS THERE ANY DIFFERENCE BETWEEN THE ENJOYMENT OF HAPPINESS BY A LAYMAN AND A SAGE?

Yes, of course. The layman's enjoyment is broken, because he takes it to be the product of objects. But the Sage's enjoyment is continuous; because he knows it to be the expression of his own Self, which never disappears.

18th November 1952

681. WHY IS NOT THE SAME *PRAKRIYĀ* APPLICABLE TO ALL ASPIRANTS?

Different people attribute different meanings to the word 'I'. This is because differences of temperament and perspective place them at different levels of understanding.

Some persons take 'I' to denote the ego, a psycho-physical organism. The 'I' of this way of thinking must be removed in order to reach the Ultimate.

But in the case of some others, the 'I' is used only to denote the witness. In their case, the 'I' need not be removed at all. For them, it is enough if the witnessed is separated from the witness 'I'. Then the 'I' stands alone as the witness, and the witnessed is no longer in the witness. Therefore even the term 'witness' becomes meaningless and the 'I' stands as the Ultimate in all its glory.

For these two different types of aspirants, different *prakriyās* are inevitable. There are many other types also, who need still different *prakriyās*.

682. HOW TO ANSWER A QUESTION AND UNDERSTAND THE ANSWER ARIGHT?

If any question is examined properly, you will see the stamp of the individual soul in it. Answering a question from the level of the question itself does not enrich you. The answer must be given from a higher plane, and the questioner must be prepared to understand such an answer.

When you say you comprehend something, you stand clearly beyond it. You can comprehend only that which is below you. The knower is always beyond the known.

683. WHY CAN'T THE REALITY BE EXPRESSED?

Answer: Can you express your feelings? *No.* If so, can you hope to express the Reality – your real nature – which is far beyond even feelings?

tannatilla 'paranuḷḷu kāṭṭuvān
onnumē naran upāyam īśvaran

[God has not given anyone
a means to show what's in one's heart
to someone other than oneself.]

Kumāran Āśān, Naḷinī

21st November 1952

684. CRAZE TO IMPROVE THE WORLD

Question: Looking around, we see individuals, communities and governments making herculean efforts to improve the world. Is this all in vain?

Answer: The question itself is spiritually ill-conceived and illogical. The question admits that you look out through your senses and see a sense world which is imperfect. You want to make it perfect by work which is also outside yourself.

Your sense world is inseparably connected with you through your senses. The apparent imperfection of the world is all the imperfection of the perspective that perceived the world. Apply the remedy at the source and perfect your perspective first. When you become perfect, your perspective also becomes perfect, and simultaneously the world of your perception will also appear perfect.

When you look through the senses, gross objects alone appear; when you look through your mind, thoughts or feelings alone appear; and when you look through Consciousness which is perfect, Consciousness alone appears and that is perfect.

The appearance of the world changes in accordance with the stand you take and the instrument you utilize. No amount of whitewashing can make your wall white, as long as you look through your green goggles. When one becomes perfect, one becomes impersonal; and the impersonal cannot attach any reality to the personal, much less come down to improve it.

685. WHEN DO *BHAKTI* AND *JNYĀNA* BEGIN TO APPEAR?

We see in some children a peculiar sense of earnestness and sincerity, even in their play. It is this same sense in some cases that develops into earnestness and sincerity for God. In due course, this earnestness and sincerity expresses itself as *bhakti* or *jnyāna*, as occasion demands.

686. HOW TO DISTINGUISH BETWEEN BEAUTY AND THE BEAUTIFUL?

Beauty is in you, always as yourself the source of all; and the beautiful is now and here. Beauty is impersonal, and the beautiful is personal.

When you are attracted by the beauty in any object, you assume there is a background for that beauty. But, on examination, you find that no such support exists. So you see that there is only beauty and not the beautiful, and that beauty is your own Self. When you become unconscious of the beautiful, you come into contact with the beauty which is your own nature, and you say you enjoy it.

Non-ātmā is never an object for your consideration. All your attention should be directed to the Truth alone, and you will slowly get established there.

687. SAGES AS WELL AS SĀDHAKAS OF ALL TYPES RADIATE AROUND THEM THE FLAVOUR OF THEIR EXPERIENCES.

In the presence of a profound devotee, you experience a trace of the happiness from the atmosphere which is charged with the happiness enjoyed by the devotee. In the presence of a yōgin, your mind, unawares, becomes slightly concentrated.

In the presence of the Sage, you feel the sublime peace that radiates from his real nature. It takes possession of you, and does not leave you even for hours after leaving his presence.

A jīvan-mukta is one who is neither bound nor free, but beyond both.

688. IS THERE ANY MEANS TO THE ABSOLUTE?

Answer: If *samādhi* could be used as a means to reach the Absolute, your daily activity here and now can equally well be made a means to reach the Absolute.

Samādhi becomes a means to the Absolute only when the content of samādhi and your real nature are expounded by a Kāraṇa-guru to be pure Consciousness and Peace. Possessing this perspective, if you examine any particular activity of yours, you reach the Absolute that way also with less effort.

> citraṁ vaṭatarōr mūlē vṛddhāś śiṣyā gurur yuvā
> gurōstu maunaṁ vyākhyānaṁ śiṣyā 'stu chinna-saṁśayāḥ

Shrī Shankara, Dakṣhiṇāmūrti-stōtram, *Dhyāna-shlōka 3*
– at start of Surēshvarācārya's Manasōllasa

This ancient verse pictures, under the hospitable shade of a spreading banyan tree, a happy group – a young Guru and some old disciples. The Guru keeps absolute silence of body and mind, and expounds thereby the ultimate Truth, and the disciples are at once enlightened.

But why is the Guru pictured as young and the disciples as old? Truth is beyond time and ever-blooming, and therefore eternally young. The disciples, by age-long study of several shāstras and diverse exercises and experiences, all worldly, have become prematurely old and grey. They were enlightened by this ever-blooming Truth one fine day; and when Truth was experienced, they found it was quite uncaused.

Truth can never be communicated by anybody. If so, Truth becomes a commodity, capable of being handled by somebody; and consequently Truth becomes inferior to him who handles it.

The enlightenment was spontaneous; and the Guru in apparent silence was Truth itself, beyond body and mind.

23rd November 1952

689. WHAT IS THE PURPOSE OF MORALITY?

Morality, if followed intelligently and with earnestness, takes one to the egoless state, just like any other path of devotion, yōga etc. The path of *pati-vratya* (service and chastity, one-pointed love and devotion to the husband) adopted by the gems of the womanhood of ancient India was nothing other than this path of morality. Ancient history abounds in stories of arrogant yōgins of great powers and reputation and even the lords of the Trinity begging at the feet of such ladies for their thoughtless misdeeds.

Morality has the touch of the Absolute in it. The outer covering is immaterial. It is the touch of the Absolute alone that matters. That attenuates the ego every time you come into contact with it. So morality has to be observed, but without any eye on its fruits.

690. DEVOTION TO THE GURU

The disciple who takes the Guru to be the formless Ultimate, is taken to the right Absolute.

However, the disciple whose sense of discrimination is less developed, but who has a deep devotion to the person of the Guru, may well take the Guru to be the form. His love and devotion compensate abundantly for the lack of discrimination; and he is easily taken through the form to the formless, and thence to the Absolute even without his knowing it. Revered Vaṭivīshvarattamma – an illiterate woman devotee near Cape Commorin, who became a renowned Sage by her sincere and earnest devotion to her Guru (*Amma-svāmi*, who was a great yōgin Sage) – is a standing testimony to this class of Sages.

Though the disciple directs his love to the person of the Guru, the reciprocation comes from the impersonal which is the abode of love. When your limited love is directed to the Guru, who is love unlimited, the limitation of your love vanishes automatically.

The result can be perfect only if the Perfect is engaged in it.

691. WHAT IS THE NATURE OF THE 'GURU-DISCIPLE RELATIONSHIP'?

From the standpoint of the Guru – who is impersonal – he has no disciple. But he allows the disciple to take him as his Guru. That is all. The impersonal is not connected with the personal; but the personal is connected with the impersonal. The Truth is the world; but the world is not the Truth.

The snake is always connected with the rope. But the rope has no connection with the snake at all.

692. I AM NOT CHANGELESS. WHY?

I perceive changes. To make this possible, I must have been the changeless background perceiving the changes.

But changelessness only means the absence of change. They are opposites. A taint of the change lingers in the very conception of changelessness. So I must transcend changelessness also, in order to be in my real nature.

Therefore, the path to the Ultimate lies from the changing, through the changeless, to the beyond.

693. WHERE IS FEELING?

'Feeling' is the generic of all feelings. The generic feeling is the oneness in the diversity. It is not in the heart. It is the right Absolute.

694. HOW ARE ACTIONS AND IDEAS RELATED?

Ideas, repeated often, express themselves as actions – we might call them 'solidified ideas'. Other ideas, which are not repeated, remain as ideas 'not solidified'. These two might look different on the surface, but in essence they are the same.

24th November 1952

695. WHY CAN I NOT SEE THE WORLD WHEN I AM IN CONSCIOUSNESS?

When you see the tree, you stand as the tree. When you think of the tree, you stand as that idea. When you stand as Consciousness, both tree and idea of tree merge into Consciousness, leaving you as you are.

You cannot see the world from Consciousness, because Truth can never see falsehood. Look at the deep sleep state and everything will become clear.

696. HOW TO ANNIHILATE THE EGO?

If you work against the ego, the ego most skilfully shifts its place to a higher ground.

Therefore direct your thought to your real nature, Consciousness, where the ego cannot reach. Then the limitations of thought disappear, and thought remains as Consciousness, pure. So you see that even as thought, it was not thought, but Consciousness in content.

This is the best way to annihilate the ego.

697. HOW CAN I BECOME A TRUE DISCIPLE?

You can become a disciple only in three regular stages.

1. You regularly set apart some part of the day to pray to your Guru to learn to love him.
2. You feel without feeling that the Guru is the background of all your actions, perceptions, thoughts and feelings.
3. You become a true disciple only at the highest level, when your personality vanishes and you stand as the impersonal Truth. Then there is no duality of any kind, like the Guru or disciple or relationship.

When you say, see or think you are a disciple, you are a witness to the discipleship and not a disciple.

698. WHAT IS CONSCIENCE?

Answer: It is really a coward. Repeated actions create habit. Repeated or condensed habit produces character often called 'conscience'. Those faults it has not strength enough to prevent, it has no right to accuse.

The appearance of a worse man makes a bad man appear a good man. Following one's artificial conscience is not the way to real progress.

699. WHAT ARE SLAVERY AND FREEDOM?

The ordinary man is a slave to the body, senses and mind. This slavery is dissolved only in the alchemy of your love for the free (the Guru or freedom).

'*Freedom*' is the surrender of slavery at the feet of the Guru (the Absolute).

Usually it is slavery or bondage that craves for freedom, but often it is found unwilling to shake off bondage itself when freedom comes.

Incessant thought of bondage is not the way to transcend it. So turn your attention to real freedom or the Absolute and the bondage dies.

700. IT IS SAID THAT I AM A LOVING AND CONSCIOUS BEING. WHAT DOES IT MEAN?

Being: It is the generic form of all one's experience; it is divorced of all qualities and distinctions. Then one comes to existence pure, which has no parts. This most expanded form comprehends all narrower denominations.

You admit that you are a loving being. Then the love goes into the being. It means that you are love itself, or that 'being' is love.

1st December 1952

701. THE NEED AND APPLICATION OF THE WITNESS ASPECT

You are asked to do deliberately what you are doing unknowingly now. Take note of the fact that you are already and always the witness.

Remembrance is the faculty which makes life appear a connected whole. Remembrance means knowing first and recalling afterwards, without considering that the agents are different. Knowing belongs to the witness and remembrance belongs to the mind. The two activities take place in two different planes.

But knowing is strictly not an activity. Usually, all activities – of body, senses and mind – are attributed to the 'I', the background. But really the 'I' can never be involved in all this. This false identification is the root of all trouble and misery.

If you can, in any way, cease to continue this false identification, you are saved. To do this, the witness aspect is brought forward. The witness is always silent and changeless. Objects or activities are not emphasized at all in the witness aspect. The witness is unconcerned and can never be brought out for evidence regarding facts. When you stand as the witness, you see that the things witnessed are not in the witness. So you transcend all duality.

Thus standing as the witness, being all alone, you stand as the right Absolute itself. The witnessing is superimposed upon the Reality, but this does not injure you.

3rd December 1952

702. IMPORTANCE OF INTELLECT

Question: Why is intellect considered all important in the world at large?

Answer: The vast majority of people in the world attribute reality to the apparent sense-world, and they live practically out of themselves. All the philosophies, sciences, arts etc. of the world are trying to explain phenomenal problems in terms of the world itself, utilizing the faculty of intellect as the instrument.

Of course the intellect is the highest faculty endowed upon man for his enquiry and traffic inside the world; and the decisions of intellect are accepted as final beyond question. This is why intellect is considered all important in the phenomenal world.

But to the vēdāntin, intellect, though subtle, is only an object like any other object; to be examined for its content (*svarūpa*) from the standpoint of pure awareness, and disposed of as mere appearance.

703. THE HISTORY OF ADVAITA

The Upaniṣhads are the oldest records of Advaitic Truth. It flourished first in North India. Subsequently, South India might have won the ascendancy over the North.

But what is true of India is true of every country; and men must have visualized the Truth in their own way in many countries. For example, the teachings of *Taoism* come very near Advaita. *Jnyānins* may differ vastly in their ways of life and in their manner of expounding the Truth; but they have much in common with Advaita.

5th December 1952

704. HAS THE WAY OF LIFE ANY BEARING UPON TRUTH?

The ways of life of Shrī Kṛiṣhṇa, Shrī Shuka, Shrī Rāma and Shrī Vasiṣhṭha were all different. But they were all equal as jīvan-muktas.

> kṛṣṇō bhōgī śukas tyāgī nṛpau janaka-rāghavau
> vasiṣṭhaḥ karma-kartā ca tēṣāṁ mukti-sthitis samā
>
> [Kṛishṇa enjoyed the fruits of life.
> Shuka renounced what others sought.
> Rāma and Janaka were kings.
> Vasiṣhṭha practiced formal rites.
> But in that freedom each attained,
> they are the same. Each is that one.]

[Source of quotation uncertain]

Answer: Yes. As individuals, they were all different. They were not Sages *as such.* The Sage was Kṛiṣhṇa, the Sage was Shuka, the Sage was Janaka, the Sage was Rāma, and the Sage was Vasiṣhṭha. The Sage is only one, and that is the Truth. But, as living entities, they were all different.

705. HOW TO MAKE ONE UNDERSTAND THE SAGE?

It is so easy. Just direct your mind to your deep sleep. The Sage is there in deep sleep. The Sage is exactly as you are in your deep sleep. If any question is put about the Sage, just ask the questioner the same question regarding his role in the deep sleep state.

Even when you are engaged in all your daily activities, does the man in you ever get disturbed? No. Similarly, the Sage is undisturbed by any of his apparent activities. When correctly examined, of course you will see there are no activities either.

Diversity can never stand scrutiny. Then why bother about activities? There is only one activity. And if activity is only one, it cannot remain as activity. It is the Reality itself.

706. HOW TO FACE ANY PROBLEM?

The appearance of questions, after one has visualized the Truth, is only the futile attempt of the ego to postpone the imminent date of its own extinction.

Your real nature has been proved to you beyond doubt. See if any problem disturbs your centre, and then alone try to solve it.

When a problem arises, even on the phenomenal level, direct your attention to the '*problem*' and lose yourself in the problem. Then you will find that the result will be not the merging of yourself in the pain or problem as usual, but the merging of the problem in the 'I'. The 'I', as sufferer, becomes the suffering itself, and no pain is experienced as such.

When a question arises in your mind, see if it has any intimate connection with – or bearing upon – your real nature or the 'I'-principle. If it has not, leave it to itself. If it does bear any connection, answer it and rise by it. If a question serves to establish duality, leave it alone.

If you feel that you would be spiritually enriched by answering a question, accept it, answer it and be enriched by it. If not, leave it alone.

6th December 1952

707. HOW DOES REMEMBRANCE FUNCTION?

How do you try to remember a pleasurable sensation that you have had? You think of all the details, like the place and circumstances which you suppose were connected with it, till the mind comes to a climax preceding the enjoyment sought. Just then, all the antecedent thoughts vanish, and you are thrown into that pleasurable sensation again.

Similarly, with regard to repeating the experience of Truth you have once had, you have to begin likewise recounting the place, circumstances etc., till at last all your thoughts vanish and you are thrown into that same experience again. Don't desire the expression, but direct your attention always to that which is expressed. Expressions ultimately die, in order that the expressed may be there as the Absolute.

708. WHEN I CONSIDER I AM IN SORROW, WHY IS THERE PAIN?

1. The reaction can take place in two ways: one emphasizing sorrow, and the other emphasizing the 'I'. In the former case, you become sorrow and emphasize the 'sorrow' part. But if you emphasize the 'I' part, the sorrow becomes you; and then sorrow vanishes, leaving you alone.

   Sorrow has parts, and you have no parts. When sorrow becomes you, it ceases to have parts and becomes one: which is Happiness – the background – your Self.

2. Because at that moment you are not that, you are not sorrow. Sorrow brings in trains of objects. When the objects are removed, sorrow is transformed into bliss, the background.

   You want others to come in, in order to sorrow.
   Sorrow must cease to be, in order to become you.

The heart that enjoys happiness is not the heart that suffers pain; because pain is something objective, and happiness is something subjective.

The consciousness which perceives consciousness of objects is not pure Consciousness.

You have been taken to the Ultimate; all questions have been solved on the way. Now ask a question – if you can – only from the level of the Ultimate.

709. WHAT IS THE SECRET OF SUICIDE?

Suicide is not the result of hate, as it is ordinarily taken to be. But it is only a crude method of dispensing with the body, when the body happens to stand as an impediment to freedom or happiness. He who commits suicide is not the one that dies. The killer can never be the killed. So the killer remains over, even after the suicide (killing). Therefore suicide – in the sense it is understood – is a myth.

710. IS THERE ANYTHING REDEEMING OR ENRICHING IN DOMESTIC LOVE?

Answer: Yes, but not in all types.

The love of father and mother for the child is selfish, because instinct and relationship of the flesh make it selfish to the core. Sentimentality is always connected with objects. If what you call love produces a limited feeling, it is certainly no love.

But the love of husband and wife can be made selfless; because they have no such things in common before marriage, and instinct does not come into play. If you succeed in loving your partner as your Self, it clears the way for the love towards any other individual likewise. Thus your love easily becomes universal and therefore objectless. This is the Reality. You will need the touch of the Guru at the last stage, and you instantly become a *jīvan-mukta*.

This was the path adopted by the *pati-vratās* (the celestials who are the ideals of chastity and husband-worship) in ancient India, and they attained their goal smoothly and effortlessly.

711. WHAT IS THE BENEFIT OF TACKLING QUESTIONS, EVEN AFTER VISUALIZATION?

If, after visualizing the Truth beyond all doubt, any question arises, you are asked to look back to the source and level of the question. You are immediately referred back to the background. Thus it takes you to the Ultimate, every time questions are answered this way. It establishes you in the background more easily than in any other way.

7th December 1952

712. WHAT IS THE ACTIVITY OF THE 'I'?

No. The 'I' has no activity whatsoever.

I am the Reality. To be active, 'I' must get out of the Reality, for the time being. Because activity is only in duality. But can you ever get out of the Reality? *No.* Then all search for Truth becomes meaningless. Has the rope ever become the snake? *No.* Then where is the problem?

Nothing you have understood in a drunken mood can ever take you out of drunkenness. Such is the question 'Why?' Get rid of the poison, and the question disappears.

713. CAN ADVAITA BE APPLIED UNIVERSALLY?

No. It is forbidden in one context alone. That is in the presence of the Guru. Everywhere else, you can boldly apply advaita and rise to the Ultimate.

It is true that advaita is the highest. But it was there all through time, and it did not come to your notice or help you in the least. It needed only a *single ray, through a word, from the flood-light of the physical Guru*, to enable you to see advaita and to visualize the Reality. The disciple, who has a throb in his heart, does not need a thought to trample down the question pertaining to the Guru, the moment it is heard. Therefore even the thought of oneness with the Guru is unimaginable to a true disciple, even from an academic standpoint.

> nādvaitaṁ guruṇā saha
> [see note 466]

Shrī Shankara, Tattvopadesha, 87

> rajjv ajñānād bhāti rajjau yathā 'hiḥ
> svātmā-jñānād ātmanō jīva-bhāvaḥ .
> dīpēnai 'tad bhrānti-nāśē sa rajjur
> jīvō nā 'haṁ dēśikō 'ktyā śivō 'ham ..

> [By misperception of a rope
> a seeming snake gets to appear
> upon the rope that's wrongly seen.
> So too, by wrongly seeing self,
> a seeming person there appears –
> created by imagining,
> from what is self and self alone.

> When the illusion is destroyed –
> by light that shows what's truly seen –
> there is no snake, but just the rope.
> So too, by what my teacher says,

I am no seeming person here.
I am just consciousness alone –
found absolute, all by itself.]

Shrī Shankara, Advaita-pancaratnam, 1.2

The higher shāstras endorse this view. So far as the disciple is concerned, the Guru is the light that firsts lights up even the Reality.

714. HOW DO I REALIZE?

You realize not by renouncing the world, nor by allowing the world to be. But you only take note of the fact that you are always standing as that Truth.

8th December 1952

715. WHAT DOES 'TAKE NOTE OF' MEAN? IS IT ACTIVE OR PASSIVE?

It is neither active nor passive. It takes place on the borderline of mind and the Reality. You may start it as a simple thought, and allow that thought to expire, leaving you as you are. You have grasped it already. Just make that grasping stronger. Hitherto, you did not recognize this fact. But now recognize it. By such a recognition, the ego is immediately transformed into the Truth.

If it is the *cure* you need, information about the composition and qualities of the medicine is not relevant.

'Taking note', at the mental level, may be taken to mean only remembering; though even remembering immediately vanishes, giving place to the Reality.

716. WHAT HAPPENS WHEN I SEE?

When you see, the seeing alone is there and not knowledge. But of course, there is knowledge in the seeing.

So far as seeing is concerned, that knowledge part is not taken into account at all. When the seeing is completed, form vanishes and knowledge dawns. Not knowledge of the form, but knowledge pure.

Thus every object ties you down not to unreality, but to the Reality itself. Therefore every activity, in fact, destroys its object by making it vanish into the Reality.

When 'I see' is examined closely, seeing vanishes and you will be forced to say 'I do not see'. But ordinarily, you do not push far enough, in order to examine the latter statement. When examined, the 'I do not see' vanishes likewise and there is only 'I am.' Thus the Truth is beyond both 'I see' and 'I do not see.'

So regarding any object, you come to the conclusion that there is 'nothing'. Here '*nothing*' is the name of the *Reality*. Therefore in order to understand the significance of any activity, one has to transcend the opposites.

717. WHEN IS LIBERATION COMPLETE?

Only when you are liberated from liberation as well. Liberation is only the end of bondage or its opposite. As such, liberation carries the taint of bondage in itself and is relative. So you have to transcend the opposites, bondage and liberation, in order to reach the Absolute.

Till then, liberation is not complete.

718. THE FALLACY OF 'TIME'

1. Time is believed to be composed of the past, present and future. Of these three, the past is past only in reference to the present and the present is present only in relation to the past, future is future only in reference to the present. So all three being interdependent, even for their very existence, it has to be admitted by sheer force of logic that none of them is real. Therefore, *time is not*.

2. Experience is the only criterion by which the reality of anything can be decided. Of the three categories of time, past and future are not experienced by any, except when they appear in the present. Then it can be considered only as present.

   Even this present – when minutely examined – reduces itself into a moment which slips into the past before you begin to perceive it, just like a geometrical point. It is nobody's experience. It is only a compromise between past and future as a meeting point.

Thus present itself being only imaginary, past and future are equally so. Therefore, *time is not*.

719. Irrelevancy of questions about Reality

When you ask why, when, where etc., in relation to the Reality, you take it for granted that why, when, where etc. are more real than Reality itself. This position is absurd. Therefore no such question can be asked, relating to the Reality.

720. Why is not the Sage always merciful?

I may admit that practice of mercy is one of the many ways suggested to enable one to become one with all others. But if one has attained that goal by other means, what more need is there for further practice of mercy in case of that one?

721. What is the clue to one's own real nature?

The only clue given to us by the unseen, to understand one's own real nature, is the 'deep sleep state'. That alone is ours in fact.

9th December 1952

722. Nescience (also called 'ignorance' or 'māyā') is a misnomer.

The only phenomenal experience we have is the knowledge of an object, gross or subtle. If the object is removed from the knowledge of the object, what remains over can only be pure Knowledge or Consciousness. Similarly, when all objects are removed from the knowledge of objects in deep sleep, what remains over is nothing but the same Consciousness, pure.

Therefore, to say that there is ignorance in deep sleep is absurd. Because ignorance can never co-exist with Consciousness. If ignorance is construed as absence of things, absence can only succeed and never precede the perception itself. For this reason also, ignorance is a misnomer. Many more arguments can be adduced to prove the same thing.

11th December 1952

723. How to fight dislike towards another?

There is no doubt that the man and dislike of him are entirely distinct and separate, one from the other. It is the dislike alone and not the man that really troubles one. That dislike is purely mental. To get over that dislike, you must necessarily transcend the mental level. That is the only possible way.

Or, if you dislike another, you can rationally analyse the dislike and prove it to be none other than yourself, and the dislike is immediately transformed into love.

724. What is beauty, and its relation to the beautiful?

Beauty is inside, and is impersonal. But inside there is only the real Self, which is also impersonal. There cannot be two impersonals inside, because the impersonal is beyond duality and therefore Beauty is the real Self.

When an object is anointed with the gild of your own Self, you like it and call it beautiful. Thus a child, however ugly by common consent, appears beautiful to its mother. You consider something beautiful, and others consider other things beautiful. But when the object is removed, the beauty stands alone and permanent. Therefore, if the beauty and the beautiful are separated by some means, beauty is left alone and supreme. Everything beautiful is only a symbol directing you to the Self, as beauty in you.

12th December 1952

725. Is a Sage's life beneficial to all?

By 'life' we mean the activities of life. They fall into three categories: physical, mental, and conscious or Ātmic.

Mental activities are accepted to be much more strong and effective than the physical.

But the last, though extremely rare, is the one pertaining to the Sage. They are self-effulgent activities of light and love, and their effect is imperceptible to the naked eye, unlike those of the preceding ones. They come from the Sage spontaneously, unasked. It is such activities alone that keep the moral balance of the world, even in the midst of all chaos.

726. WHAT IS THE TEST OF MY PROGRESS TOWARDS THE TRUTH?

Your increased sincerity and earnestness for the Truth, which you alone can know, is the best test possible.

727. THE SAGE SOMETIMES SEEMS TO COME DOWN TO A LOWER LEVEL IN ANSWERING QUESTIONS. IS IT A COMPROMISE?

No. Never. Though the level of the answer might appear lower when looked at from lower down, it is not so; because the Sage is all along emphasizing that Reality which the questioner has never noted. So the answer, unknowingly, takes the listener to the goal; and therefore the result is not a compromise at all.

728. HOW TO FACE PAIN

Avoiding pain, by directing the mind away from the pain, is yōgi*c* in character.

But becoming the pain, or standing as witness to that pain, is purely *jnyānic*.

729. WHAT IS THE DIFFERENCE BETWEEN THE DEATH OF A LAYMAN AND A JNYĀNIN?

If you concede that a Jnyānin has a body, no other concession likewise can legitimately be denied to him. Speaking from the relative level, in the case of the layman, only the gross body dies and the subtle body along with its samskāras is supposed to take another body on rebirth. But in the case of the Jnyānin, the mind also dies or dissolves in the Absolute and nothing remains over for rebirth.

730. WHO ANSWERS ONE'S PRAYERS?

It is admitted by all that prayer, to be effective, should be sincere and deep. It means that one's identification with the inner being should be deep, although unknowingly. Therefore, evidently, it is that *being, the Self* that awards the fruits and not anything else.

731. WHAT IS THE SIGNIFICANCE OF THE KINGDOMS ON EARTH?

The kingdoms are mineral, vegetable, animal, man and God-man: in order of progression. They are all but layers of ignorance, viewed from the spiritual standpoint.

732. WHAT WAS THE METHOD EMPLOYED BY SOCRATES?

The method of Socrates was to follow the lines already laid down. But he would say something more about the Truth, when he found that his followers were landed in a dilemma and could not proceed.

His followers did not aspire for the ultimate Truth, in the vēdāntic sense. They erred in so far as they failed to reckon their own part in their questions. They did not ask themselves who was to decide in solving the questions and who was to judge. They say: '*One is.*' The '*is*' is superfluous, since that '*is*' – which represents the subjective element – is already in the '*One*'.

Socrates did not attempt to expound the whole Truth to his followers in a regular order (as is done by the vēdāntic teachers of India). We do not know why. Even his followers, in their comments on and interpretations of his teaching, do not seem to have done full justice to the sublime stature of Socrates. This has been the experience all over the world (particularly in India), wherever the words of a Jnyānin have been explained or interpreted by persons of lesser experience. The conflicting commentaries on the Upaniṣhads are an example of this evil.

733. How is the world established?

When one says that the world is, the Self does not come in to prove it. It is the senses and mind, which form part of the world, that strive to establish the world.

734. What exactly is the heart?

Heart is not the seat of emotions and feelings alone, as is the usual view. It is the whole being, viewed through the faculty of feeling.

Where the heart of the Gopīs of Vṛindāvana turned to Kṛiṣhṇa, their heart was their whole being: including the head, intellect etc. So, that heart could easily rise to the Ultimate.

735. Who is in illusion?

It is only the man in illusion who thinks that he is in illusion. I have never told you that you will never be reborn. I have only said that you will be rid of the illusion that you were ever born or will die.

736. How to proceed

It is but wise to prepare yourself, before starting on a bold venture. Even before proceeding to cut down a tree, you must first examine whether the axe is sharp, else the effort will be futile and a waste of energy.

So also, when you proceed towards the Truth, you must first carefully examine the instrument and see that the real subject is utilized.

Very often, it is not so. The real subject is ignored. Then failure is inevitable.

737. What are birth and death?

'Nothing' can never be the source of 'something' – 'I'. If 'I' am born out of 'something', that 'something' is still with me. So I was never born, and so there is no death for me or for anybody.

You can cease to fear death only by the strength of your conviction of a solid and permanent something within you.

738. WHAT IS HUMAN EFFORT?

Human effort consists in creating bondage for oneself, clinging fast to it, and wanting to become free without giving up bondage itself.

14th December 1952

739. WHAT IS THE DIFFERENCE BETWEEN YŌGA AND VICĀRA?

Yōga is one-pointed attention and concentration upon a set ideal.

Vicāra is concentration without giving up variety. You should not be carried away by the idea that there is anything to be attained by such strenuous effort as demanded by yōga. Vicāra makes you catch the right perspective to see the Truth as it is. You are not asked to do anything new. You are perfectly in order, even when engaged in worldly activities. Only take note of this fact. See that everything is perfect, and that you are there behind all. As Shrī Aṣhṭāvakra, the ancient Sage, sings:

> sama-duhkha-sukhaḥ pūrṇa āśā-nairāśyayōḥ samaḥ .
> sama-jīvita-mṛtyuḥ sann ēvam ēva layaṁ vraja ..
>
> [You are that being which is perfect:
> just the same in pain and joy,
> the same in hope and in despair,
> the same in living as in dying.
> Only thus, as perfect being
> may you come to be dissolved.]

Aṣhṭāvakra-samhitā, 5.4

You are not asked *to be* the same in both. But you are only shown that you *are* the same in both.

740. HOW TO DISTINGUISH BETWEEN HAPPINESS AND PEACE?

> *Happiness* is momentary.
> *Peace* is happiness continued.

Happiness, as seen by the disciple, is apparent and time-limited.

Happiness, in the eyes of the Guru, is nothing other than absolute Peace itself (Happiness unlimited). It transcends even happiness. It is *sat-cit-ānanda*. Or better still, *sat-cit-shānta*.

741. IS IT IN ORDER TO SPEAK OF THE KNOWLEDGE OF AN OBJECT?

No. It is wrong. The statement presupposes the existence of objects even before knowledge. This is impossible. Knowledge of the object is the only proof by which we can establish the existence of the object. Therefore, without establishing the existence of an object by some other means, the statement cannot stand. So objects are not, and knowledge is only pure Knowledge.

742. THE MYTH OF BONDAGE AND LIBERATION

I know myself (I know I am). This is the only fact that does not want a proof.

Everything has to be reduced to knowledge before I can know it, or absorb it into me as knowledge; because I am knowledge myself. Therefore I can know nothing other than myself.

Bondage comes in when I do not know myself. This position is absurd. Therefore there is no bondage, and no liberation either. Knowing this, be free, and be at Peace.

743. WHAT IS WITNESSED?

Only illusion. In the illustration of the figure in the rock, the 'figure-illusion' is witnessed by the rock. Similarly, everything other than Consciousness is witnessed by Consciousness. So actions, perceptions, thoughts, feelings etc. are all witnessed by consciousness. But these do not really exist. Neither does the figure. The figure-illusion alone is witnessed by the rock, and the object-illusion alone is witnessed by consciousness.

744. WHAT HAPPENS WHEN YOU THINK OF CONSCIOUSNESS?

All thought of Consciousness annihilates thought, like a moth in the fire.

745. HOW TO TALK ABOUT THE TRUTH?

In talking about the Truth, you (the ego) must cease to talk, and allow it (Truth or the real Self) to talk or express itself in its own language.

746. HOW IS THE SAGE BENEFICENT TO SOCIETY?

Is the Sage beneficent to himself? Yes. If so, he is beneficent to the world which is in essence himself.

Is he beneficent to humanity? Yes. He is beneficent to man as man. He proves to man that he is one with animals, vegetables and minerals. What higher form can love take than feeling one with another? This is the highest service, and this the Sage does in full.

You say one must love his neighbour as himself. When the Sage does it in full, you find fault with him. When one loves his neighbour as himself, he cannot stand separate to do service to him. So to do service, from the standpoint of a Sage, is impossible.

You can never become one with another with the body or with the mind. Beyond mind, there is no duality of any kind. One has only to rise to that level and all problems vanish. The Sage stands there in Peace.

747. HOW TO BECOME PERFECT?

Some try to become one with God, in order to become perfect. But, I say, become 'man' and that itself makes you perfect. By 'man' I mean that which is common to all men, and that is impersonal and Absolute.

748. HOW TO APPLY THE ILLUSTRATION OF THE THIRSTY ONE IN QUEST OF WATER IN A MIRAGE?

The thirsty man goes to the mirage for water and discovers that it is a mirage. But you ask why he still feels thirsty. This is the usual incompetency of an objective illustration for a subjective problem. Here, you must understand that everything other than himself is mirage. The thirst, the elsewhere etc. are all mirage. Therefore the water can no longer appear separate and you find yourself alone in your own glory. Stand in the Reality, your nature, and examine the mirage of the world.

17th December 1952

749. WHEN CAN ONE SEE THAT ONE IS A TRUE DISCIPLE?

Never. Because, in order to see that, one must stand separate from the disciple.

The crucial point is, what is it that one wants? Is it to see that worldly life proceeds successfully, or get established in the Ultimate? If it is the former, it is impossible. If it is the latter, the former question does not arise.

750. WHAT IS ĪSHVARA?

The aggregate of everything that prevents the accomplishment of your desires is *Īshvara*. Suppose you want to fly. Everything other than that desire is opposing the desire. The desire is also Īshvara. The body is Īshvara.

He who destroys everything other than himself is Īshvara.

All-knowingness is attributed to Īshvara; which means that Īshvara knows the past, present and future and also knows that one which knows the principle that knows these. It can be nothing other than pure Consciousness. The *all-knowing* can never be part of the known world. It is pure knowledge. It is not the principle that knows. That principle must also be known.

18th December 1952

751. WHAT IS THE MEANING OF THE SUBDIVIDING OR GRADING OF CONSCIOUSNESS?

Usually, Consciousness is divided into the sub-conscious, conscious and super-conscious – all being based upon Consciousness. Pure Consciousness is equally present in all the three states. It is from the standpoint of Consciousness itself, and not from the standpoint of him who is conscious, that these different states are to be considered.

The services of pure Consciousness have to be indented upon, to connect the three states; and in that light there is no difference between these states. You can compare the states only by standing outside them, as their perceiver. The perceiver can never be the perceived. The perceiver is pure, impersonal Consciousness alone. It is *Consciousness* and not '*conscious*'.

All the three are expressions of Consciousness, and all the three are 'sub' or inferior from the position of Consciousness. What you call 'super' from the mental level in the waking state is 'sub' from the level of pure Consciousness. So they are only empty words.

752. WHAT IS THE MOST IMPORTANT PART OF MY LIFE?

Deep sleep. It really saves you from going mad.

753. CAN I DIE GLADLY?

Of course you can! What is the object of your life? Happiness. If you can get it even now and here, would you not die gladly? Not by ending this life, but by knowing death. That is how all Jnyānins die. Therefore, know yourself and transcend death.

754. HOW TO MAKE THE BEST USE OF DEEP SLEEP?

If you merely direct attention to the deep sleep state, you are thrown into the deep sleep state. But, under the instructions of a Kāraṇa-guru, if you direct your attention to the Happiness aspect of the deep sleep state, you are thrown into the Happiness aspect, i.e. your own real nature. Then all nescience drops away, as the material parts of the ego do when you emphasize the consciousness aspect, and you remain in all your glory.

755. WHAT IS THE SECRET OF FORM AND SEEING?

> Form exists alone (let us suppose).
> Seeing = Form + Consciousness

So, when form merges in seeing, form disappears and Consciousness alone remains over. That was the real part of seeing.

You do not actually see form. It is *form forming form*. The fleshy eye is nothing but form. It is this fleshy eye that *forms form, as if it was outside*.

756. WHAT IS WISDOM?

It is not increase of knowledge, as some persons take it to be. Knowledge does not increase or decrease, as you know more objects or less. *Knowledge without object is wisdom proper*.

757. HOW IS OBJECT RELATED TO SUBJECT?

The object exists only in relation to the subject. But the subject is self-evident. It is wrong to bring in the object to prove the subject.

The subject is Consciousness – the Self – and self-luminous by nature. It is really *Knowledge, objectless*.

Even from the standpoint of the ignorant man, no object can be known and no object is ever known.

758. IS THE SPIRITUAL EDUCATION OF THE MASSES POSSIBLE?

No. Not by extending amenities or adjusting external objects. Spirituality is directed from diversity to non-duality. But by your question, you want to keep on the diversity – by calling it 'masses' – and turn your back on true spirituality.

It is a change of heart and a change of perspective that are sought by spirituality. Education cannot provide these. It can only give information to the mind and multiply diversity. There is no such thing as spiritual education. What ordinarily passes for 'spiritual' is only ethical or religious education. This has nothing to do with real spirituality, which pertains only to absolute Truth.

Absolute Peace is the goal of spirituality. This goal, at any rate, is not outside. Spirituality helps you to find permanent peace and live in it. Your conduct and contact thereafter will improve all those who come near you.

Platform lectures or classroom instructions cannot help you much. When you are at the centre, your perspective is so completely changed that the usual questions of the ordinary man never arise in you. The ordinary man might find it difficult to understand this.

Can the dreamer ever be made to understand that all he perceives, including himself, is a dream? *No.* Not till he wakes up from the dream. And then no proof is needed, nor is the dreamer anywhere.

20th December 1952

759. WILL SATISFACTION OF PHYSICAL NEEDS ENHANCE SPIRITUALITY?

No. It will only distance it (render it still more distant). It is rightly said: 'When a savage is converted to Christianity, really it is Christianity that is being converted to savagery.'

760. HOW COULD A PATRIOT TURN TO SPIRITUALITY?

The question is itself a bundle of illusions and inconsistencies, which puts the cart before the horse. To become a real patriot is the goal of spirituality, and not the other way round. The patriot has nothing to seek. You might take it to be a paradox. I will make it clear.

1. Who is a patriot? He is one who has dedicated his life to the service of 'his' kingdom. Which kingdom please? You owe allegiance to different kingdoms in different states and leave them without a thought; because these kingdoms really do not belong to you and you cannot cling on to any of them as you desire to.

   Therefore, first find your real kingdom. Jesus calls it the kingdom of heaven and says it is within you. But I say it is the ultimate Truth – your own real nature. Discover that kingdom which alone is yours, before calling yourself a patriot. Then you will find that what is denoted by that '*kingdom*', '*yourself*' and '*patriotism*' are all one and the same Reality, perfect in itself.

Therefore you have nothing to achieve and nothing to do. Thus the real Jnyānin is the only patriot worth the name. Therefore, become a true patriot and you are free. The path that leads one to real patriotism is called spirituality.

2. What do you mean by 'patriotism'? Love of the country of one's birth. Of course you presume to love the people more than everything else in the country. What is the basis of this love? A feeling of oneness with others. Is it possible on the physical level to feel one with another? *No*. Is it possible on the mental level? *No*.

   So the goal is clearly beyond the mental level. Rise to that level and then look at the problem. The question, the country and your ego all disappear, giving place to perfect self-luminous Peace. That is your country for ever. Be a patriot to it, if you still want to be one, and be at Peace.

761. WHAT IS INSIDE AND OUTSIDE?

To the individual soul (ego) everything is outside. To God, everything is inside.

To the Sage (Jnyānin), there is neither inside nor outside. He is beyond both.

762. WHEN SHALL I BEGIN TO WORK FOR OTHERS?

Working for oneself and working for others are distinct and separate, one from the other. You will begin to work for others only when you have finished all your work for yourself. You can help the sick only by yourself becoming a doctor first. Otherwise you will only misguide others.

All the work you have to do for yourself is only to discover your real nature or centre. Therefore establish your own centre first and then try to work for a world, if you can then find a real world demanding service.

Selfless workers have toiled to uplift humanity from time immemorial. But the world is not a jot the better for all of them. Of course those workers themselves reaped the full benefit of their own labours, by attenuating their own egos considerably by self-sacrifice, however partial.

The Jnyānin alone can help another to the ultimate Truth and Happiness.

763. What is our obligation to the Sages who have attained liberation and departed?

Every Sage leaves a rich legacy behind, to help us reach the Truth. It is as a result of that legacy that we have been able to meet here today. We are ungrateful wretches if we do not recognize it.

We greedily grasp at the chaff and ignore the grain of Truth.

764. What does divine Līlā mean?

It is not the absolute Truth. Let us take an illustration. What is ice? You may say it is water. Next you say it is vapour. All these are only partially true. Similarly, *līlā* [divine play] expresses only the partial truth. It is a patchwork explanation which may convince you for a short time.

But from the standpoint of Truth, partial truth is as good as untruth. Because Truth has no degrees.

765. What is the purpose of the intellect?

The intellect is given to man only to measure the variety in the world.

766. How to find out a real Guru?

One who follows the path of devotion to a personal God in a *sāttvic* manner, his ultimate goal being the absolute Truth, invariably places upon his deity the responsibility of finding him a Kāraṇa-guru. The deity within gives the suggestion at the proper time and it never fails; because the suggestion emanates from his own *sāttvic* nature, which is very close to the background Truth.

But if the aspirant is one who follows the path of discrimination alone, the conditions are different.

It is never safe to accept a Guru merely on grounds of appearance and worldly reputation. Both are equally deceptive.

To test another, to see if he is competent to guide you to the Truth, is also impossible; because you will have to be higher than the other, to apply such a test. Therefore a regular test is out of the question.

The only reasonable recourse, left to you, is to put all your doubts and difficulties before the proposed Guru; and to listen to his answers patiently, relying more upon the response of your heart than upon the intellectual satisfaction that you receive from his answers. If he is able to satisfy you both ways, you may without hesitation accept him and follow his advice and instructions.

When once you have accepted a Kāraṇa-guru, you must unconditionally and unreservedly surrender your ego to the Guru: who represents the ultimate Truth. Remember the words of Shrī Shankara.

> … jīvō nā 'haṁ dēśikō 'ktyā śivō 'ham ..
>
> *Shrī Shankara,* Advaita-pancaratnam, 1.2

I am not the jīva. But I am Peace, because my Guru has said so.

767. IS GOD THE SAME TO ALL?

No. It changes according to what one identifies oneself with, in life. To the man who identifies himself with his body, God is also embodied. To one who identifies himself with the mind, God is also possessed of the best of all attributes.

To him who transcends even the mind, God is the right Absolute.

768. HOW TO VISUALIZE THE REAL GOD?

Conceding God as the creator of the universe, God must have existed even before creation – all alone as the impersonal.

God in his real nature cannot be seen from or through any created thing. So body and mind are incapable of understanding God. We are forced, therefore, to look out for some principle in man which was not created.

The real 'I'-principle, defying all the three states, is found not to have been created. So, by taking to this 'I'-principle, you may be able to visualize the real God. This is what Vēdānta tells you. Vēdānta does not deny God at all.

Standing as that 'I'-principle, you see that you are all alone in deep sleep. There is no other God there. So this 'I'-principle is the God they mean.

769. HOW TO ENHANCE THE RESPECT AND REGARD FOR THE ULTIMATE TRUTH AMONG THE PEOPLE?

If an individual, already respected and revered by the general public, is made to know the Truth, the public also will gradually begin to look upon Truth with the same respect and regard. Gradually, many of them will make themselves ready even to accept his guidance to Truth. This will be a highly beneficial turn in their life and a great service to humanity.

This was the reason why, in the vēdic age, there was a comparatively higher degree of respect and regard for the ultimate Truth, its exponents and followers than at present. Many of the ruling kings and queens of that age were Jnyānins, and some of them were the authors of the Upaniṣhads and other vēdāntic texts. Such kings have proved to be the most ideal of kings in history.

Similarly, someone who has visualized the Truth and is established in it, will be the ideal citizen in every way.

770. CAN ANYONE IMPROVE THE WORLD?

No. Who will undertake the work? The individual. He is but a part of the world which has to be improved. From where does he get the ideal or the urge to improve the world? Of course from the inner Self, which is perfect.

Before improving oneself and becoming perfect, any attempt to improve another is meaningless. Therefore, rise to that Self and make yourself perfect first. Then, to your surprise, you will find the world also perfect.

The individual worker being part of the world, he is not in a position to comprehend the world as a whole. To do that, he must necessarily stand out of the world. Then your perspective is changed, and the world also appears entirely different and perfect in itself.

771. WHAT WORK CAN A JNYĀNIN UNDERTAKE?

A Jnyānin can take to any vocation in life he chooses, in accordance with his former habits and samskāras; because he knows that the activities of life have no bearing upon his real nature. He does not act for individual pleasure or happiness, but purely out of a spontaneous urge coming from deep below.

772. CAN DEMOCRACY FUNCTION?

No. You may say the majority rules in the present day world. But, if you examine the facts impartially, you will find that in practice, in every country, it is the few that govern the many, and that few are guided by the one. So democracy, in practice, is a myth.

773. CAN I REMEMBER A DREAM?

You can remember only your past experiences. You can think of your dream experiences only by standing as the dreamer for the time being. But you, as the waking subject, were never the dreamer. Therefore the waking subject can never remember the dream.

774. WHAT IS ĀTMIC URGE?

Unconditional freedom, deathlessness, Knowledge, Happiness etc. are your very nature. These surge up as the desire in the embodied man to become free, to defy death, to know everything, and above all to be happy etc. But no embodied being can possess any of these qualities in full.

775. WHAT IS MORALITY AND WHY?

Morality, as at present in vogue amidst us, is of a peculiar social type, calculated only to enable man to live up to his own ideals and lead a contented life. But you are not told why you should observe morality.

Every law curtails your individual freedom to a certain extent. That means so much of self-sacrifice is called for; and that attenuates the ego, little by little. Therefore, the ultimate goal of every law, including laws of morality, is the annihilation of the ego, resulting in the realization of the Self.

Thus the ultimate Truth is the source and goal of morality, and true morality can be observed only by understanding that source – the Truth. In this sense, all talk of petty, relative morality is futile.

Therefore, morality is only that thought, feeling or action which attenuates the ego and leads you on to Truth.

776. WHAT ARE FEELINGS OR EMOTIONS?

Every feeling is said to be a wave in the ocean of Peace. The analogy is not strictly correct. Here we must understand that there is wave only in the ocean and that there is no wave in Peace. In Peace, there is neither ocean nor wave, as there is neither ocean nor wave in water. Similarly, there are no thoughts or feelings in me, the real 'I'-principle. Understanding feelings in this manner, we can enjoy even the feeling of misery, by emphasizing the real content of that misery and dismissing the illusory name and form.

Thus every emotion is a clear pointer to that permanent background Peace. So you can very well lose your apparent self at the upsurge of any emotion; not in the emotion itself, but in its permanent background.

We have all had the occasion of witnessing tragic dramas brimming over with pathos and cold cruelty towards the righteous, at which we have wept from start to finish. But the next day again we are prepared to pay in order to witness the same drama, so that we may continue to weep. What is the secret of this? Is this not the enjoyment of misery? This shows you that there is something inherent in the so-called misery that tempts you to court it again. It is nothing but the background, Peace, which is behind all emotions.

Therefore, see through every emotion and perceive that Peace alone is there. This is what every Jnyānin does. So he enjoys every feeling which you so carefully separate from Peace and thereby suffer.

777. WHAT IS THE CAUSE OF THE WORLD, IF ANY?

A cause implies that without which the result cannot appear at all. For example, the serpent cannot appear if the rope is not there already. But we know that the rope never undergoes any change. Similarly, the world can never appear if Ātmā is not behind it, without undergoing any change. Therefore, if any cause is to be posited for the world, the most correct answer would be '*Ātmā itself*'.

Thus, in fact, there is no creation; and if creation is taken for granted, Ātmā is the only cause of it. But causality can never exist in Ātmā.

26th December 1952

778. THE 'CHILD IN KNOWLEDGE'

Some statements made in a transcendental mood as the '*child in knowledge*', with their explanations added later on.

The child asked:

1. 'If Happiness assumes the form of riches, what does it give rise to? Bondage or liberation. Of course *bondage*!'
2. 'If riches assume the form of Happiness, what will be the result? *Liberation*.'

Explanation: So you have only to reverse the existing order of perception. Usually, you see yourself as things outside. But instead, bring everything inside you and see them all as yourself.

1. In the former, the happiness aspect is forgotten and it appears disguised as riches; hence it binds you.
2. If you understand that richness by itself is not Happiness, that when you desire for Happiness the sense of riches vanishes and that Happiness manifests in its own glory, it is *liberation*.

Now apply this principle subjectively to *bōdha* or Consciousness. Here also there are two perspectives.

1. Consciousness assuming the form of objects. This is bondage. Here, Consciousness is forgotten and the object sense alone is emphasized.

2. The object assuming the form of Consciousness or seen as nothing other than Consciousness. This is liberation. Here the object is forgotten and you get established as Consciousness, your real nature.

    Consciousness to object is bondage.
    Object to Consciousness is liberation.
    Look behind you and you will always see the Truth.

779. TRUTH AND MIND

Truth transcends both reality and unreality. But the mind can conceive only these two opposites. So the real nature of Truth is not understandable to the mind. The real 'I' down to nature is covered by both the reality and the unreality. Your memory, intelligence etc. are all in the plurality and never *one*.

780. PERCEPTION AND SENSE ORGANS

'See with your ears.' It may look a paradox. But it is exactly the way that you see, with your eyes also. You do not ever see anything with your eyes; and yet you believe you see with them. So, you can as well say you see with your ears.

781. DELIGHT AND SAYING

If you delightfully say anything, delight becomes the saying and remains over still. If you have delight in you already and you begin saying, the delight will cover up the saying and remain over.

But if you take delight in saying, the saying covers up the delight. Or, in other words, if you have not got the delight in you already and you simply begin to say and enjoy, the saying covers up the enjoyment and the enjoyment disappears immediately.

782. THE CHILD

The child asked: 'What do you see in me?' Finding us puzzled, he himself answered.

'You do not see the Reality in me. Nor do you see the unreality. So you see the "child in knowledge" in me. I am not going to explain these to you yesterday, today or tomorrow. Because I am the ever-present. I am beyond time. At last I disappear in you.' And he disappeared.

783. 'IS THE REALITY STATIC OR DYNAMIC?'

Answer: 'It transcends both static and dynamic, expressing itself in both and standing independent of both. But the static and dynamic cannot exist without me. I am none of these, but am all these.'

784. WHAT DO YOU LOVE?

Answer: 'You can love only the right Absolute, represented by the life principle in others. You can love nothing else.'

28th December 1952

785. SNAKE IN THE ROPE

In applying the illustration of 'the snake in the rope', in order to establish yourself in the rope (the Self), you are taking the services of the snake (the mind) which is not the rope.

786. HOW ARE YOU THE BEST KNOWN AND SELF-LUMINOUS?

Answer: It is in and through you that you know anything else. So the 'I' is clearly better known than anything else known, and nothing else is required to make the 'I' known.

So the 'I' is the most concrete (real) of all things and self-luminous. The essence of a thing is 'the thing in itself' (self-luminous). It is the ultimate background.

787. SIGNIFICANCE OF GIVING A SPIRITUAL NAME

The spiritual aspirant, all along, considered himself to be a jīva, possessing a name pertaining to his body. But when he is made to visualize that he is not the body, but Ātmā itself, he is given a spiritual name, which denotes only Ātmā and nothing else.

This name, which is always a synonym of the ultimate Truth, helps him to counteract the old samskāras of the jīva, which occasionally raise their shadows to drag him into the basic error. But when he understands that all names point to the Absolute, he gets established in the Ātmā.

788. FRIEND AND FOE

Your revilers are your real friends, and your flatterers your enemies. Phenomenally, the former are supposed to relieve you of half your sins, and the latter to deprive you of half your virtues.

But a spiritual aspirant on the direct path of knowledge has nothing to do with virtue or vice. Even he is helped more by his revilers than by his flatterers, to turn his attention introspectively to his real nature.

789. THE EGO, ĀTMĀ AND THE GURU

It is an invariable truth that Ātmā suffers recognition when the ego enjoys, and the ego suffers when Ātmā shines (is recognized). But this has a happy and lonely exception. When the ego thinks of the Guru and enjoys even in the mental plane, Ātmā (Guru) also shines simultaneously and delivers a pleasant death to the ego.

790. HOW TO THINK OF MY GURU?

Think of your Guru only in the dualistic sphere. Don't apply your intellect to it. It is far beyond your intellect. Apply your heart to it and get lost in the Guru. Then the Ultimate dances like a child before you.

But when you think of the real 'I'-principle or 'Consciousness', think that they are the absolute Reality itself, beyond name and form.

All these are but synonyms of the ultimate Reality. But Guru alone has the revered place of honour and veneration in all planes. It is an experience that sometimes when you go deep into pure Consciousness and get lost in it (nirvikalpa samādhi of the Jnyānin), you see the person of your Guru there, and this vision throws you into an ecstatic joy taking you even beyond *sat-cit-ānanda*. Blessed indeed are you then.

29th December 1952

791. HOW TO APPROACH AN INTRUDING THOUGHT?

When a thought arises in you, you invariably try to discriminate whether it is good or bad. Thereby you attribute more reality to the thought and make it abide and bind you more.

But instead, if you examine the content of the thought irrespective of the object concerned, and see that it is nothing other than your own real nature, the thought vanishes as such, leaving you in your real nature.

So adopt the latter course and be happy.

> 'You have only to take the non-existent from the non-existent and be ever free.'

792. WHO IS YOUR ENEMY?

If you find anybody else your enemy, your lower instinct tells you to destroy him first. But don't heed to it. Instead, destroy first the ego which discriminates you from him, and you will find that both of you stand in essence as one and the same Reality, the 'I'-principle. The enmity also becomes equally objective and vanishes.

In fact, eliminate the subject and the object from their false appendages.

1st January 1953

793. HOW AM I DEATHLESS?

Death takes place in time. Time is made up of the past, present and future. These do not affect the 'I'-principle in any way. Therefore, from one standpoint, it may be said to be an eternal present for the 'I'-principle.

Strictly speaking, even this is wrong. Because time exists only in connection with the apparent 'I'. The activities of the apparent 'I' may be divided into five classes: actions, perceptions, thoughts, feelings and knowing. Which of these five functions do you prefer to be?

If you choose any one of the first four, you will automatically die after every such function. But experience is that you do not so die. Therefore you must be the last one – the knower – which alone continues through all activities and never dies.

You know even death. Therefore you transcend death as well.

794. HABIT CHANNELS AND REALITY

The habit channels of the mind distort the Reality, and therefore they have to be destroyed. This can be done only by directing your attention to the ultimate Reality.

The Reality is in the thought itself, as its background. So thought need not go outside itself to realize the Reality.

When you direct your attention to something blank, your mind also becomes blank. Similarly, when you direct your attention to the Reality, your mind becomes the Reality at once.

795. CAN THE SAHAJA STATE BE CALLED A CONTINUOUS SAMĀDHI?

No. If you are so particular about using the word 'samādhi', you may say you are then in a permanent samādhi.

But be where you are and know what you are.

4th January 1953

796. WHAT IS A DREAM?

Everything other than your real nature (the Self, the ultimate Reality) is a dream.

797. WE OFTEN SEE NO COHERENCE IN A DREAM.

No. The reason obtaining in the dream state is different from the reason of the waking state. Hence the apparent incoherence.

798. WHAT IS THE MEANING AND PURPOSE OF SURRENDER?

To '*surrender*' means strictly to 'disown'. When all untruth is surrendered, you stand as the Truth itself.

799. TO BE NEAR OR AWAY FROM THE GURU – WHICH IS MORE ADVANTAGEOUS?

Each has its own advantage and disadvantage. When one is near the Guru, the obstacles that come up are transcended immediately, in spite of the retarding influences of the ego. When you are at a distance from the Guru, the progress might be slower but will certainly be steadier, being dependent on 'yourself' alone.

800. WHAT IS THE SIGNIFICANCE OF '*KARMA-SANNYĀSA*'

It is composed of two words: '*karma*' [action] and '*sannyāsa*' [renunciation].

Karma has meaning only when it is related to the 'I'. The real 'I'-principle is indivisible. You claim all activities to be yours. So no activity can be part of your real nature. So 'you' can have no activity. How can you renounce what does not belong to you? Then what is your relationship with activity? You are the knowing principle or the witness of the activity. The sense of permanence is given to the individuality by that Consciousness which is your real nature. Therefore '*karma-sannyāsa*' is strictly a meaningless term.

But *sannyāsa* is meaningful in another sense. You surrender your sense of separateness from the Reality, to that Reality itself (sattil nyasikkuka). This is real *sannyāsa.*

801. WHAT IS INTENSE THOUGHT?

No thought which does not merge in the background, the Reality, can be intense. It is only the one that has visualized the Reality behind all appearance who can take an intense thought. Its process is to repeat the arguments to prove one's real nature.

14th January 1953

802. WHAT IS THE RELATIONSHIP BETWEEN THE EGO AND LIBERATION?

It is the whole ego that seeks liberation and strives for it. When it is directed towards the ultimate Reality, the material part automatically drops away and the Consciousness part alone remains over as the real 'I'-principle. This is liberation.

803. IS WORK A HINDRANCE TO SPIRITUALITY?

Not always. It is a hindrance if the ego is present. It is a help if the ego is absent.

804. WHO CAN BE FREE?

Neither the body nor the mind can ever be free. Because they are dependent upon the real 'I', even for their very existence. The 'I' alone is always free, and real freedom is its monopoly and its alone. The urge for freedom springs from that source and is usurped in vain by the body and mind.

805. WHAT IS THE BENEFIT OF STANDING AS THE WITNESS?

By standing as the witness, you establish yourself in the unity in diversity.

806. HOW TO EXORCIZE THE PHANTOM OF IGNORANCE FROM DEEP SLEEP?

See that either end of your sleep is saturated with the thought of your real nature, your native home.

15th January 1953

807. WHAT IS THE RELATIONSHIP BETWEEN GOD AND *BRAHMAN*?

God is conceived with the attributes of omnipresence, omnipotence, omniscience etc.; and therefore he has to possess a cosmic mind, and there must be a cosmic world also for the mind to function in.

But the real 'I'-principle in man goes beyond mind and therefore beyond everything objective. In the sphere of the real 'I'-principle, there is absolutely nothing else existing beside it. It is therefore attributeless.

Brahman is also supposed to be attributeless. Therefore, for God to become *brahman*, he has to give up all the attributes attached to him.

808. WHAT ARE LIFE AND DEATH?

Life is the real 'I'-principle. When you are life itself, how can you die?

809. HOW TO CHOOSE BETWEEN THE WITNESS ASPECT AND THE CONSCIOUSNESS ASPECT IN PRACTICE?

When your mind is active, you may take the witness thought with advantage, to eliminate yourself from objects. But when your mind is free and passive, the thought of your real nature is better.

16th January 1953

810. HOW DOES CONTINUITY COME INTO PLAY?

Continuity is the characteristic of the 'I'-principle alone. Memory is its expression in the realm of the mind. Memory is the last and mental link that seems to connect the phenomenal with the Ultimate.

811. ARE EXPERIENCES RECORDED ANYWHERE?

A man under certain drugs speaks of his past experiences. How then can we prove that experiences are not recorded anywhere?

Am I to accept half your story or the whole? Certainly, the whole. You have many such experiences in your dream. Are those experiences to be explained individually? *No*. The explanation of the whole dream explains every part of it.

812. HOW TO CLASSIFY EXPERIENCES?

They are generally of two types – *relative* and *in identity*. Relative experiences are again divided into:

1. *Objective* – physical and outward going
2. *Subjective* – psychic or mental and inward going

But from the stand of Consciousness, all relative experiences are objective. The only experience *in identity* is the experience of the Self, as in deep sleep.

813. WHAT IS THE SIGNIFICANCE OF NORMAL AND ABNORMAL?

In ordinary parlance, the distinction between the normal and the abnormal is an attempt at measuring the more changing in terms of the less changing. This cannot have any fixity in itself. The ultimate standard of normality is the really changeless 'I'-principle itself. So the Self is the only thing normal and everything else is abnormal, in relation to the Self.

From this standard, the waking state is the most abnormal.

17th January 1953

814. WHAT IS INDIVIDUALITY?

The word 'individuality' is ordinarily used in a very loose sense, to denote a personality which is purely physical and mental, pertaining to the waking state alone.

To understand the significance of individuality, your own stand in life must first be defined. Where do you stand, in activity or in inactivity? When there is mental activity, you stand as the background, in relation to that activity. But between two such activities and in deep sleep, when the mind is supposed to be inactive, you stand as the absolute Reality – your real nature.

Now let us examine individuality. By this word, we mean the characteristic of the individual. Here, the individual is not the small, insignificant embodied being you may seem to be. This individual is the centre, which projects, through the five senses, the five sense-worlds which we call the universe. Thus the individual is characteristic of the universe as well. Now let us examine this individual. The characteristic of the individual should be the same throughout his three states, throughout his whole life and in both activity and inactivity. The only principle that stands unchanging in this way is the ultimate Reality (one's own real nature). Personality is always changing and individuality is changeless.

18th January 1953

815. STAGES OF PROGRESS OF THE DEVOTEE

> ... ārtō jijñāsur arthā-'rthī jñānī ca bharata-'rṣabha ..
>
> *Bhagavad-gītā, 7.16*

The regular order of progress of the devotee is (1) arthā-'rthi, (2) jijnyāsu, (3) ārta, (4) jnyāni.

Of these, the third stage (ārta) is the forerunner of the jnyāni, the perfect state. It is characterized by a restless desire to attain the Truth, or in other words, a thirst for knowledge. This is pure Love itself. This thirst does not come from the heart. It comes from deeper below and it takes you to the very source.

The mind and intellect only cleanse the road and pave the way for the royal procession of the heart to the Ultimate.

816. HOW TO PROVE THAT NOTHING EXISTS EXCEPT WHEN KNOWN?

> ajñāta sattayilla
> [There is no existence that's not known.]

An examination of the dream experience is the easiest way to prove this. The whole dream world becomes an illusion when the state changes. This is clear when you look at it from the waking state or from the Reality in the relative sphere.

Similarly, there is no evidence to prove that the waking state is not also an illusion. You may ask where does the dream world come from? If there is *something*, it might have come from something. But if it is nothing, where is it to come from? So, if it is an illusion, how could it have come from anything?

Even in the waking state, can you connect two thoughts, perceptions or objects? *No*. Because things appear and disappear one after the other and none of them can be given permanence. No two things can exist simultaneously and nothing can be connected. When this is the case even in the waking state, why do you go so far as the dream state to prove the illusion? You are the One and so you can have connection only with that One. The mind is the father of all illusion.

> tiriyunnoravastha mūnnuma-
> sthiramanyōnyamavēdyameṅkiluṁ
> śariyāyavayētuśaktīyāl-
> aṙiyāmāsthirasākṣitanne ñān
>
> [Of the three states, each comes and goes
> unsteadily; and each can't know
> the other states. But by what
> capability can they be rightly
> known? The changeless witness that
> remains. Just that is what I am.]

Shrī Vidyānanda-tīrttha, Bhagavad-darshanam

19th January 1953

817. HOW IS A SAGE ALWAYS IN SAMĀDHI?

Question: Is the Sage ever in samādhi?

Answer: Yes, always.

> dēhābhīmānē galitē vijñātē paramātmani
> yatra yatra manō yāti tatra tatra samādhayaḥ

Shrī Shankara

Because, in the case of the Sage, the activities of the mind do not leave a virile trace behind, and that makes each one of them a samādhi. Of course, the trace is there, but under complete control and it will come up only if he wants it to. If he does not want it to, it will not. If he *wants* to think, feel etc., he can very well do it. If he does not want to, no. This is the *sahaja* state.

When a Sage remembers, the memory is non-responsible and purely objective, whether it concerns a thought or a feeling. But to an ordinary man, all this is subjective. Involuntary thoughts will never come in for a Sage.

> nānābhautika vastuyōgajanitānandaṁ nijānandam-
> ennanyūnaṁ manatārar̲iññu var̲ipōlbōdhiccuṇernnīṭukil
> dṛśyattinnu vidhēyanenna nilapōy˘, tal svāmiyāy˘, śāntanāy˘,
> paṫṫillāte jalattil aṁbujadaḷaṁ pōlatra jīvicciṭāṁ

Shrī Ātmānanda, Ātmārāmam, 1.50

This means: If you properly realize from the depth of your heart that the happiness you enjoy on your contact with objects is nothing but your own real nature of Happiness, you become awakened. Thenceforward the tables are turned. You become the master of the objective world of which you had been a slave so far; and your life becomes unattached, like the lotus leaf in water.

To the Sage, all things of world – gross as well as subtle, including time, space and causality – are objective in their own relative sphere.

818. WHAT IS THE PLACE OF LAW IN THE PATH TO THE TRUTH?

The law deals with logic. So one who takes to law has a good chance of rising to higher logic leading to the Truth, which is but logic in a higher form.

20th January 1953

819. WHAT IS THE NATURE OF THE WORLD?

The world is perfect. But it appears imperfect because you use fallacious instruments of sense organs and mind and a wrong perspective of subject-object relationship. Get rid of them first. Take hold of the changeless principle of awareness in you and then examine the world. Then you will find the world perfect and entirely different from what it appears now.

820. Is death liberation?

Not always. Death is liberation if it is ultimate death, that is the death of everything objective including even samskāras. But ordinary death is only partial, being the death of the gross body alone. It is no more than a change and does not deserve the name of death.

Real death is a shift of your centre from the ego to the witness.

821. What should be my attitude towards social customs and conventions, even after my visualization of Truth?

The original customs and conventions in Hindu society were based upon advaita in some way or other. But their real significance is not known to all. You should not consider them meaningless merely on that score. You must observe those customs strictly and faithfully.

From the spiritual standpoint, it might be immaterial to you whether you observe them or not. But then you have an obligation to the less fortunate members of society, who are really in need of every one of those customs and conventions to help them through the moral and righteous way of life.

If a man respected in society – for whatsoever reason – were to break such laws of society, many others would follow him regardless of consequences; and society would disintegrate. An enlightened man will not violate any of the healthy conventions and customs insisted upon by shāstras and the great men of old.

Therefore, you must perform the rites for your departed ones as is prescribed by your society. They might be meaningless from the standpoint of the absolute Truth. It is wrong to apply the perspective and the tests of absolute Truth to the objective outside alone, leaving the subjective untouched.

If you mean to examine society from that standpoint, first examine the subject (the ego). Attributing reality to the body is the most meaningless of all our acts, and the conception of society is only an offshoot of this error. Therefore transcend that mistake if possible, and then all other problems vanish.

822. WHAT IS LIBERATION?

From one standpoint, it may be defined as going beyond birth and death. But that is not the whole Truth. Strictly speaking, it must be defined as going beyond the delusion of birth and death.

823. WHAT IS THE DIFFERENCE BETWEEN PERCEIVING THE PERSONAL AND THE IMPERSONAL?

In principle, both are the same. You perceive both by becoming that for the time being.

You direct your attention to the impersonal and you stand as that impersonal.

But for perceiving the personal or objects, you also use the instruments of the sense organs and mind. You concentrate your mind (the apparent 'I') upon that object, and as a result you stand as that object for the time being. So much so that when I am there as the object, I am not here in the body.

824. WHAT DOES *PRATYAKṢHA* (DIRECT) MEAN?

Pratyakṣha (direct) means that which does not demand a proof. The real 'I'-principle is alone direct.

825. WHAT ARE THE ENDS OF LIFE?

Life has two ends: (1) the body (matter) which is the wrong end, and (2) the real 'I' (Consciousness) which is the right end. Spiritual aspirants alone take hold of the right end, and others take hold of the wrong end of life.

The Sage ignores matter and knows light. The ignorant man ignores light and knows matter.

The Sage sees light and matter both as light. The ignorant man sees matter and light both as matter.

There is ignorance on both sides. The Sage ignores ignorance (what is non-existent), and the ignorant man ignores what is really existent.

21st February 1953

826. WHAT IS THE SECRET OF LANGUAGE?

The language of the body, gross or subtle, is the only kind of language ordinarily known. This is governed by grammar, rhythm, harmony of sound and the superficial dictionary-meaning of words (padārtha).

But there is an infinitely higher language called the language of Truth. In relation to this language of Truth, the authors of its writings are called *akṣhara-jnyānins* or *jnyānins* who have visualized the absolute Truth, who have discovered the ultimate goal or background of alphabets composing the language and who have discovered the infinite potentialities of alphabets or sounds.

This language is governed by the inner harmony of the Ultimate, known and experienced by the Sage alone and by the ultimate meaning of words (paramārtha). They do not make any effort to observe the rules of grammar or rhythm. But the grammar and rhythm being the gross expressions of the ultimate harmony, they come in uninvited to support what comes from the Truth, direct, through the lips or the pen of a Sage. If grammar fails to agree with any usage of the Sage, it is the incompleteness of grammar alone; and the learned grammarians immediately recognize it and readily incorporate it into their science.

Every sentence or verse that comes from a Sage is a *mantra*, perfect in itself. To attempt to measure, criticize or correct such lines from the level of the superficial literary men of the world is nothing short of sacrilege.

(The exceptional few among such Sages, who were also born poets, have contributed poetic works to literature expressing the divine harmony in different stages. For example, look at the works of Shrī Ātmānanda.

1. His poetic work called *Rādhā-mādhavam* abounds in the harmony of words pointing to the divine harmony.

2. His other poetic work called *Ātmārāmam* abounds in the harmony of ideas touching the divine harmony.
3. His purely vēdāntic works *Ātma-darshanam* and *Ātma-nirvṛiti* directly express the harmony of Truth.)

827. WHY CAN'T I ANSWER DIVERSITY FROM DIVERSITY ITSELF?

The question on diversity arises in the realm of causality itself, and you stand in that realm seeking the answer.

Suppose I give an answer by way of a cause of the diversity. The answer and the question create a new diversity. This process of multiplication of diversity will continue indefinitely. Such a solution does not serve any purpose.

So, for a real solution of the problem you must go beyond the realm of diversity, and then the question disappears as illusion.

22nd February 1953

828. SYMPATHETIC SAMĀDHI. HOW DOES IT HAPPEN?

It is narrated in the *Mahābhārata* that once lying over *Shara-shayanā* [his bed of arrows], when Shrī Bhīṣhma went into a casual samādhi, Lord Kṛiṣhṇa who was just then talking to the Pāndavas far away, was also thrown into a sympathetic samādhi. How did this happen? Shrī Tuncat Eṟuttacchan describes the process thus:

> karaṇaṅṅaḷil viṣayaṅṅaḷe layippiccu
> karaṇaṅṅaḷeppunarātmani cērttu nannāy˘
> gōvindan samādhiyiluṙappicciḷakāte …
>
> [With objects merged back into sense-
> perceptions, and with sense-perceptions
> then completely joined back into
> self, Lord Kṛiṣhṇa came to be
> absorbed in a samādhi state.]

Mahābhāratam – Shānti-parvvam, 374-6

Just before going into samādhi, Shrī Bhīṣhma took a deep thought about Lord Kṛiṣhṇa, whose Truth Shrī Bhīṣhma knew more or less.

This thought suddenly arrested the attention of Lord Kṛishṇa, who knew it immediately. But Bhīṣhma straightaway went into the regular jnyānin's samādhi, which is the real nature of Lord Kṛishṇa himself. Therefore naturally, Lord Kṛishṇa, whose attention was already attracted by Shrī Bhīṣhma, happily glided in to a sympathetic samādhi.

The process, adopted by Shrī Bhīṣhma for disposing of the body, senses and mind before samādhi, was the same as the one adopted by Lord Kṛishṇa also for initiation. This prakriyā is object-senses-consciousness (viṣhayam-indriyam-prajnyānam) – object, senses, knowledge. This is exactly the method adopted by us here.

829. THE SOLUTION OFFERED BY THE UPANIṢHADS ON FINDING EVEN THE TRINITIES IMPERFECT

In the Purāṇas and other ancient texts, *Brahma* is represented as still studying something higher. *Viṣhṇu* is represented as in incessant *yōga-samādhi* showing that there is some higher principle, and *Shiva* in *tapas* and meditation on something higher. So none of them can evidently take you to the beyond.

Understanding this imperfection of the trinities, the Upaniṣhads come forth showing the way to the ultimate Truth subjectively, through direct *vicāra.*

> parāñci khāni vyatṛṇat svayaṁ-bhūs
> tasmāt parāṅ paśyati nā 'ntarātman .
> kaścid dhīraḥ pratyag-ātmānam aikṣad
> āvṛtta-cakṣur amṛtatvam icchan ..
>
> [The world that happens of itself
> has excavated outward holes,
> through which perception looks outside
> and does not see the self within.
>
> But someone brave, who longs for that
> which does not die, turns sight back in
> upon itself. And it is thus

that self is seen, returned to self,
to its own true reality.]

Kaṭha Upaniṣhad, 4.1
[See also notes 180 & 497]

830. WHOSE IS THE RESPONSIBILITY FOR ACTION?

The instrument is dead and inert. It can never be made to share responsibility for any deed. It is not the chopper that cuts the tree. It is the '*living-ness*' you transmit to the chopper that cuts it. Similarly, body, senses and mind are mere instruments under the true living-ness or awareness, the 'I'. That 'I' is alone responsible for all action.

Action is only *tripuṭī* [triad of doer, doing and deed, or subject, activity and object]. Knowledge pertains only to the 'I'. When you examine the *tripuṭī*, it vanishes in its due order, leaving you as knowledge. Thus when the 'I'-principle thinks, it is that that is called the mind (manvānō manayiti). I am called mind when that particular function is there.

831. WHAT ARE *SAT*, *CIT* AND *ĀNANDA*, AND HOW ARE THEY THE SAME?

Sat, *cit* and *ānanda* are *lakṣhaṇas* or pointers to the 'I'-principle. They are ignorantly attributed to body, senses and mind; and you say 'I exist', 'I know' and 'I am happy' – just as the aspects of the rope are attributed to the snake you create in illusion.

Existence is permanent and cannot be attributed to the perishable body. Existence is experienced or it shines; and in shining, Consciousness comes in. In the light of pure Existence and Consciousness, no duality can appear. Non-duality is Peace or Happiness. So *sat*, *cit* and *ānanda* are the three aspects of the one and the same Reality.

832. WHAT IS THE CONTENT OF SPEECH?

It is different at different stages:

1. In the case of a child, *words* speak.
2. In the case of an adult, *ideas* speak.
3. In the case of the Sage, *Truth* speaks.

You become so familiar with certain ideas that they form part of the integral 'I'-principle for all practical purposes. These ideas sometimes come out like a flash, surprising even you. Ideas come out as though by instinct, as your hands come out to protect your head or eyes in the face of sudden danger.

In the case of the Sage, when a question is put, there being no ego present, the Truth comes out spontaneously and the talk that follows is not really eloquent, but is eloquence itself.

833. HOW TO OBTAIN 'JNYĀNA SAMĀDHI'?

It is possible only after listening to the Truth directly from the Guru. First, the mind is taken away from sense objects and not allowed to go after the happiness of passivity either in deep sleep or in samādhi. In this steadiness of the mind (madhyagatāvastha), you experience afresh that the happiness expressed is your real nature. Then the mind is mildly persuaded to take to Ātmā, which alone is real and is your real nature. Slowly the potential desires, which were not killed, all drop away and your real nature shines in all its glory. This is jnyāna samādhi. The mind itself is transformed into Ātmā in course of time.

You desire the happiness of samādhi because you have given up sense objects, not out of your own free will but by behest, without a substitute. Therefore objectless pleasure is welcomed. This tendency for the pleasure of samādhi can be successfully given up only by knowing your real nature from the Guru. Enjoying happiness in samādhi often strengthens your desire for it over again. The enjoyership does not die even in samādhi.

It is only the wrong notion, which prevents one from realizing one's own real nature as pure Happiness, that has to be corrected.

834. WHAT IS THE RELATION BETWEEN LEARNING AND KNOWLEDGE?

Learning is darkness, and knowledge is light. Learning pertains to objects of ignorance. Its result is sharpening the intellect and accumulating information. The mind does not get a ray of light or knowledge by all this.

Knowledge takes up higher reason as its instrument, takes up the mind itself for examination and discovers its real nature to be Consciousness, the 'I'-principle. In the light of knowledge, all learning disappears as illusion.

835. WHY DOES A JNYĀNIN WEEP?

Why should he not weep? Why should he laugh? What prohibits him from weeping alone? He does everything else: acting, perceiving, thinking and feeling, apparently like an ordinary man. But there is a world of difference between the activities of the two. The ignorant man acts as a slave to his passions; the Jnyānin as a master, the passions being his slaves. Therefore the Jnyānin can weep or not weep as he chooses.

But there is happiness even in weeping. The mere thought of the departed gives happiness. But that thought cannot be ordinarily separated from the allied aspects. So both together are helplessly accepted by the ordinary man. He begins to think of the agreeable aspects of the departed and gradually gets lost in the less happy aspects and weeps profusely.

But the Jnyānin knows perfectly well that his real nature Peace (objectless Happiness) is the background of all emotions, and welcomes grief and weeps like anybody else, but not for a moment does he lose sight of the background Peace.

836. WHAT IS THE DIFFERENCE BETWEEN THE APPROACHES OF THE YŌGIN AND THE JNYĀNIN TOWARDS HAPPINESS?

The yōgin asks you to withdraw from objects in order to enjoy happiness. He uses the mind as his instrument and enjoys only the happiness reflected in his blankness of the mind. This is only pleasure.

But the Jnyānin asks you to withdraw not only from objects of mind but from the mind itself, in order to enjoy not reflected but pure Happiness. Here you use awareness or higher reason as the instrument.

The happiness of the yōgin is experienced only in concentration or oneness, and misery is experienced only in diversity.

20th March 1953

837. WHAT IS THE MINIMUM THAT AN ORDINARY MAN HAS TO DO TO ATTAIN PEACE?

Shrī Aṣhṭavakra answers this question in the verse:

> yadi dēhaṁ pṛthak-kṛtya citi viśrāmya tiṣṭhasi .
> adhunai 'va sukhī śāntō bandha-muktō bhaviṣyasi ..

Aṣhṭāvakra-samhitā, 1.4

This means: 'Throw away your body first in idea and take rest in pure Consciousness. You shall at once be free and at Peace.'

When you stand as body, you are a *jīva*. When you stand as mind, you are *God*.

When you stand as Truth, beyond both body and mind, you are the *Absolute*.

How to throw away the body? By simply becoming aware of it.

838. WHAT IS THE USE OF ARGUMENTS IN SPIRITUAL DISCOURSE?

Only to expel the samskāras, which are the only impediments to understanding the Self aright. Otherwise the samskāras will safely lurk behind and create havoc afterwards.

839. WHAT IS THE ROOT CAUSE OF ALL MISUNDERSTANDING?

Answer: Name and its misuse.

The generic name which denotes only the Absolute is indiscriminately used to denote the particular. Thus the generic or Absolute is forgotten and the particular or the appearance is emphasized. What more is needed for misunderstanding?

22nd March 1953

840. WHY IS CONSCIOUSNESS INVISIBLE?

The nature of Consciousness is 'experience' itself. The 'I'-principle is the only experience. The tests of experience are permanence and self-luminosity. Experience can never be experienced. It is '*anubhava-mātrā-'tmā*' (of the nature of pure experience alone).

To become visible, it must stand as an object of perception, which Consciousness can never do. To know, to enjoy, and to become it are all functions of the ego. But '*to be it*' is alone yours. *You were and are that always.*

841. WHAT IS PURITY?

Purity is getting away from all that is extraneous to your real nature.

842. HOW DO I SEE?

Seeing is an expression of Consciousness. Consciousness first expresses itself inwardly. It is only afterwards that it expresses itself outwardly. Unless you see yourself inwardly, you cannot see yourself outwardly either. The latter is only a corollary of the former.

23rd March 1953

843. WHAT IS MEANT BY 'GETTING ENRICHED'?

It really means getting enlightened. It means you do not come out of an experience just as you went into it. You have gained some spiritual profit therefrom.

24th March 1953

844. WHAT ARE GOOD AND BAD SPIRITUALLY?

Association with objects makes one *bad*. Association with the 'I'-principle makes one *good*.

2nd April 1953

845. WHAT IS REALIZATION?

The ordinary man is alive to the illusion that he is bound. Therefore he has only to become alive to the fact that he is free. Realization is only this.

846. WHAT IS THE PURPOSE OF ILLUSTRATION IN A SPIRITUAL CONTEXT?

An illustration from the phenomenal is often indented upon, to clarify a particular position beyond the sensuous. An illustration should never be completely applied, but only to light up the particular aspect in question.

An illustration from the objective sphere should straightaway be applied to the subjective in you.

847. CAN I UNDERSTAND ANYTHING TILL THE EGO DIES?

No. In the question, you are putting the cart before the horse. You are emphasizing the ego more than the understanding.

However much you may try to kill the ego, it will only become stronger. So you have to approach it from the other end. Everybody understands in spite of the ego. The truth is that the ego automatically dies when you understand anything.

You will never succeed in bringing in light, if you insist upon removing all the darkness from your room before you do so. Therefore simply ignore the ego and try to understand, and the understanding itself will remove the ego.

848. WHAT IS FREEDOM AND HOW TO ATTAIN IT?

The first scent of freedom is obtained from the urge for freedom coming spontaneously from deep within you. But you are unable to locate it and so think it comes from the outside. The ego takes up this urge and seeks for solution in its own way. You try to be free with body, senses, mind and objects and fail miserably.

At last, you discover that the urge comes from within and so look within subjectively, along the line of the heart. Following the track closely and earnestly, you reach the real 'I', behind the heart itself. Then you discover that the sense of bondage was an illusion, and that you were never bound at all. Coming out, you declare this to the world outside.

849. WHAT ARE THE FUNCTIONS OF CONSCIOUSNESS?

Like fire, it has two functions:

1. It illumines objects at a distance.
2. It destroys them on contact.

3rd April 1953

850. WHY DOES MAN GO TO WAR?

Because there is war already inside him. He has not found subjective Peace and so cannot escape from either war within him or the war without, which is a corollary of the former. So try to attenuate your ego and find permanent Peace within you. Then alone will you be able to transcend all war outside.

851. HOW DOES ONE ATTENUATE THE EGO WHEN ONE HAS TO FIGHT AGAINST A STRONGER ADVERSARY?

It is your selfish interest that tells you to keep away. But when you choose to fight, you sacrifice the ego and prefer even death. What greater attenuation of the ego can you have?

852. HOW TO DECIDE MY CONDUCT UNDER PERPLEXING SITUATIONS?

Examine first what reigns in you, in the situation. If it is Peace, yield. If it is cowardice, well, stand up and fight. Kill your enemy (subjectively, the desire first; and then the objective enemy next, if needs be). The fight within you is between Peace on one side, and the different feelings, thoughts and emotions on the other side.

853. HOW TO TRANSCEND FEAR?

Bhītir nāma dvitīyād bhavati

Nārāyaṇabhaṭṭa, Nārāyaṇīyam, 91.3

Duality is the parent of fear. The moment you think that there is another existing beside you, fear sets in; and the only remedy against fear is the understanding that you are the one without a second, the ultimate Reality. Therefore, visualize the Reality and get back to fearlessness. To know that you are the silent witness to all mentations is also an equally successful remedy to eradicate all fear.

Witness thought is the surest panacea for all ills.

854. HOW TO DEAL WITH ANGER AGAINST AN ENEMY?

Anger arises only because you imagine that the enemy stands against the Peace you seek to achieve by the accomplishment of certain desires. So the anger itself is the greater and nearer enemy to you.

Therefore, turn to that anger first, and examine it independently of its objects. Then you find it to be nothing but the Peace you were seeking for. The anger as such disappears, and all enemies are given a hearty send off.

855. WHAT IS THE ABSENCE OF A THING?

The absence of anything is not directly perceived. It is only the background that is really perceived, and the absence of a thing is superimposed upon that background.

4th April 1953

856. HOW TO WAKE UP THE HIGHER REASON?

If the outward going tendency of the intellect is curbed and the inward going tendency is encouraged, the lower reason itself is transformed into the higher reason.

857. WHAT IS IT THAT TAKES PLACE HERE, DURING THESE TALKS?

The Truth is that it is the Truth that talks to the Truth, all about the Truth. The Truth goes into you undressed, not through language at all.

5th April 1953

858. HOW DOES A SAGE HELP ONE?

It is one of the fundamental laws of nature that every action has a reaction. If you love someone, your affection is usually reciprocated.

So if you love even the person of a Sage, the Sage reciprocates from the right Absolute or the impersonal; because there is no trace of the personal in the Sage. What seems personal in the Sage is indeed the impersonal itself. (You have heard the story of the travellers dying with hunger and thirst. They saw some monkeys on the tops of some coconut trees. They threw stones at the monkeys. Immediately the monkeys pelted back with tender coconuts. The travellers appeased their hunger and thirst with tender coconuts and went on.) Similarly, you get knowledge if you approach even the person of a Sage.

859. CREATION AND DISSOLUTION OF THE WORLD

Creation: 1. Consciousness objectified is thought, and
2. Thought objectified is the gross world.

The reverse process is *dissolution:*
1. Gross world subjectified is thought, and
2. Thought subjectified is Consciousness.

860. IS EVERY DESIRE AN OBSTACLE TO TRUTH?

Every desire rises in duality and so is generally considered an obstacle to Truth. But there are some exceptions.

Desire for freedom, desire for *mukti* etc. are not obstacles. Freedom is the characteristic of the real 'I'-principle. So by desiring freedom, the desire together with the ego merges into the 'I'-principle and you rest in Peace.

Mukti is selflessness. So, to desire *mukti* is also to desire selflessness. That can never be selfish either.

6th April 1953

861. DIFFERENCE OF APPROACH BETWEEN VĒDĀNTA AND SCIENCE

Vēdānta always takes the generic of all things for discussion, and disposes of them with reference to the ultimate background. But science takes the particular objects and their mutual relationship alone into consideration, and does not at all consider the background.

862. RANGES OF ACTIVITIES OF THE SAGE AND THE LAYMAN

To the Sage, all activities spring from the background, traverse the mental realm and end in the background itself. But to the layman, all activities start in the mental realm and end in the mental realm.

863. WHAT IS THE SIGNIFICANCE OF THE STATEMENT 'I KNOW IT'?

The statement only means 'I know.' The 'it' disappears even with the function of the sense organ. When I actually know, there is only myself as knowledge.

7th April 1953

864. WHAT IS IMPROVING A THOUGHT?

The question arises out of ignorance of the content of thought. You can look at thought in two ways – from the inside and from the outside. When you look at a thought-form from the outside, you call it a thought-form: as you call water a wave when you look at it from the outside. In whatever way you see it, and whatever you call it, its content does not change.

You see only the material side or the boundary of thought. It is the boundary alone that makes it a thought. The boundary of thought is time. But time is itself a thought. It is impossible to limit one thought by another thought. So thought is not limited by anything. Its content is Consciousness.

One who is concerned with the content of thought, ignores the boundaries, and knowing that the content is ever perfect never attempts to improve it. 'Improving thought' only means the rearrangement of the boundaries. You are not enriched by such improvement.

Still, you should beware of thoughts. Voluntary thoughts you may well take. But involuntary thoughts should never be allowed to come in unawares, to overpower you and guide you or to devour you.

865. THE LIGHT BEFORE THE EGO AND THE SAGE

The ego never sees the light, though he always uses light. The Sage sees that light alone (the most vital part) in every perception. He is great who sees the light alone in all perceptions.

The 'I' is the first part of every perception. This is the light which manifests the object. But this part is usually ignored. You can speak of anything only as dead matter. I alone possess Consciousness. Even God is to be taken only as dead matter. No human being has ever reached the Ultimate, though sages may seem to live. The human being is transformed into the Ultimate itself, just before reaching it.

If you are able to stand as your real nature even for a second, and know that you were beyond time during that experience, you were really in the timeless. There is no need to lengthen the duration of that experience. That tendency is a vicious yōgic samskāra.

866. WHAT IS THE RELATIONSHIP BETWEEN ART AND A GENIUS?

Art is an attempt to express the inner harmony of the ultimate Reality through the outer harmony created by the senses and the mind – for example music, beauty, poetry, painting and all the other arts. Everything can be made into an art, provided the ultimate goal is the inner harmony of the Absolute.

Beauty in nature is the ultimate Reality. But it has to be understood that it is not outside but within you as the real 'I'-principle.

What you call a *genius* is a personality in whom a limited expression of the Ultimate is evident. It may express itself through one of the arts or in some other manner.

8th April 1953

867. WHEN AND HOW DOES HIGHER REASON FUNCTION?

Higher reason is always ready to help you, provided you want earnestly to know the Truth. It is on hearing the Truth from the Guru that the higher reason is equipped and set in motion, and it does not stop till the goal of Truth is reached. The function of the higher reason is to dissolve the mind, and then the higher reason stands transformed into Ātmā itself.

The higher reason is the fire (the Guru) that has gone into you, through the words of the Guru. It consumes the creations of your mind and vanishes at last, becoming Ātmā itself.

868. WHAT IS LONELINESS AND ITS REMEDY, IF IT CALLS FOR ANY?

You are the ultimate Reality, the one without a second. Therefore, loneliness is inevitable and you welcome it; because every activity of yours is meant to make you lonely. You want Happiness, which is yourself alone, and when you are in your true nature you cannot share it with any other, because there is no other there.

When there is duality, there is always fear. Fearlessness obtains only in non-duality or loneliness. In fact, you are that always. Its nature is Peace or pure Happiness and therefore you never want to lose it. So, naturally, no remedy is called for.

869. WHAT IS THE BEST WAY TO TRUTH?

Love prepares the way to Truth. Knowledge takes you straight to Truth. It is made possible for you to accomplish both by listening to the talks of the Sage. In love, the ego is lost and you get to Peace.

Sincerity is to be true to oneself.

9th April 1953

870. THE SAGE TRANSCENDS ALL LIMITATIONS OF LANGUAGE.

Language, of course, has its own limitations everywhere. But the luminous presence of the Guru compensates for all limitations of his language, and you are taken straight to the Truth.

To be nearer the Truth, it may even be said that the Self knows the Self, or Ātmā knows Ātmā.

871. HOW TO LIVE?

Live in this world knowing full well that all the limitations there are self-imposed; and that you, as the creator and imposer of the limitations, stand above all the limitations themselves. So the world can never bind you.

872. WHAT IS MEANT BY 'TO TAKE NOTE OF'?

'To take note of' = to recognize.

In trying to recognize the Truth deeply, you happen to be placed there (to stand as that) and the recognition dies. So it takes you to a non-dual experience in identity.

10th April 1953

873. HOW IS THE WORLD A THOUGHT FORM?

Take the mind away from the world. What remains? You can neither say that it exists or that it does not exist. So you alone remain.

Therefore, the world is only a thought.

874. WHAT IS THE PERMANENT BACKGROUND?

The permanent background of everything, whether of sense organs or mind, is Ātmā itself.

Sense organs or mind, if they become permanent or changeless, are Ātmā itself. That permanent principle which stands behind perceptions, thoughts and feelings – beyond perception and non-perception, beyond thought and non thought etc. – is the real 'I'.

That which gives you light, or that which enables you to see, think etc., is the 'I'-principle. That is the permanent background.

Samskāras are habit-channels of thought, or dormant tendencies.

875. WHAT DO I LOVE? AND WHY?

Your love is directed only to the real substratum or Self. You happen to love the qualities in one, simply because they belong to the substratum you love. You love, because love is the real nature of the real Self and you cannot help loving even for a moment.

876. HOW TO LOVE?

Love is the feeling or sense of oneness with another.

If you correctly understand yourself to be beyond body, senses and mind, your love for another will also be for that self in him. Because there are no two selves, and love is its nature.

If your understanding is incorrect, you love the incorrect self in him; and as a result of that incorrectness, you hate others.

Genuine love absorbs everything into you, and then duality dies. But in conditioned love, or gratitude, duality persists in giving and taking. Even this gratitude, if directed to the Guru, goes deep into you, takes you beyond duality and is transformed into objectless love.

11th April 1953

877. WHEN DO I BEGIN TO LOVE MY GURU?

When that which has been given by the Guru is accepted wholly, love for the Guru springs up within you.

878. THERE IS NO MOVEMENT. WHY?

A vacuum is necessary to make movement possible. Something can move only into a vacuum. Nature abhors a vacuum. The real Self, as existence, infills all. If there is no vacuum and if nature is already full, how can anything move?

879. How to be awake in deep sleep?

> Not seeing the Reality or forgetting the Self is *sleep.*
> Seeing the Reality or visualizing the Self is *waking.*
> In this sense, the present waking state is sleep or *a dream.*

To be really awake is not to be awake with sense organs or mind, but with Consciousness. Give up the waking dream and be awake to the real Self.

880. What do I mean when I say 'I walked'?

I mean I never walked.

I cannot say I walked without knowing I walked. Then 'I walked' was the object, and 'I' was the witness. Walking does not go into the make of me. I was that principle which was witness to walking and non-walking. Therefore I never walked.

881. How does the mind become pure?

The mind becomes pure by its own death. The attempt to purify the mind by any amount of other effort is futile.

882. The sahaja state

The sahaja state is the state where you maintain that certainty or deep-rooted conviction that you never leave your real nature of Consciousness and Peace.

16th April 1953

883. ALL THE WORLD IS RELATIVE. I AM THE ONLY ABSOLUTE.

> karmaṇy akarma yaḥ paśyēd akarmaṇi ca karma yaḥ …
>
> [One who sees actionlessness in action,
> and action only in actionlessness,…]

Bhagavad-gītā, 4.18
[see note 272]

To give a meaning to any activity, reference must be made at least unconsciously to its opposite. These opposites depend upon each other for their very existence. Strict laws of logic however enjoin that, in such cases, both are non-existent. Two opposites cannot exist side by side, at the same time. They say that it is exactly like saying, 'A is the father of B and B is the father of A', where the fallacy is evident.

Thus birth is birth only in relation to death, and death is death only in relation to birth. So both are non-existent, and you stand beyond both.

884. WHAT ARE THE DISTINCT STAGES OF PROGRESS TO THE ULTIMATE?

First from bondage to liberation, and from liberation to pure Consciousness. You have only to come to a deep recognition of the fact that you have always been, that you are, and that you shall ever be the witness. That is all that is needed.

> First you *know* that you are the Reality.
> Then you *become* it.
> Then you *be* it.

In the being it, both the knowing it and the becoming it expire. The first two were misunderstandings of the 'being it', at different levels.

The first knowing had an object, the last being is objectless knowledge.

17th April 1953

885. WHAT IS THE RELATION BETWEEN THOUGHT AND FEELING? DOES THOUGHT MERGE IN FEELING?

No. Nor the other way round. Both merge directly in Consciousness. The question is not of much spiritual significance. Both being sensations, they may be disposed of together. But I answer it only out of academic interest.

From another perspective, it may be said that feeling is nothing but a *deep* thought. Here '*deep*' signifies the heart element. When you take a particular thought over and over again, the heart begins to function and craves for that thought. Thus thought begets feeling and descends into the heart.

886. WHAT IS THE PURPOSE OF LIFE?

It is only to know the Truth and to be it. You can never be happy; you can only be Happiness.

All phenomenal workers try to make others happy.

But the vēdāntin tries to make them Happiness directly, or enables them to see themselves as Happiness itself. The vēdāntin cares for the inside of the 'he'. Others cater for the outside of 'him'. I ask such advocates of work for humanity: where, in deep sleep, is the world they wish to elevate?

To become universal is the goal of another set. It is well-nigh impossible. Even if you succeed in that attempt and become universal, the fact of becoming still remains and then the individuality also remains. You find no means to transcend the universality and the individuality (together called duality).

887. IS IT RIGHT TO HATE THE EGO?

Yes. Because the ego is something which does not exist. So you hate the non-existent because you want to be the existent Reality.

The best way to annihilate the ego is not to think frequently of annihilating it. This will thereby only strengthen the ego. You need only to ignore the ego at every turn, and the ego will die a natural death.

See what Lord Kṛiṣhṇa contrived at the end of his career. He made his kith and kin fight between themselves and completely exterminate the sect, leaving Kṛiṣhṇa alone. Similarly, allow the body, senses and mind and objects to fight between themselves and die, leaving You alone.

18th April 1953

888. WHAT DOES YŌGA MEAN?

Yōga is a word which is used in a very broad and comprehensive sense. It is used with a different meaning in different contexts. Generally, it means only a 'path'.

'Yōga', in any context, must be understood in accordance with the level of the person who uses it and the person who listens to it. When a Sage uses the word 'yōgin', he means a *jnyāna-yōgin* or a Sage. When a *rāja-yōgin* or a *bhakti-yōgin* uses the same word, he means another yōgin of his own type.

The Sage is that principle upon which all opposites and paradoxes appear and disappear.

889. WHAT DIFFERENTIATES LOVE FROM KNOWLEDGE?

Knowing with your whole being is Love itself. In thought (which is knowing with the mind alone) you do not lose yourself. But in love you lose yourself. So love entails the sacrifice of the ego.

890. WHAT IS COURAGE?

If love of any kind prompts you to action and sacrifice of any degree, courage comes in. If pure love (objectless love) prompts you to action and sacrifice, that is real courage. But if love of any object prompts you to sacrifice, your courage is not genuine – but secondary and worldly.

891. How to use feelings as a means to reach the ultimate?

Love for objects is a feeling. It consists of love and the object, which are distinct and separate. In that feeling, if you turn your attention to the love part ignoring the object part, you are free.

Every feeling is obstructed love. So, see every feeling as obstructed love and fix your attention on the love part, and you are free.

892. Eliminated from objects, has knowledge any attraction?

Yes, certainly.

You love objects for enjoyment. So you love enjoyment more than objects. You have more interest in self-love than in love for objects. And you love Love itself or the Self more than self-love. So you love the Self most.

When objects are eliminated from knowledge of objects, what remains over is knowledge, your real nature or Self, and you love that most. What else can have a greater attraction for you?

893. Why are texts interpreted differently?

Shrī Shankara, Shrī Rāmānuja and Shrī Madhva stand for Advaitic, Vishiṣhṭādvaitic and Dvaitic sections of Indian philosophy respectively. All of them unanimously accept the prasthānatraya tripod of Hindu philosophy as their authority. This tripod of texts consists of the *Brahma-sūtra*, the *Dashōpaniṣhads*, and the *Bhagavad-gītā*.

All these texts abound in statements and verses made from the standpoint of all the three schools. Instead of being satisfied with choosing and adopting the particular verses most favourable to each school, they went out of their way and, by far-fetched argument and much straining of the intellect, attempted to read the sense of their own school into the verses more suited to the others. Shrī Shankara also has committed the same mistake, by trying to twist purely dvaitic texts into the advaitic sense. The shāstras were written to suit all grades of people in society. This is how the sacred texts came to be tortured.

20th April 1953

894. WHAT DOES THE EGO WANT?

It is wrong to say the ego always wants enjoyment of objective pleasure alone. If so, why does he desire deep sleep where there is no thought or feeling? So it proves that he wants to be alone in his real nature.

The ego's activities are:

You perceive it. Then you know it. Then you enjoy it.	All three take place in the realm of the mind alone.
Then you *become* it.	On the borderline between mind and self.
Then you *be* it.	In the Reality or Self.

895. HOW ARE LIFE'S ACTIVITIES CONNECTED?

It is through the witness alone that your varied thoughts, feelings and perceptions are connected. The real you are not connecting them at all.

Your life-eternal is ego's death – eternal. True life begins when the ego dies and consciousness dawns.

21st April 1953

896. HOW DOES A THING AFFECT ME?

Things affect you both by their presence and by their absence. Both of them hide you.

897. TRYING TO IMPROVE THE WORLD IS A SACRILEGE. HOW?

If there is a God who created this world, he knows and has powers to maintain it. For a creature to try to improve the world is to usurp God's own responsibilities and to correct God himself. Is this anything short of sacrilege to God? It is like the stupid railway passenger who carried his baggage on his own head all through the journey, and alighting claimed that it was he who carried it through.

The poor fool forgot that it was the train that was actually carrying himself and his baggage.

898. WHO HAS ESTABLISHED HIMSELF?

He who has deeply known Consciousness (though it is ridiculous to say so) has established himself in Consciousness. He is a *jīvan-mukta.*

899. IS THERE ANYTHING HIGHER STILL?

Yes. Not in content, but in the naturalness of control. Though born, as a child in ignorance, it is the highest goal to become a '*child in knowledge*'. All *jīvan-muktas* do not rise to that state and it is not necessary for their own purpose either.

900. HOW DO THE HEAD AND THE HEART FUNCTION?

In spiritual matters alone, the head and the heart work harmoniously together. But in the phenomenal sphere, they often work each divorced of the other.

901. WHAT ARE THE ACTIVITIES OF LOVE AND KNOWLEDGE?

Love creates an object for its enjoyment. Immediately, knowledge destroys that object, leaving love objectless. Being objectless, it is one with love Absolute. Love is enriched not by taking but by giving.

> iṭatumiṟiparattunniprapañcaṁ samastaṁ
> palatumiṟi vamikkuṁ vahniyil bhasmamākkuṁ
> karumanapalatēvaṁ kāṭṭiyātmasvarūpē
> śiśutaviśadamākkuṁ vastuvē satyamāvū

Shrī Ātmānanda, Ātmārāmam, 1.42

The verse means: The left eye representing love creates all this world for enjoyment; but the next moment the right eye representing knowledge destroys all that in its consuming fire. This is indeed one of the manifold divine līlās of the 'child in knowledge' in the field of the Ultimate, through which it explains the world and establishes the Truth.

22nd April 1953

902. It is said, I am alone, in the interval between mentations. When the interval is mentioned, does not time come in?

The interval is visualized by that principle standing beyond. To him there is no time. For he is beyond body, senses and mind. So from his stand, he was perceiving in identity. But to make you conceive it in some manner, time is merely given as a starting point. The interval being really timeless and objectless, when you make the attempt, you are thrown into the beyond – where time disappears.

A means, which is an illusion, is first adopted from the relative sphere, which is all illusion. But reaching the goal, when you look back, you find that the world-illusion has disappeared, and the means-illusion along with it, leaving you all alone in your own glory.

23rd April 1953

903. What is a spiritual thought?

Thought is an exercise of the mind, in relation to objects of the world. Thought about the Truth is not a thought in the real sense. Because Truth can never be an object of thought. So spiritual thought is a misnomer. What is actually called a spiritual thought is only a deep recognition of an established fact regarding the real 'I', beyond all subject-object relationship.

904. What is recognition?

Recognition is an acceptance of the fact of Truth. Repetition of it makes the recognition deeper and deeper.

Recognition, remembrance and hope are the three props that maintain the continuity of individual life. Of these three, recognition stands nearer the 'I'-principle than the other two.

905. WHY SHOULD I AVOID SIDDHIS (POWERS)?

Because they create a newer and subtler world which binds you even more strongly than the waking world, and weans you away from the path of the Reality. So the spiritual aspirant should scrupulously shun *siddhis* of all kinds.

> viṭa-saṁsargavat siddha-saṁsargaṁ mōha-varddhakam
> mōhāya bhayaṅkaraṁ jñātvā siddhāṁ styajati yō naraḥ
> tasya nirvighnam ēkānta kalpayā nirvikalpayā
> anāyāsami hai 'vā 'tma-jñāna-siddhir bhavēd dhruvam

[Source of quotation uncertain]

906. HOW IS THE WITNESS TRANSFORMED?

The witness is the highest limit to which one can go, on the way to the Ultimate. When you reach the witness, your understanding it as the witness disappears. But what appeared as the witness continues still, as the Reality.

10th May 1953

907. WHY DO I SEE DIVERSITY?

Because you are diversity yourself. When you think you are body, senses and mind, all constantly changing, you are diversity yourself and you see nothing but diversity outside. When you see you are that changeless principle, you are no longer in diversity and then you see no diversity either.

14th May 1953

908. WHY WAS SĪTA-DĒVĪ MADE FIRST TO EXPOUND THE TRUTH OF RĀMA AND SĪTĀ TO HANUMĀN?

In spite of the extreme flight of devotion to the person of Rāma and Sītā, and the profound but objective study of all the shāstras, the higher reason or *vidyā-vṛitti* had not yet awakened in Hanumān. Therefore, the word expounding the Truth, as it came from Shrī Rāma, was apt to be misunderstood.

Therefore Sītā was made to expound first the Truth of Rāma, explaining his impersonal and self-luminous aspects, extolling the glory of the Guru. Next, she expounded the truth of herself and the world, to be appearing and acting by his mere presence. Thus was Hanumān transformed into an uttamādhikāri (earnest aspirant) by having his attention directed to the impersonal in Rāma. Her part was only a preparation of the ground.

The crowning conclusion of tattvōpadēsha was given by Shrī Rāma himself in a few words and Hanumān became a *jīvan-mukta* then and there.

23rd May 1953

909. WHY AM I GIVEN A SPIRITUAL NAME?

This is done in response to an urge from deep below. When everything (body, senses and mind) changes, you have to be shown that you are changeless by clinging on to something at least relatively changeless. So a changeless name is given to you to show that you are changeless.

14th June 1953

910. HOW DO I SEE BEAUTY IN THE MOUNTAINS?

You see only the mountain and superimpose beauty from your own nature upon the mountain. So beauty is your own projection. Now do *you* really see the mountain? If so, a child also must see the mountain. But it does not. It simply sees. Neither do *you* see the mountain. *You* too simply see. Seeing is Consciousness, the Self. Therefore you see only yourself.

911. HOW IS TRUTH TRANSMITTED?

When you are angry, you lose yourself in anger and so you transmit it to another who gets angry with you in return. Similarly, when the Guru talks about the Truth, the Guru gets lost in Truth and, through the words that he uses, takes you to the Truth. So it is anger that transmits anger and Truth that transmits Truth or enlightens one.

25th June 1953

912. WHAT IS REAL EXPERIENCE?

You say that you have understood the Truth. It means you stood one with the Truth.

(The very word 'understood' is significant. It means you stood under. Under what? Under the phenomenal. Under body, senses and mind, as their background. Whether the godfathers of the language meant the word to mean this, is a different question. It easily yields itself to this interpretation, and it is also the perfect truth. Then why not accept it?)

That was real experience. It was not experienced by anybody. Experience is the very nature of Reality. You stood as that Reality; but you do not often take note of it. Sometimes that deep conviction of the Truth expresses itself in the realm of the mind. Ignorantly, you call that expression an experience.

Real experience you first have on hearing the whole Truth direct from the Guru. Immediately you endorse it with your whole being. To say that you experienced it, is wrong. It is the language of duality, and experience is non-dual. Experience itself is the ultimate Reality, Truth, Background, 'I'-principle, Consciousness, Love, Peace, Beauty, Harmony and whatever else you may call it.

29th June 1953

913. WHAT IS THE TEST OF THE RIGHT LINE OF THINKING?

It is to see whether it takes you to the witness. If so, you are on the right line. That which expresses itself in the witnessed as well as in the witness is alone the Truth.

914. THE IGNORANT MAN AND THE SAGE

The ignorant man does not experience anything other than the body, and is blissfully ignorant of the 'I'-principle.

The Sage does not experience anything other than the 'I'-principle, and knows the body to be only an illusion.

30th June 1953

915. HOW DO OBJECTS HELP ME TO KNOW THE TRUTH?

Adṛśyō dṛśyatē rāhur gṛhītēnē 'ndunā yathā,
tathā 'nubhava-mātrā 'tmā dṛśyēnā 'tmā vilōkyatē

[Source of quotation uncertain]

The invisible Rāhu is perceived through the eclipsed moon. In the same way the *Ātmā* who is mere experience is perceived through objects.

Translation by Shrī Ātmānanda, Ātma-darshan, *Preface*

Objects being known help you to understand first that there is an independent principle in you called 'knowingness'; and then, when under instructions from a Guru you eliminate objects from the knowledge of objects, you stand as pure knowingness or Consciousness itself. This knowledge is the all-pervading Reality, yourself.

So don't look down upon objects, but utilize them intelligently as a means to the Ultimate.

2nd July 1953

916. HOW TO KNOW THE UNIVERSE?

To talk of the universe, a cosmic ruler etc. is all gibberish. The mind cannot conceive anything bigger than itself. The universe comprehends the individual and his mind. So the individual mind, as such, can never comprehend its own holder – the universe or the supreme power. In order to be able to conceive them, the mind must first transcend its own limits of time and outgrow the universe. Then the mind ceases to be mind and stands as the ultimate Reality. Looked at from that stand, the universe as such disappears and stands transformed as the Reality itself. Therefore the attempt is in vain.

917. WHERE IS SUBJECT-OBJECT RELATIONSHIP IN LOVE?

When you say you love yourself, you yourself and love stand as one. So also when you love another, you become one with the other. The subject-object relationship vanishes, and the experience is one of identity. In order to *'love thy neighbour as thyself'* you have to stand as Ātmā itself.

The disappearance of subject-object relationship is a natural corollary of the experience of love. So also of the experience of knowledge. This actually happens in all experiences in the plane of the relative.

Instead of taking note of the sublime Truth, after the event the ego tries to limit, misrepresent and possess it. Whenever any doubt arises, refer to the deep sleep experience. There is no subject-object relationship there.

In the experience of Happiness, the mind dies. There is neither enjoyer nor enjoyed in it. There is only Happiness. It is an egoless state; but this is usurped subsequently by the ego. You are not getting Happiness by loving all, but loving all is itself Happiness. The humanitarian worker emphasizes the 'all' and misses Happiness; the vēdāntin emphasizes Happiness, his own nature, and misses or loses the 'all'.

8th July 1953

918. WHAT ARE OBSTACLES TO SPIRITUALITY AND HOW TO REMOVE THEM?

The thought that some things are obstacles is the first obstacle to you. The best way to remove them is to look straight at them and examine them. What you consider an obstacle consists of the material part and the Consciousness or Reality part. Direct your attention to the Reality part alone and ignore the material part. Then the thing ceases to be an obstacle and becomes a help instead.

919. SINCE HAPPINESS IS MY REAL NATURE WILL NOT MY WORK SUFFER FOR WANT OF AN INCENTIVE?

No. The question touches the Absolute and therefore you should not expect an answer from the intellectual level. The answer can only be from the level of experience. Your work will become objectless and something other than happiness will take the place of the incentive. The work will continue to be done perfectly even to the minutest detail, unknown to the mind, and in all such work you will enjoy yourself.

25th July 1953

920. WHAT IS IT THAT REALLY BINDS ME?

It is not the outside that binds you, but it is something inside. It is only your ignorance of what you are and your identification with the wrong thing (body, senses and mind) that really binds you.

> svayame tanne lākkappil sukhamāy˘ viśramicciṭuṁ
> inspekṭaŕ ennapōl dēha-pañjarē vāṟka saukhyamāy˘
>
> *Shrī Ātmānanda*

The Inspector of police and the thief may be sleeping or resting in similar and adjacent cells in the police lockup. The Inspector does not feel bound but the thief does. Thus the liberated, though in apparent bondage, is free beyond doubt.

921. WHY DO I NOT VISUALIZE ĀTMĀ?

Who asks the question? If it is the ego, he can never visualize Ātmā. If it is the 'I' in you that asks the question, that 'I' is Ātmā itself and shall neither want nor be able to visualize Ātmā. Because you cannot be the subject and object simultaneously.

26th July 1953

922. WHAT ARE RULES TO A SAGE?

The Sage does not follow any rules. I do not mean rules like those of the road or society, but rules of spirituality. Rules are really meant to take one to the Sage or Truth. Therefore rules humbly follow the Sage and do not dare to overtake him. Because the Sage does not need their services and they are dissolved or become meaningless in his presence.

923. WHY WAS THE ARTIFICIAL STATE OF NIRVIKALPA SAMĀDHI INVENTED?

The pioneers of the traditional (cosmological) jnyāna path understood and interpreted the spontaneous state of deep sleep as the seat of causal ignorance. It was with a view to avoid or remove this ignorance by human effort that the *nirvikalpa samādhi* was invented. They succeeded in their goal only partially; because when they came out of the samādhi state, the shroud of ignorance engrossed them once again. So a permanent solution had to be sought again.

924. HOW DO YOU EXPERIENCE BEAUTY IN AN OBJECT?

Beauty, as the world conceives it, is nothing but the harmony of discordant things. The discordant notes in the object first attract you. Slowly, the notes die away and you become aware of an external harmony; which in its turn leads you to the inner harmony in which you yourself are lost. This inner harmony is itself beauty – your real nature.

925. DOES THIS NOT TAKE AWAY THE RELISH OF LIFE?

No. Never. It only enhances the relish. At first you enjoy beauty. But then you desire to be that enjoyment which is beyond that joy, and thus you are taken to that harmony itself. You put that question because you have not experienced beauty or harmony in its fullness.

926. HOW DO THE SAGE AND THE IGNORANT MAN SEE BEAUTIFUL THINGS?

The Sage sees first pure degreeless harmony and then he sees the object. So he may be said to see the object in the beauty. But the ordinary man, who stands only at the body level, sees the object first; and only then does he see something of the beauty or harmony expressed in the object. This helps him to have a peep into the beyond and nothing more.

27th July 1953

927. DEEP SLEEP AND SAMĀDHI – CAN THEY BE COMPARED?

The deep sleep experience, as it is understood by the ordinary man, is a mixture of a positive and a negative experience. Samādhi of the yōgin is a positive experience alone and both take place in the realm of the mind.

928. HOW CAN SAMĀDHI EXPERIENCE BE MADE THE ULTIMATE EXPERIENCE?

The samādhi experience is that '*I was happy.*' But when you understand, from a Kāraṇa-guru, that Happiness is your real nature, you come to realize that you are yourself the goal of samādhi. With this understanding, all hankering after samādhi disappears; though samādhi might still come upon you sometimes merely as a matter of course or samskāra. But you will never again be attracted by the enjoyment of happiness in samādhi.

If there is a general agreement with regard to anything objective, it is only an expression of the higher reason. If there is any sense of permanence or changelessness appearing anywhere, it can only be that of the ultimate background.

28th July 1953

929. WHAT OBSTRUCTS THE REALITY?

The presence as well as absence of the object. When you see the wall without the usual picture hanging on it, you form a percept and a concept together – the concept getting the better of the two. The percept is the absence of the picture and the concept is the idea of the presence of the picture. It is clear that the wall, as it is, will never be perceived if your attention is directed to either of the two. Similarly, the Reality behind the world is obstructed both by the presence of the world in the waking and dream states, and by its absence in the deep sleep state. You have to transcend both in order to reach the background.

930. WHAT IS MEANT BY 'DIRECTING ATTENTION TO'?

You have grown up from a baby to a man. It is a fact in itself. Can you say you remember it? *No*. You can only recognize it deeply. That is directing attention to it. Direct attention to your real nature also in a like manner.

31st July 1953

931. WHAT IS THE MISCHIEF OF TIME?

Time is only an idea. World is built upon the plurality of ideas, depending upon time which is but an idea. Therefore time is not. Idea is not. Both are nothing but the ultimate Reality. This time is the arch-deceiver of all. You rely upon him to establish the world and its religions.

What you recognize is here already. But what you remember has to be brought or created by a thought depending upon the illusion of time.

You are the changeless principle. So you need only recognize that fact.

1st August 1953

932. WHAT DO I SEEK BY LIBERATION?

Your own individuality, which is that changeless principle in you.

933. WHY HAS THE 'I'-PRINCIPLE NO ACTIVITY?

Because the 'I'-principle has neither organs nor mind.

But it is not dead. It is ever-present and it is from it that everything else gets light.

934. HOW DOES A TATTVŌPADĒSHA HELP ME AFTERWARDS?

You first listen to the Truth direct from the lips of the Guru. Your mind, turned perfectly sāttvic by the luminous presence of the Guru, has become so sensitive and sharp that the whole thing is impressed upon it as if it were a sensitive film. You visualize your real nature then and there.

But the moment you come out, the check of the presence of the Guru being removed, other samskāras rush in and you are unable to recapitulate what was said or heard. But later on, whenever you think of that glorious incident, the whole picture comes back to your mind – including the form, words and arguments of the Guru – and you are thrown afresh into the same state of visualization you had experienced on the first day. Thus you constantly hear the same Truth from within.

This is how a spiritual *tattvōpadēsha* helps you all through life, till you are established in your own real nature.

935. WHAT DOES THE WITNESS PERCEIVE?

The witness perceives only the material part of the activity, and never the Consciousness part of it.

936. HOW TO SEARCH FOR THE TRUTH?

It is usually undertaken in two ways. One way is by following an ascending order as in the traditional method, and the other in a descending order as in the direct method.

The former process is adopted by scientists, slowly ascending from the world, always attributing reality to the objective. Proceeding this way, they knock against a blank wall of ignorance, because they find no way to transcend duality.

The latter is a process of descent from the Ātmā down to the world of objects. Here you retain your perspective of non-duality, which is the characteristic of Ātmā, and from that stand you find it easy to discover the Truth – even behind the diversity of the world.

If you want to see the world in the correct perspective, you must first see yourself correctly and then the world will automatically shine in its true nature.

937. WHAT ARE TRIGUṆAS?

Tamas [passivity] and *rajas* [activity] are two distinct and separate qualities or attributes – each with a good proportion of the other mixed with it. But *sattva* [peace] is not a positive quality like the other two. It is that principle which keeps the balance between the other two.

Let us take an example. If a man walks and walks, without wanting to stop at all, that amounts to sattva, though on the surface it may appear to be rajas. Similarly, if a sleeping man, when he wakes up, is inclined to return to that sleep again rather than take to the activities of life in spite of all kinds of temptations for active life, that is also sattva, though it might appear on the surface as tamas itself.

So there is tamas in rajas and rajas in tamas – sattva balancing the two. If the ego does not come in to interfere, indolence is the Reality itself. It may also be said that there is only sattva. When it is divided into two, it appears as rajas and tamas. Sattva is the ultimate Reality itself (*shuddha-sattva*).

938. HOW DOES THE WORLD VANISH?

You cannot accept the evidence of form, in order to establish form. The evidence must be provided from a higher level.

Therefore, to examine the gross world, you have to rise to the next higher plane – the mental plane. Then the idea of space and along with it the idea of outside vanish.

Next, when you begin to examine the mental plane, you have to rise to the Consciousness plane, when the sense of inside also vanishes and the world disappears completely, leaving you as the 'I'-principle.

The mind can never conceive the 'generic'.

3rd August 1953

939. HOW TO APPLY THE ILLUSTRATION OF THE SNAKE IN THE ROPE?

The 'this'-ness of the rope stands for the 'I' in me, and the snake stands for body, senses and mind. This 'I' is attached to the illusion as well as to the Reality beyond.

10th August 1953

940. MEMORY AND OBJECTIFICATION OF TIME

Memory and objectification of time are the obverse and the reverse of the same coin, and upon that springs up the world.

Desire for liberation or Truth is not the function of the ego, but is the expression of the being in you. If one says sincerely that he takes a delight in being bound, surely he is liberated. (Of course 'bound' being used not in any limited sense but in the most comprehensive way.) He must be so deeply convinced of his real nature of Peace being the background of the bondage (misery) of every kind.

941. A SAGE IS IN REAL SAMĀDHI EVEN IN ACTIVITY. HOW?

When you see a thing, actually you become it. The 'it' vanishes or merges in you. This is nothing but samādhi [absorption]. This is equally true in respect of other sense organs also. This is the truth regarding the activities of the ordinary man. Much more so is it true of the Sage, who is every moment conscious of it.

942. WHAT DOES MAN DESIRE – COMPANY OR LONELINESS?

Only loneliness.

There is no denying that you like only Happiness, and it is to obtain Happiness that you seek company. But when Happiness dawns, you leave all company and stand alone. There you are in absolute loneliness. Even when you are deluded that your company gives you Happiness, if you carefully examine this you will find that you give up the objects including your own body, senses and mind the moment you begin to be happy. Do you like or welcome company in deep sleep, where you are all alone and happy?

943. HOW IS POWER AN OBSTACLE TO TRUTH?

The yōgin takes to Consciousness as power and thus the way to Consciousness as Truth is blocked. Power is objective and you become enamoured of that power, never wanting to get beyond.

944. HOW IS A SAGE EQUIPPED TO BE A KĀRAṆA-GURU, AN ĀCĀRYA?

Every Sage cannot be an Ācārya. It needs certain special qualifications to equip oneself to be an Ācārya. He must have the experience of all the different paths, particularly of those of devotion and yōga, so that he can guide the aspirants that come to him (sometimes with perverted experiences) without cutting the ground off their feet. These qualifications he can acquire by dint of exercises in the earlier stages of his spiritual life. In the light of the ultimate Truth, later on, he would be able to see the correct significance of such experiences.

There are Sages who, though they have had no such previous training, cannot help taking the role of the Guru; because they have been explicitly ordered by their own Gurus to do so. In such cases, all the necessary qualifications of the Guru come to them, as and when required. Whatever they are lacking will be supplied instantly by the *word* of their Guru. Look at the exalted certitude of Shrī Shankara when he declares:

> … jīvo nā 'haṁ dēśikō 'ktyā śivō 'ham ..
>
> *Shrī Shankara,* Advaita-pancaratnam, 1.2
>
> By the *word of my Guru*, I am not the jīva, I am Peace itself.

945. HOW IS THE EGO TRANSFORMED?

It is your thought, that every object is distinct and separate from you, that constitutes the waking state with the ego full-blown. If you stand separate from any object, that separateness will also exist between objects.

Gradually, you discover that your body is also an object like any other, and you begin to look upon it as something separate from you. Then you become a mental being. This is the first stage of progress when the ego loses its grossness.

The mental stand is next given up and then your stand is in the 'I'-principle. Then the whole of the objective world appears as a single mass and that whole mass stands transformed into pure Consciousness. Grossness vanishes first and subtleness vanishes next.

Then you stand as pure Consciousness. This experience may happen either in the dream state or in the waking state; but the result is the same. Sometimes in your dream you feel it is a dream; in a few seconds, without any further effort, the whole thing dissolves into pure Consciousness.

24th August 1953

946. WHY DOES NOT THE EXPERIENCE OF DEEP SLEEP HELP ONE SPIRITUALLY?

Because the ordinary man looks upon deep sleep objectively. If deep sleep loses its sense of objectivity and becomes subjective, you are free.

947. WHAT DOES 'I KNOW IT' MEAN?

First the 'it' stands for form or object. Next, 'it' stands for seeing. At last, 'it' stands for knowledge.

Thus the statement means 'I know knowledge', i.e. 'I know I', i.e. 'I. I. I.'

948. WHAT IS A PERCEPT?

That which is perceived. If you emphasize the 'that' part of it, the percept becomes 'that' and ceases to be a percept.

25th August 1953

949. HOW DOES THE WITNESS STAND HELP ME?

The witness stand helps you to renounce everything in effect, without renouncing anything physically or mentally.

950. HOW TO SEE THE FORM OF THE LORD?

You see the Lord through his pranks or deeds or mischief in his story. So also see the Lord in and through his form.

31st August 1953

951. WHAT ARE FREE CHOICE AND FREE WILL?

They are both contradictions in terms. Freedom cannot have anything beside it; so choice is out of the question. The real 'I'-principle alone is, always, free. If anything stoops to choose, it is the ego that does it. The ego is itself not free, its choice cannot be free and it cannot help another to be free. The same applies to free will. They are both misnomers.

952. ARISTOTLE SAYS THAT MAN IS A SOCIAL ANIMAL AND ABHORS SOLITUDE. IS IT JUSTIFIABLE?

The remark is superficial and made from a purely social standpoint. The truth on closer examination is just the opposite. I say: 'Man is always in solitude and can never be otherwise.'

Can you share with another any part of your pain or pleasure? *No.* Even your company has to come at last to 'you' in loneliness in order to be recognized. They are also a projection of yourself.

Really there is no enjoyment in company. In company the mind is always dissipated. The mind must die in order to be happy.

Samskāras = Innate tendencies.
Witnessing = Disinterested perception.

1st September 1953

953. HOW TO EXAMINE AN ACTION (DOING)?

It has to be done subjectively and not objectively. Then the doer and the deed both vanish, not being present in the doing.

> draṣṭra-darśana-dṛśyēṣu pratyēkaṁ bōdha-mātratā …
>
> [The see-er, seeing and the seen –
> of these, each is pure consciousness.…]

Shrī Shankara

2nd September 1953

954. TRIPUṬĪ IS A MISNOMER.

Even to say that two things exist simultaneously, you must admit that you can conceive or perceive two things simultaneously. This is impossible. So the tripuṭī [the triad of see-er, seeing and seen] cannot exist simultaneously.

15th September 1953

955. WHAT IS RENUNCIATION?

Your real nature is renunciation itself. Renunciation of doership and enjoyership from all your activities is real renunciation. Renunciation can never be made. It is the natural effect of directing your attention to your real nature.

956. FALLACY OF OPPOSITES

You cannot attribute activity or inactivity to another, from the standpoint of the onlooker. If you can perceive an activity without making reference to its opposite, which is only a concept at a different point of time, you are safe.

At one point of time the opposites cannot exist together. Nor are they opposites as such. Thus each is independent and complete in itself. So each is the ultimate Truth. Thus reference to opposites is impossible at the same point of time.

What you call non-walking is in fact only another form of walking. Therefore there is neither walking nor non-walking.

957. THE EGO IS LIKE A GHOST. HOW?

The ghost, having no form of its own, takes possession of somebody else's form. When exorcized from there, he takes possession of the form of still another.

Similarly, the ego has no form of its own. It claims the form of doer, perceiver or enjoyer after the activity. The best way to kill the ego is to refuse to give it any of these forms. The ego will then be starved to death.

Directing attention to your real nature is the only sure means of killing the ego.

17th September 1953

958. WHY IS NOT BEAUTY SEEN IN THE SAME OBJECT BY DIFFERENT PERSONS?

Because different persons have such different perspectives and different stands, setting up different standards, and they look at things also differently. So recognition and appreciation of beauty differs from person to person.

959. WHAT IS BEAUTY AND ITS RELATION TO OBJECTS?

Some see beauty in the mountain. A mountain is a concrete object of perception and beauty is the experience. You cannot separate the two. So you make the mountain the possessor of beauty and call it beautiful.

But the Truth is just the opposite. Beauty possesses the mountain, because beauty exists beyond the body, senses and mind and so can exist even without the mountain or any other object. That which transcends body, senses and mind is only the 'I'-principle or Truth. So beauty is yourself.

960. HOW DO THE JNYĀNIN AND THE IGNORANT MAN PERCEIVE BEAUTY?

1. The Jnyānin sees the mountain as beauty, keeping beauty as beauty, sublime to the core.
2. The ignorant man sees beauty in the mountain, keeping the mountain as the mountain gross and inert.

The Sage sees the body as *Ātmā* and the ignorant man sees *body* as Ātmā, each emphasizing the part italicized, and ignoring the other part.

In the first case, beauty appears as the mountain, mountain-ness vanishes, and beauty alone remains.

In the second case the mountain appears beautiful; mountain-ness is emphasized; and beauty comes and goes.

22nd September 1953

961. WHAT IS SUICIDE?

You find it impossible to get what you want with this body. So you hope to get it elsewhere. You consider this body to be an obstacle to the attainment of that which you desire. So you try to remove that obstacle (your body) hoping thereby to achieve your desire.

24th September 1953

962. WHAT IS THE ULTIMATE REALITY?

It is that principle which denies everything else. It cannot refuse existence to itself. You cannot say it is Consciousness. Who says so? The mind cannot. You cannot say it exists; because then it and existence must be different. You cannot say it is existence; because then you must have perceived it. Therefore you cannot say anything about the Reality.

28th September 1953

963. HOW DOES ONE LIVE?

We see two distinct ways of living. They are:

1. The ignorant man's life, and
2. The jīvan-mukta's life.

Life consists of the relationship of objects and knowledge. Objects and knowledge are distinct and separate. The ignorant man attributes reality to objects alone and lives in them. His life begins with the mind and ends there. Therefore, he is bound. His activities begin from the ego and end in the ego.

But the jīvan-mukta knows that objects are nothing but Consciousness and lives in Consciousness. He knows that life begins in him, beyond the mind, in Consciousness and ends there. Therefore what ordinarily affects an ignorant man does not affect the Sage.

Thus the Sage is not upset by apparently conflicting thoughts, feelings, perceptions or actions. He sees them all as nothing but Consciousness, the Self. That is the reason why activities do not leave any samskāra in the Sage. The Sage knows that even the ego rises from Consciousness and ends there.

So the difference comes only with regard to the centre. To the ignorant man, the centre is the ego; and to the Sage, the centre is Consciousness.

Know that your relationship with an object is only 'knowing'. The jīvan-mukta is a living commentary of the Truth you have visualized. So knowing that life is Consciousness, live in Consciousness and be free.

2nd October 1953

964. WHAT IS IDOL WORSHIP?

You cannot worship anything but a form. Concepts and percepts are all forms. Brahman and the infinite are also forms. An idol is only something known particularly. It is the symbol of the Absolute. But in fact nobody worships the idol; because, in practice, after looking at the idol for a few moments, you invariably close your eyes and contemplate that of which the idol is only a symbol. Nobody worships the idol, and nobody can worship without an idol.

15th October 1953

965. WHAT IS NOTHINGNESS?

Nothingness can never be perceived by the sense organs nor conceived by the mind.

bhāvāntaram abhāvō 'nyō na kaś cid anirūpaṇāt

[Source of quotation uncertain]

Nothingness is only the change from one positive thing to another positive thing. You become what you perceive. You are not nothing and therefore can never become nothing. So you cannot perceive nothingness. Nothingness is never perceived but only otherness.

18th October 1953

966. WHAT IS REAL BHAKTI?

It is not merely the adoration of the form of the personal god. It is the resulting mobility or melting of the heart that is the real goal. You have to get that melting of the heart even in *tattva* as it comes from the lips of the Guru. This melting should happen, not in any of the lower levels, but in a higher level and by something pertaining to the right Absolute.

21st October 1953

967. WHAT IS MADNESS?

Variety is madness. See the unity (witness) behind the variety and you transcend madness. Be the knower and you are sane and free.

968. HOW TO EXAMINE THE TRIPUṬĪ (TRIAD)?

Tripuṭī is constituted of the doer, doing and the deed. Of these three, the doing and the deed alone are perceived. But the doer comes in only after the function, and the doer is never perceived at all. So there is no separate doer. This so called 'doer' is the witness itself, but apparently limited or misunderstood.

draṣṭra-darśana-dṛśyēṣu pratyēkaṁ bōdha-mātratā …

[The see-er, seeing and the seen –
of these, each is pure consciousness....]

Shrī Shankara

969. WHY CAN YOU NOT SEE THE DOER?

Because the witness alone can see the doer. But the witness has no eyes to see; and the doer is not in the witness. So you can never see the doer.

25th October 1953

970. HOW DOES THE SAGE TALK?

The Sage always talks through *your* instruments. But there is something of the Sage even in those statements. Take note of that part with advantage and benefit yourself. The statements by themselves leave no mark behind.

8th November 1953

971. TEARS AND SAMĀDHI

A great man has said that a devotee *goes into* samādhi with tears in his eyes and that a Jnyānin *comes out of* samādhi with tears in his eyes. But I say that this is not yet the whole truth. One can very well *both* go into *and* come out of samādhi with tears in his eyes. This is definitely higher than the former experiences. The experience of the devotee was the result of contemplation (bhāvam) of his iṣhṭa-dēva. The second was the result of a short contact with the ultimate Truth. The third is the characteristic of the sahaja state of the established Jnyānin.

5th December 1953

972. WHO WANTS AND TAKES TO SHĀSTRAS?

It is only the ignorant man, who had not had the good fortune to be blessed by a living Sage (a Guru), that usually takes to shāstra – somewhat helplessly. Knowledge (Consciousness pure) is the parent of the shāstras. As such, the shāstras can never be the father of knowledge, nor can they awaken knowledge in the aspirant. One who is being guided by a Kāraṇa-guru will never need the service of any shāstra. The ultimate purpose and utility of all shāstras is only to convince the aspirant about the supreme need of a Kāraṇa-guru and to help him to seek one.

> uttiṣṭhata jāgrata prāpya varān nibōdhata .
>
> [Arise! Awake! Find those who are
> the best, and realize the Truth.]

Kaṭha Upaniṣhad, 3.14

20th December 1953

973. PROFESSOR EINSTEIN HAS SAID: 'WE CANNOT SAY THAT THERE IS AN "I" BEYOND THE REALM OF MIND AND INTELLECT.' WHAT DOES IT MEAN?

That certitude itself is the nature of that 'I' or Truth. So Einstein's own statement actually proves that 'I' beyond. Further, can Einstein prove that there is anything in or below the mental level? *No*. Then he has to deny himself everywhere. That certitude, which declares that I cannot say I exist beyond intellect, is itself the svarūpa (nature) of Truth.

21st December 1953

974. ALL PROBLEMS RISE IN THE MENTAL PLANE AND THERE IS NO PROBLEM IN THE PLANE BEYOND. THEN HOW IS ANY SOLUTION POSSIBLE?

Problems exist in the gross, sensual and mental planes. Each is solved not from its own plane, but only from the plane above it. Thus problems in the mental plane can be explained only from the plane beyond. For example take the palace on the stage curtain. The verdict of the eye is corrected by the intellect behind it. Similarly the experience of the mind and intellect are corrected by some principle from beyond the intellect.

23rd December 1953

975. THE KEY TO THE ULTIMATE TRUTH

Can there be a key to the ultimate Truth? Yes, of course. The interval between two mentations and deep sleep, if rightly understood, are keys to the absolute Truth.

25th December 1953

976. HOW TO PERFORM AN ACTION UNATTACHED?

Worldly actions can be performed in two ways:

1. By identifying yourself completely with body, senses and mind. Then the action is spontaneous as in the lay-man.
2. By standing behind and controlling body, senses and mind in order to achieve certain results, as in the case of the yōgin. You are still the apparent I, but more detached from the body, senses and mind.

There is still a higher kind of action which is not strictly worldly.

3. Stand beyond the mind as the witness of all the activities of the mind. As witness you are unaffected by objects or actions and so you are unattached in your action.

28th December 1953

977. WHAT IS BONDAGE AND HOW TO BE LIBERATED?

Diversity is bondage and non-duality is liberation.

When you, yourself, stand as the many, you cannot help seeing many outside. But when you stand as the only *one*, you can never see the many. The many in you are body, senses and mind. Stand as the one subject in yourself, and the world will also stand reduced to the one Reality. This is liberation.

If anyone says he is in trouble, ask him, 'Are you one or are you many?' He will certainly reply, 'I am one.' Then say, 'Be that one always', and all trouble will vanish at once.

978. HOW TO SEE THE FLOWER AS IT IS?

You see the things possessed by the flower through the senses and mind possessed by you. But to see the flower as it is, you must stand by yourself, dispossessed of senses and mind. Then you see the flower as yourself, pure Consciousness.

8th January 1954

979. PLEASURE

Pleasure (or a sigh of relief) is a prelude to the state of Peace and is often mistaken for Peace itself.

980. THE BODY

The body is the cell in which both the Sage and the ignorant man seem to sleep. The one feels free and the other bound.

> svayamē tanne lākkappil sukhamāy˘ viśramicciṭuṁ
> inspekṭaŕ ennapōl dēha-pañjarē vāṟka saukhyamāy˘

> [As in a cell in his own lock-up,
> an inspector of police
> may rest content and be refreshed;

> so also in this cage of body,
> one who is in charge of it
> may live refreshed, at one with that
> which is contentment in itself.]

Shrī Ātmānanda
[see also note 920]

12th January 1954

981. WHAT IS THE 'IT'?

The 'It' in our transactions is the real part of the world. What is this 'It'? That alone can be permanent or real which answers equally to your perception, thought, feeling and knowing. That which answers to all these four alike is only the 'I' or Consciousness. That is itself the 'It'.

982. WHAT IS THE DIFFERENCE BETWEEN LISTENING TO THE WORDS OF THE SAGE AND READING THE SAGE'S WRITINGS?

When you read the works of a Sage you read your own sense into his words. You try to illumine the writings of the Sage with the distorting light of your puny intellect, and you fail miserably. But, on listening to the Sage, because the Sage himself gives the full blaze of his light of pure Consciousness to the talk, his words are understood by you in the *correctest* manner, in spite of all your resistance.

Doing good to the world by itself is no criterion to prove that an individual has realized the Truth.

983. GRADATION OF LOVE

> Love is *conditioned* (kāma) when it is limited to your physical body.
>
> Love is *gratitude* (snēha) when it is attached not so much to the body as to your subtle being.
>
> Love is *prēma*, where there is no consideration of the lower self at all. The ideal goal of Hindu marriage is to be wedded in love as *prēma*.

Why does a Sage take pains to talk in order to enlighten others? It is for the self-satisfaction of the Sage, himself, and not of the apparent 'I'. The self-satisfaction of the Sage covers the whole world including the listeners. Therefore it is pure love that speaks to love. The love of the Sage is not conditioned and has no purpose. It is that love that talks.

14th January 1954

984. STATES OF GOD

As the individual soul has three states, so has God.

> The gross universe is God's waking state.
> The cosmic mind is God's subtle word (or dream state).
> *Pralaya* (deluge) is God's deep sleep state.

15th January 1954

985. WHAT IS YOUR PLACE IN AN ACTIVITY?

An important statement is often made by you. You say, '*I stand here.*'

Who says that? Certainly not the dead inert body which is standing, but someone who has seen the standing. He, the witness, can only see and cannot say. This sayer is the ego, who identifies himself with the witness and claims the witnessing for himself.

Therefore in every statement which concerns your activities, there are three different entities involved, namely the body, the ego and the witness. Of these three, know that you are always the witness. Be there, and you are free.

986. WHAT IS THE GOAL OF MUSIC?

Harmony outside takes you to harmony inside, and harmony inside is the 'I'-principle itself. Thus music takes you to the harmony behind it, and that takes you to the harmony inside which is Truth itself.

16th January 1954

987. WHY DOES NOT THE SAGE WORK FOR THE UPLIFT OF HUMANITY?

Answer: Where is the humanity please, for whom I am to work?

Questioner: This humanity we see.

Answer: Why don't you then work for the suffering humanity you perceived with an equal sense of reality in your dream state?

I am working for it in my own way, not by doling out material comforts, but by examining the correctness of this apparent humanity and its apparent suffering; and proving that the whole of humanity is myself, the real 'I'-principle, and that the appearance is all an illusion.

But you are trying to reach the same goal through your organs of action. These, being products of the waking state, can never take you to the goal of Peace and Happiness which is clearly beyond the waking state.

22nd January 1954

988. FORM AND SEEING

You say that all forms you see are seeing alone, because form and seeing are one. Why can't you assert for the same reason that all is form?

The basic method employed in all examination is the verification of distant things by instruments nearer and better known to you. Therefore you cannot take your stand in form and examine seeing, since seeing is nearer to you than form. So form merges in seeing and not the other way round. In examining the world, the object first reduces itself into the known. In the next step the known is found to be nothing but knowledge itself. So the world is nothing but knowledge.

23rd January 1954

989. FORGETFULNESS BY FAR EXCELS GRATEFULNESS

> mayy ēva jīrṇatāṁ yātu yatvayō 'pakṛtaṁ harē
> naraḥ pratyupakārā 'rthī vipattim abhivāñchati

[Source of quotation uncertain]

Meaning: If you have done me any good, may all thought of it die in me, and let me not long to help you in return. Because otherwise that would actually be longing for misfortune to befall upon you, in order to give me an opportunity to do you good in return.

31st January 1954

990. HOW TO CONDUCT ONESELF AFTER VISUALIZING THE TRUTH?

You may conduct yourself in everyday life exactly as you have always done. But there will be a world of difference between your activities before and after visualization of Truth. Formerly you lost yourself in the objects, but now it is their turn to lose themselves in you.

991. WHEN DO YOU KNOW YOURSELF?

You know yourself when there is neither something nor nothing to be known.

3rd February 1954

992. BRAIN IS INACTIVE BETWEEN MENTATIONS

The state between two thoughts is the same as the state when you appear to think, 'I am' or 'I know I am.' Then the brain cells do not function even though you appear to think. If you ask the doctor to examine you at that time, he can only say that the brain is still, or not perceptible.

993. BACKGROUND

The apparent variety must prove the existence of something changeless as its background. Analysing the variety and reaching the so called background, its background-ness also vanishes and you stand Absolute in your real nature, which was merely called the background in relation to the appearance.

4th February 1954

994. WHAT IS EXPRESSION?

The real 'I'-principle is not the expression. It is the Reality itself (the expressed). But when you consider it in terms of its characteristics as happiness or knowledge, with a beginning and an end, that is what is called an 'expression'.

995. WHY DO BHAKTAS NOT LIKE ADVAITA?

Strictly speaking they are also seeking advaita. But they do not know what they are doing. They want enjoyment and do not want to give it up. They are afraid that they will loose their enjoyment in actual advaita. But when they are made to understand that the happiness, which they assume they enjoy, is but an expression of the real 'I'-principle (advaita), the bhakta becomes an advaitin and realizes the

Truth. So the real 'I'-principle is the expressed and the happiness aspect a mere expression.

Lord Kṛiṣhṇa is the happiness in the vision of the Lord. If you admit that you want that happiness in all the three states, without a break, it is only that principle that is persistently present in all the three states that can provide it. There is only one such principle, and that is the real 'I'-principle, and its real nature is pure Happiness. Therefore get beyond the name and form of the Lord and you are in advaita.

996. What is getting beyond name and form?

Understanding name and form to be but an expression of the impersonal, and then meditating even upon that name and form, takes you beyond name and form. Then, the reaction that comes is from the impersonal, and that spontaneously raises you to the impersonal.

This is the way to get beyond name and form. Understand God to be impersonal and then meditate upon any of his names and forms to get beyond all appearance. Worldly knowledge expires in 'enjoyment'; 'enjoyment' expires in 'becoming'; and 'becoming' expires in 'being'.

997. Some say that it is only after death that one can become one with God. Is it true?

At the moment of every enjoyment of happiness you are really momentarily dead, and have become one with God (whose real nature, *svarūpa*, is objectless Happiness). Then your body is relaxed, the sense organs refuse to function, the mind ceases to think or feel, and you enjoy happiness as you call it. All the principles that claim to live have, for that moment, died.

Therefore, you are actually dying every moment, to become God. So don't wait for the last death of the body, but know that you are doing it every moment and you become God himself (real advaita).

6th February 1954

998. APHORISMS AND THEIR INTERPRETATIONS

'*Thou art that.*' (Tat tvam asi)

None but a Sage can understand the real significance of this aphorism or discuss its meaning. In order to understand anything, you must stand at least one step higher than the level of the object concerned. Thus in order to understand the correct meaning of '*thou*', you have to stand beyond the '*thou*'; and to understand the meaning of '*that*', you have to stand beyond the '*that*'. Therefore all remarks, in books by those who are not Sages, about the meaning of such aphorisms can only be short-sighted and wrong.

999. HOW TO REALIZE *BRAHMAN*?

Brahman is conceived as remote and big by the relatively small, apparent 'I'. It has to be brought into the present and experienced by the 'I'. To this there are two obstacles: the smallness of the 'I' and the farness or distance of *brahman.*

The idea of smallness of the 'I' is removed by contemplating the aphorism 'I am brahman' (Ahaṁ brahmā 'smi).

After experiencing identity with brahman, by deep contemplation, you are asked to contemplate another aphorism 'Brahman am I' (Brahmai 'vā 'ham). This process brings brahman nearer and establishes its identity with the ever-present 'I'.

But the sense of bigness attached to brahman still continues. This limitation has to be transcended by contemplating still another aphorism 'Consciousness is brahman' (Prajñānaṁ brahmā).

Thus you reach the state of pure advaita. But this can be attained directly, even at the very outset, by seeing the 'I' to be nothing but Consciousness.

1000. WHAT DO YOU ACHIEVE BY PRACTISING YŌGA?

By yōga one achieves only such things as can be achieved by other means and that only after involving much more time and effort. It is foolish to waste one's life on such things.

Realization of Truth cannot be achieved by yōga. Realization is possible only by approaching a Sage and surrendering yourself unconditionally to Him. Therefore devote your life to the attainment of that end and to nothing else.

8th February 1954

1001. CAN IT BE SAID THAT ART COMES OUT OF SUFFERING?

Many artists suffer intensely. Still, profound works of art come out of them. Of course art is the expression of Truth. So can it be said that art comes out of suffering?

Let us first examine the question itself. From what level does the question arise? Certainly from the level of duality. Art is the expression of harmony. Where there is harmony, there are no words or any other kind of duality. So through the harmony of words, get to the harmony beyond, which is your real nature. Art is the expression of that harmony.

Or in other words, look at the question subjectively, find out your relationship with that question, and try to solve it from that level. Then you will find that at your own level, the question does not arise at all. This alone is the ultimate solution of all such questions. Approach every question in this manner.

Discord and harmony are both related only to you and not to each other. If you go to either and remain there alone, it ceases to be what it is called and becomes the Truth itself.

1002. ORIGIN OF SPACE AND TIME

You yourself are the permanent substratum, and the urge naturally comes from deep within you to give a similar substratum to all changes outside.

The substratum of changing objects is space; but space is as dead and inert as an object itself. Just give Consciousness to space and it becomes the Absolute.

So also, time is the permanent substratum of thoughts and feelings and is dead and inert as well. Give Consciousness to time and it also becomes the Absolute.

By 'give Consciousness to it', I mean either see it subjectively or see it as possessing consciousness.

> dvayōr madhya-gataṁ nityam asti-nā 'stī 'ti pakṣayōḥ
> prakāśanaṁ prakāśyānām ātmānaṁ samupāsmahē
>
> *Yōga-vāsiṣhṭha* [unverified]

I stand between 'is' and 'is not', explaining or illuminating both. When you understand that light as the being itself, the non-being disappears.

1003. How to view 'I am all'?

The all should merge in the 'I' and disappear, leaving the 'I' absolute. But if you begin to expand the 'I' into the 'all', you go wrong and still remain as the object. The objectivity must disappear completely.

If you say that 'Nothing *is*', it does not mean that non-existence is the end of all, but that existence is the end of all; because the 'is' at the end of the statement stands for being or existence alone.

14th February 1954

1004. What is *ahankāra* and how to rise above it?

Ahankāra [ego] is the sense of one's separateness from everything else. You can rise above it only by reaching the background Truth, where all sense of separateness vanishes. One of the tests of having annihilated the ego is a genuine sense of humility, expressing itself by never trying to exploit or even recognize your position of vantage and perfection.

1005. Why are people (and even gods) fond of flattery?

All flattery is directed to the Reality behind the ego. Even though you do not know it, you are that Reality. The false identification of the ego with the 'I'-principle enables you to be pleased, and the ego wrongly claims for himself all praise.

1006. WHY DON'T 'I' KNOW MYSELF IN DEEP SLEEP?

In deep sleep you are all alone. In that state, you can never split yourself into two – one part knowing the other. You had no knowledge even of yourself there. Hence you can never know that, when you *are* that.

1007. WHAT HAPPENS WHEN I SAY 'I ENJOY HAPPINESS' OR THAT 'I KNOW OR PERCEIVE ANYTHING'?

It is all a lie. It is a distortion created by the ego, by interpreting the Truth in the ego's own terms. So, whenever you say you perceive, know or enjoy anything, you are really in your own background, the Truth. When you say you see anything, you are seeing the mind assuming that form. If you are seeing the mind in that manner what is your position? You can only be the witness of the mentation.

15th February 1954

1008. ARE MIND AND SENSES PRESENT IN CONSCIOUSNESS?

'Some people say that mind and senses are not present in Consciousness. That position is wrong. They are present in Consciousness. Are you not aware of the existence of mind and senses?'

'Yes, of course.'

'So are they not in your awareness which is pure Consciousness?'

'Yes.'

3rd March 1954

1009. WHAT IS THE RIGHT WAY OF UNDERSTANDING?

Through the expression to the expressed is the right way of understanding. When you are listening to his teaching, you are accepting the teacher as your 'self'. The expressed is always the teacher.

You are never asked to look out – through the senses or mind. Looking in, you are yourself alone as the 'I'-principle, which is another vision of the teacher. The teaching is only a means to make you look in. The teaching takes you beyond body and mind where you get a vision of the teacher himself. There you see the teacher in the whole. No part of him is left behind.

> teḷivāy˘ oḷivāy˘ nilkkum oḷiyāṁ poruḷ aśramaṁ
> mama kāṇicca mal svāmi caraṇaṁ śaraṇaṁ mama .

Shrī Ātmānanda, Ātmārāmam, 1.19

(It means: 'My Lord has most graciously and effortlessly revealed to me the self-effulgent Truth which though ever shining was unnoticed so long. His holy feet alone are my eternal solace.')

Here the teacher, the teaching and the taught are one. The understanding is also the real 'I'-principle. To teach anything, the teacher must stand above the teaching. So the teacher, standing beyond the mind, is helping the disciple to come to that level, through the medium of teaching which takes him beyond body and mind.

You can never remember what *you* do understand. You can remember only that which the mind has understood. Here understanding the truth means becoming the Truth. If you want to repeat the same experience, think of the teacher along with the teaching and you will easily be led on to the same experience (the expressed). You cannot express yourself as you wish. So never desire that. But if the expressed (the Truth) ever chooses to express itself at any moment in any manner, enjoy it. That is all.

In all phenomenal teaching it is only '*his*' that is transmitted, often in parts, through the teaching. But in spiritual teaching it is '*he*' that is taught or transmitted and that not in part but in *full.* The Guru's form is the only object in the universe which, if contemplated upon, takes you directly to the real subject – the Reality.

12th March 1954

1010. WHERE DO YOU WAKE UP FROM A DREAM STATE?

(In the dream itself or in the waking state?)

If the waking act is an act in the waking state, the waking state must have existed even before the waking act. Then it is no waking act. Nor can it ever take place in the dream state either. So the waking act is timeless. The timeless is the Ultimate, or the 'I'-

principle. So you wake up into the interval between the states, where you are alone and timeless.

7th April 1954

1011. SOLIPSISM

Solipsism is a cult developed in the west. They hold the 'self' as the only knowable or existent thing. According to them the ego is the 'self'. Solipsism may well be accepted by Vēdānta if the word 'self' is interpreted to mean the real 'I'-principle, which remains over even after the annihilation of the ego.

8th April 1954

1012. WHAT DO YOU KNOW IN DEEP SLEEP?

You do not know anything objective in deep sleep.

But you might say you know Happiness. No, not even that. You do not know Happiness. It is unknowable.

But it may be said that you know the limitations placed on it by time or the boundaries of Happiness, which belong evidently, not to deep sleep or Happiness, but to the other states immediately before and after deep sleep. These boundaries are perceived only in the dream or waking states, and then you call the interval deep sleep and its content Happiness, since the opposite of happiness was not experienced.

Suppose that the deep sleep continues. Would you be able to recognize it? No. Still you would perceive only the very same boundaries when not in deep sleep. Therefore you do not know anything in deep sleep.

1013. INTERVAL BETWEEN TWO MENTATIONS

Unable to refute the argument that Peace prevails in the interval between two mentations, some imitation teachers – possessing mere book lore – advise their unfortunate followers to endeavour to extend the period of the interval, hoping thereby to extend the Peace in time. Poor souls, they understand neither Peace nor the interval.

It is only a *Jnyānin* that can draw your attention to the interval between two mentations. In so directing your attention to it, the purpose of the Jnyānin is not to show you the limitations of the interval, but its content. The limitation is mere time, and the content of the interval is beyond both time and mind. When you perceive that content which is your own Self, you go beyond mind and time, and the limitations belonging only to the mental sphere disappear at once. Thus what appeared as interval ceases to be an interval, but stands as the Absolute.

So the advice to endeavour to extend the period of the interval is absurd. It amounts to advising you never to allow the mind, as such, to disappear.

1014. SHIVŌHAM

> rajjv ajñānād bhāti rajjau yathā 'hiḥ
> svātmā-jñānād ātmanō jīva-bhāvaḥ .
> dīpēnai 'tad bhrānti-nāśē sa rajjur
> jīvō nā 'haṁ dēśikō 'ktyā śivō 'ham ..
> [see note 713]

Shrī Shankara, Advaita-pancaratnam, 1.2

This verse is often quoted to establish that Peace or Happiness is your real nature. The phrase 'dēśikō 'ktyā', meaning 'by the word of my Guru', is the heart and soul of the whole verse. That word starts from the Guru, the background of *Ātmā*; and it has certainly the aroma of Ātmā in it. It is that word or sound carrying that aroma with it that drills itself into the disciple and makes it impossible for him to escape from visualizing Ātmā at once.

When once the Truth is thus visualized, you can repeat that experience as often as you want, by trying to recollect the circumstances antecedent to it which throw you into the same experience beyond all circumstances. This experience you can never remember, since it is beyond the mind. But you can remember only the antecedent circumstances which led you on to that experience. So Happiness alone is experienced and the antecedents alone are remembered.

1015. Efficacy of the spoken word of the Guru and the written word

When the Guru talks to you about the Truth there is no doubt that it is the words that you hear. But the words disappear at once. Nothing remains for you to refer to or to depend upon, except the Guru himself. So in case of any doubt you approach the Guru again any number of times; and every time he explains it in a different set of words. Each time you understand the same sense, more and more deeply. Therefore it is evident that it is not from words or their meaning that you understand the sense, because the words used each time are different. From this it is clear that something else also follows the words, from the Guru. It is this something that penetrates into the inmost core of the disciple and works the miraculous transformation called experience.

When you read the written word before listening to the Truth from the lips of the Guru, that something, which follows the spoken word of the Guru, is entirely absent; and you have to depend upon the dead word which is still before you and its meaning as your ego is inclined to interpret it, in the dark light of its own phenomenal experiences. Naturally, therefore, you miss that divine experience when you only read the written word; though it is so easily and effortlessly obtained in the presence of the Guru, or after even once listening to the Truth from him.

When you listen to the spoken word of the Guru, even on the first occasion your ego takes leave of you and you visualize the Truth at once, being left alone in your real nature. But when you read the same words by yourself, your ego lingers on in the form of the word, its meaning etc., and you fail to transcend them. To visualize the Truth, the only condition needed is the elimination of the ego. This is never possible by mere reading, before meeting the Guru. Therefore listen, listen, listen and never be satisfied with anything else. After listening to the Truth from the Guru direct and after visualizing the Truth in his presence, you may well take to thinking deeply over what the Guru has told you. This is also another form of listening and takes you, without fail, to the same experience you have already had in his presence.

9th June 1954

1016. Dr. H. and his wife asked: 'WHAT BOOKS ON PHILOSOPHY SHALL WE READ'?

Books will not help you much to understand the Truth. Sometimes they may even do you much harm. Suppose you read the *Bhagavad-gītā* which is recognized as one of the tripods of Hindu religion. Your only help is the existing commentaries. You do not know whether a particular commentator was a man who had realized the Truth or not. If he had not, he will misguide you. You can read only your *own* sense in a book, be it the original or a commentary.

A Sage alone can show you the Truth. But after understanding the Truth from the Sage, you may read only the few books he suggests, to keep you in the groove he has chalked out. After some time, when you are established in the Truth yourself, you may read any book, good or bad.

Every book has some nuggets of Truth in it. You will yourself be able to pick these out and throw away the dross. If nothing in the book attracts you, accept it for its existence value and thus find it an expression of the Ultimate.

1017. WHEN DOES THE HIGHER REASON COME INTO PLAY?

When you want to know something beyond the experiences of the body, senses or the mind, then the higher reason comes into play.

1018. PHILOSOPHY WESTERN AND EASTERN

Western philosophy is all speculation in the realm of the mind. But Indian philosophy is '*darshana*', meaning visualization or direct experience.

1019. METHODS OF SELF-REALIZATION – (COSMOLOGICAL AND DIRECT)

The cosmological method consists of three distinct stages:

1. Shravaṇa – listening to the Truth from the lips of the Guru.

2. Manana – thinking over it with concentrated attention over and over again.
3. Nididhyāsana – thinking profoundly about that Truth with the aid of reason.

This last exercise leads you to a state called nirvikalpa samādhi, where the mind remains in a state of stillness, and you stand as witness of everything. By getting accustomed to this state, by dint of the prolonged practice of samādhi, one day the seed of Truth, received from the Guru in the form of the aphorism 'Prajñānam asmi' (I am Consciousness), bears fruit and you realize your real nature of Consciousness. This is Self-realization.

Direct method: You listen to the Truth from the lips of the Guru, and you visualize your real nature the 'Truth' then and there. Then you are asked to cling on to the Truth so visualized, either by listening to the Guru as often as possible, or by repeating the same or other arguments to prove your real nature, over and over again. This last course is also another form of listening to the Guru and takes you, without fail, to that very same experience you had at first. Therefore listen, listen, listen to the Guru. This is the direct method.

11th June 1954

1020. PHENOMENAL KNOWLEDGE

Phenomenal knowledge is the inherent 'knowingness' within you, coming out occasionally through the mind or senses.

18th June 1954

1021. WHAT IS PRACTICAL?

The term 'practical' literally means that which is concerned with practice. By practice we mean habitual action. So 'practical', in the ordinary sense, involves body or mind.

But practical and impractical both depend for their very existence upon the fundamental Truth involved in the statement or experience: 'I know I am.' It is an assertion of the fact that I exist. Is there any mind or sense involved in this? No. It is pure experience or direct knowledge. It is more real and so more practical, if by 'practical' you mean real.

1022. WHY IS THERE DIVERSITY?

Really there is no diversity. This is the correct answer. But it can also be answered in other ways.

1. Because the 'why' is there. The 'why' is diversity itself. One thing is divided into two by mere words and kept separate. Here begins diversity. Take for example, the earth and the pot. There is the earth in the pot, and there is earth and earth alone. 'Pot' is only another name for the particular form temporarily assumed by the earth.
2. Because you stand as diversity yourself. See what you are in your phenomenal life. You are the body, senses, mind or anything else you please. But please tell me, which 'you' in this medley am I to address? Each of these has its corresponding objects outside. So it is only when you stand as diversity yourself that you perceive diversity outside. When you stand as the indivisible beyond the mind, as the real 'I'-principle, there is no diversity at all, anywhere.

1023. A PEEP INTO THE HEART OF YŌGA

Yōgins say vaguely that they are trying to control the mind by dint of vairāgya (dispassion) and exercise. This is easily said. But who is it exactly that controls the prāṇa and the mind?

Certainly not the mind itself; because the purpose of the exercise itself is to still the mind, and the same mind can never be simultaneously the subject and the object of the same activity. So some independent principle beyond the mind must be guiding the yōgin to control the prāṇa and the mind. Is it not better to be that free principle itself and cease bothering about the mind or anything else?

Leave the mind to itself. This is how the mind is dealt with in the direct method.

29th June 1954

1024. WHAT IS THE SIGNIFICANCE OF FRONT AND BACK IN SPIRITUAL CONTEXT?

Question: In *Ātma-nirvṛiti*, chapter 18 (verses 5-7), addressed 'To the mind', it is said: 'You should first look behind and see me there, and then I will draw you into the inmost core of your being.' What does this mean, and what is the significance of 'front' and 'back', so far as the mind is concerned?

Answer: The mind moves only in the realm of the body-samskāras. So by 'front' the mind means objects, and by 'back' it means absence of objects.

The mind is asked to look back, in its own language. Therefore it has to give up objects as a whole, when it gives up the front. But then it does not realize that the back – which is just the reverse of the front – has also simultaneously disappeared with the front.

So when the mind has given up objects and tries to look back, it is really left within itself – which is the inside of the mind, in the mind's own language. This is how the mind is drawn into the inmost core of one's being.

1st July 1954

1025. WHAT SHOULD I EMPHASIZE IN MY ACTIVITIES?

Every man has three distinct and progressive perspectives of the world: through the senses, the mind and Consciousness.

Through the senses, you perceive only gross objects. As you transcend the first and reach the second stage, you perceive only subtle objects or ideas. In the last stage, everything appears as Consciousness.

The Guru wants you only to recognize and emphasize sufficiently this last faculty (if faculty it may be called) or Consciousness. If you succeed in doing at least this much after listening to the Truth from the Guru, you will without doubt get established in the Reality. Emphasis on any one or both of the first two perspectives ties you down as a jīva.

1026. WHAT IS THE MEANING OF THE INDISPENSABLE 'IT'?

We usually say: 'I saw it', 'I thought about it', and 'I know it.'

The first 'it' is form.
The second 'it' is thought-form or idea.
The third 'it' is pure Consciousness.

Here our attempt is to establish a changeless 'It' behind all the three experiences. This shows that the thing is changeless (Consciousness).

dṛṣṭīṁ jñāna-mayīṁ kṛtvā paśyan brahma-mayaṁ jagat

[Converting sight of objects into
seeing that just knows, that very
seeing is none other than
the world's complete reality.]
[see note 1056]

Shrī Shankara, Aparokṣhānubhūti, 116

1027. WHAT IS WITNESS KNOWLEDGE?

Witness knowledge is pure Consciousness. But mentation knowledge always appears in the form of subject-object relationship. When you stand as witness, you are in your real nature.

Mentation appears in the light of the witness. *The light in the mentation knowledge is itself the witness.* There is no mentation in the witness.

The state of the witness is the same as that of deep sleep and Consciousness pure.

4th July 1954

1028. WHEN DID YOU WAKE UP?

If in your answer you refer to the waking time, it would mean that the waking state existed even before the so-called waking. In that sense waking has no meaning, and waking becomes merely an incident in the waking state. So also deep sleep becomes part of the waking state. Then the problem of waking does not arise, since deep sleep cannot be established as a separate state.

But waking is our experience, and this definitely precedes the waking state. In that condition, which we call waking, which separates the two states, waking time has not come into existence, and deep sleep has no time of its own. Therefore it is timeless, and the experience is not of a subject-object nature. This is your real nature of pure Consciousness.

Therefore every state appears in you and vanishes into you. Thus you do not wake at all, since you have never gone out of your own Self.

But speaking from a lower level, you can say that you wake up from every state into that so called interval which is your real nature, or you wake up into yourself, where there is no time and so the question 'when' does not apply to it.

It has been proved that you are in your real nature in between two mentations. The states are mere expanded mentations. Therefore, the interval between two states is also your real nature; and therefore you wake up into that unqualified wakefulness which is your real nature, and it is only subsequently that the next state appears.

Within the waking and dream states you are awake to the world. But between the states you are awake to your own Self.

13th July 1954

1029. RELATIONSHIP BETWEEN JĪVA-HOOD AND THE REAL NATURE

The jīva has a nine-fold samsāra, namely:

The doer	The doing	The deed
The enjoyer or perceiver	The enjoyment or perception	The enjoyed or perceived
The knower	The knowing	The known

One's jīva-hood and one's real nature can never be perceived by each other. But standing in the jīva itself, and accepting a small taint which is neither detrimental nor instrumental to the Truth, you can visualize the Reality; and this method is the method of the witness.

21st July 1954

1030. METHODS FOR SELF-REALIZATION

The methods usually adopted for Self-realization are of two kinds:

1. The absorption process (the traditional method).
2. The separation process (the direct method).

The yōgically minded jnyānins usually adopt the first method – that of *absorption.* Here you try to purify the mind and make it more and more sāttvic, until at last you make it fit to be absorbed into your own Self. There is still another application of the process of absorption. The object is at a distance. You bring it nearer by seeing. You bring it still nearer by loving. Lastly, by knowing, you absorb it into you.

The real jnyānins adopt the second method – that of *separation.* The ordinary man's self is a crude mixture of the real Self with a lot of accretions, viz., body, senses and mind. By proving, with the aid of reason and your own experiences, that you are not the body, senses or mind. Shown thus standing separate from all these, you remain in your real Self. According to this process, everything – from the intellect down to the body and the world – become objects to be separated from you.

1031. DISTINCTION AND NON-DISTINCTION

Non-distinction is imperceptible and is one's real nature. It expresses itself as distinction, which alone is perceptible. Therefore, in the attempt to visualize the non-distinction of Truth, distinction which is perceptible is made a means. It merges in the non-distinction at the last stage, and then the Truth shines in its own glory.

27th August 1954

1032. WHAT BINDS ME?

The world of forms is never the cause of bondage. It is the world of names alone that binds you.

A perception, left to itself, dies out naturally; but if you give a name to it, the perception becomes an idea. Then it becomes capable of being remembered, and only then does it begin to bind you.

1033. WHY DOES THE *BHAGAVAD-GĪTĀ* ENCOURAGE ALL PATHS?

It is proclaimed by all great men that one should not discourage an aspirant from following any path, unless one has something higher and easier to offer him. Therefore, no true shāstra discourages the pursuit of any path, even if it only serves as a preparation course.

The shāstras have varying degrees of applicability. Some have a very narrow field of scope, and others cover a very broad field. The *Bhagavad-gītā* is one with the broadest scope and so it is accepted as one of the tripods of Vēdānta. Its purpose is to point out the best and the most useful aspects of all the paths leading to the ultimate Truth. Every path has some nugget of Truth in it. The *Bhagavad-gītā* only picks them out and places them before you, for what they are worth. This is why the *Bhagavad-gītā* does not seem to decry any of the legitimate paths to the Reality.

30th August 1954

1034. ACTIONS

Two distinct kinds of actions have been employed in order to visualize the Truth. They are called *voluntary* and *involuntary*, with reference to the attitude of the mind.

1. The *voluntary* action makes the mind active and tries to comprehend Truth as its object. This path is evidently doomed to failure, since it can never take you beyond objective truth.

   Nirvikalpa samādhi is the highest experience that can result from such action. It is preceded by an intense effort. In the relative level, this effort may well be considered to be the cause and nirvikalpa samādhi its legitimate effect. So nirvikalpa samādhi is limited by causality. The yōgin admits that he goes into nirvikalpa samādhi and comes out of it. Therefore it is also limited by time. In order to get into nirvikalpa samādhi, the body is necessary for the yōgin to start with. Therefore nirvikalpa samādhi is also limited by space.

Thus nirvikalpa samādhi clearly forms part of the phenomenal.

2. The *involuntary* action is the other type. This is spontaneous and objectless. It comes over you involuntarily; you yield to it and merge into it. In its progress, the mind gets relaxed and ultimately disappears, leaving you to yourself all alone.

   This experience denotes the real significance of the term 'deep sleep'. The interval between two mentations is another instance of involuntary action. You stand as yourself alone in both these experiences, but you do not cease to be the same Reality, yourself, in the so called dream and waking states. Therefore you do not ever go into or come out of deep sleep, and it is uncaused.

   Hence deep sleep, if correctly understood, is evidently your real nature. It is, strictly speaking, no state at all; and is far beyond any samādhi.

2nd September 1954

1035. WHERE IS THE WITNESS?

A thought can never be remembered; but you can think of the object of your thought once again, or you can remember the fact that you had a thought. So you think only of the objects of your former thought.

Thought by itself is object of the witness alone. The object of the witness can never be remembered by the mind. Thought, divested of its objects, is the witness itself. So the witness is in the thought itself and not outside.

1036. HOW IS THE INDIVIDUAL RELATED TO THE COSMOS AND TO THE REALITY?

Strictly speaking, the individual comprehends the cosmos. The cosmos depends upon the individual, for its very existence. The conception of ourselves as embodied beings expands until it reaches the broad generality of ourselves as *living beings*. This is the highest concept of the human mind. Here, you comprehend the whole animate kingdom.

But you can look even beyond, though the mind cannot conceive anything higher. Besides the animate kingdom, there is the inanimate kingdom, which has also to be comprehended in your further expansion. Thus, when you try to be one with the inanimate kingdom as well, you can only say you exist. But this is not conceivable.

> *Life* is the first expression of the *sat* aspect of the Reality;
> *Thought* is the first expression of the *cit* aspect of the Reality; and
> *Feeling* is the first expression of the *ānanda* aspect of the Reality.

A strict examination of any expression through any of these aspects takes you to the Reality itself.

3rd September 1954

1037. A DISCIPLE ASKED: HOW SHOULD ONE LEAD A PROPER LIFE?

Before answering this, life has to be first defined. In order to perceive or define life you have to transcend duality. Life is that unknown something which enables even the prāṇa to function. Therefore neither prāṇa (the vital energy), nor any principle below that, can perceive life. The only moment I live is when I direct my attention to my real nature, the right Absolute.

So to visualize the Truth constantly is the only way really to live or to lead a proper life. Hence understand the Truth and try to live it. Then life becomes a synonym of Truth.

14th September 1954

1038. WHAT DOES THE JĪVA WANT?

The jīva is experience which is limited, and it also wants limited experience; but wants it for all time. That is, it wants it to be limited and unlimited simultaneously; in other words it wants limited experience itself to be unlimited. This is self-contradictory and impossible as long as you remain a jīva (a limited being).

Therefore what the jīva really wants is to become experience itself, which is unlimited and your real nature.

19th September 1954

1039. HOW DOES AN OBJECT SERVE ME?

An object is innocent in itself and serves you in accordance with the perspective through which you view it.

1. If you view it as dead and inert and as distinct and separate from you, it takes you from the centre of your being to the world outside.
2. But if you look upon it as something appearing in Consciousness and if you emphasize that Consciousness aspect of it, immediately it points to you – the source of that appearance – Consciousness being your real nature.

1040. HOW TO LOVE MY RELATIONS?

You have been shown that you are that permanent, changeless principle beyond your body, senses and mind. Consider your relation also as that principle.

You cannot love a changing thing, but you love only love or Consciousness. So it is that permanent principle in you that loves the same permanent principle in the other. Love is the real nature of both.

For this you have only to recognize, deeply, that love is your own real nature. No more effort is needed for its application. It follows automatically and does not stop till the whole world is absorbed into that love.

20th September 1954

1041. WHAT IS THE PURPOSE OF LANGUAGE?

It is to show the way to the Reality. This ideal, however, is miserably thwarted in its application. Language is made up of words. Each word has two meanings.

1. The literal meaning (padārtha); and
2. The ultimate meaning (paramārtha).

The literal meaning of every word pertains to name and form alone and the ultimate meaning pertains to the Reality. If you cling to the former you get lost in the world of illusion, and if you cling to the latter you are taken to the centre of your own being, the Reality.

1042. WHERE IS CONSCIOUSNESS IN GREATER EVIDENCE?

Consciousness is in greater evidence in the absence of the object than in the presence of the same.

Suppose an empty space is shown to you for you to sit down. At once you recognize the absence of a seat there and refuse to sit. But in the case of the actual chair pointed out, no active thought is called for and you safely ignore the part played by Consciousness. Relatively speaking, the play of Consciousness is more evident in the former than in the latter.

21st September 1954

1043. WHY DO YOU GIVE A THING A NAME?

Because you want the transient to be always associated with a permanent background; since you are, yourself, that permanent changeless principle behind the body, senses and mind.

So, that name denotes the unknown background, the Truth, which is in fact the best known.

25th September 1954

1044. WHEN I ANALYSE THE WORLD THE 'I'-NESS IN THE THINKER DISAPPEARS. THEN HOW CAN THE ANALYSIS CONTINUE?

Prakriyās or processes should never be mixed up. This question arises out of the confusion of the processes of absorption and separation.

The jīva is a part of the world and, as such, cannot analyse the world as a whole or any part of it. It is only the higher reason that can do this. Therefore when the thinker drops away as you say, it does not affect the analysis at all; it is Ātmā itself as the higher reason that does the analysis and continues to be. It is always the higher reason that analyses anything, gross or subtle. It utilizes instruments, like the mind and senses, to analyse other objects. But thoughts and feelings (mentations) are analysed by the higher reason without an instrument.

1045. WHAT IS 'I'-NESS?

It is used in two senses:

1. In the phenomenal plane, 'I'-ness distinguishes you from others. It contains the samskāras of body, senses and mind and is intended only for worldly purposes.
2. In the spiritual sense, it is the impersonal and changeless background of the apparent 'I'. It takes you to the ultimate Reality.

29th September 1954

1046. HOW IS INDIFFERENCE RELATED TO TRUTH?

Indifference can be sāttvic or tāmasic, as the case may be. Indifference leading you to the ultimate Truth can be said to be sāttvic, and that leading you to mere inaction and sleep can be said to be tāmasic. Indifference must always have an object.

If your indifference encompasses the universe, in part or whole, gross as well as subtle, it is sāttvic and brings you nearer the Truth.

But if you become indifferent in the least to your real nature, that indifference is tāmasic and must be shunned.

2nd October 1954

1047. HOW ARE THOUGHTS, RECORDED IN THE MIND, REMEMBERED?

First of all, the question does not arise. Because no question of why, where, when and how can ever arise in relation to the Absolute. Between objects themselves the question is quite relevant; but this question refers to some principle beyond the mind, which is nothing but the Absolute. Any question which has the slightest reference to the Absolute cannot be answered in the relative and the question does not arise in the Absolute.

The mind or memory is nothing but a thought. One thought cannot record another thought. Therefore it is wrong to assume that past thoughts are recorded in the mind.

> smṛti-rūpaḥ paratra-pūrva dṛṣṭāvabhāsaḥ
>
> *Shrī Shankara,* Adhyāsa-bhāṣhya (Introduction to Sūtra-bhāṣhya), 3.1

Seeing an object for the first time and taking it to be something you perceived some time ago is what is called *memory*. Look at your dream experience, if you feel any doubt. Therefore memory does not prove anything in the past.

Thought is illuminated by a ray of light. It cannot be recorded by dead matter. It can be recorded only by Consciousness. If you take the mind to be the container of all thoughts, it must be infinite and eternal. But there cannot be two infinites or eternals. Therefore that mind is Consciousness itself and changeless. As Consciousness, it can never record anything else. Therefore memory is *not*.

Another approach: When you think that thought is recorded, you attribute an independent reality to thought. Thinking is nothing but subtle perception. It has been proved that there is no form without seeing. So in the subtle perception called thought, the same process goes on. When the sense organs – gross and subtle – are shut, the mind can no longer function. (Can you think about Truth without indenting upon the services of sense objects? Thinking in an abstract manner is impossible.) When seeing is withdrawn, the form is no longer present.

Therefore it is wrong to suppose that you are recalling the same thing, once again, by memory. The same is true about recording and recollecting thoughts.

Still another approach: You stand out as the witness of your mental activities. What is witnessed by the witness cannot be said to be past; because the witness is beyond time. But, as a result of its closeness to the witness, the ego takes up the information from the witness and claims it as a past experience of the ego. The ego twists every information which it has usurped from the witness and gives it an objective expression.

Consciousness can never be witness to anything other than Consciousness. The sense organs can never be witness to anything other than sense objects. Everything recorded in knowledge becomes knowledge itself.

1048. CHANGELESSNESS AND CHANGE ARE BOTH CONSISTENT.

A changeless thing can never be changing, even for a short time; and a changing thing can never be changeless, for however short a time. So if anything has been admitted to be changeless within a period of time, it must be the ultimate Reality alone. Through memory, thought, feeling etc., you only recognize your own real Self.

> yat tvaṁ paśyasi tatrai 'kas tvam ēva pratibhāsasē .
> kiṁ pṛthak bhāsatē svarṇāt kaṭak-āṅgada-nūpuram ..
>
> [In what you see, just *you* shine forth, alone.
> What else but gold shines out in golden ornaments?]

Aṣhṭāvakra-samhitā, 15.14

> udicca bōdhaṁ prabala pramāṇāntaram enniyē
> naśikkayilla, vēdāntaṁ pramāṇaṁ sakalattinuṁ
>
> [Without some other means of knowing
> that somehow predominates,
> awakened knowledge cannot die.
> It cannot suffer any loss.
> Vēdānta is that means of knowing
> which applies to everything.]

Bhāṣha Pancadashi, Mahābhūta-vivēka, 121
(Malayalam translation)

1049. WHAT IS IT THAT YOU REMEMBER?

If you remember anything, the thing remembered must be changeless, at least between the two incidents. All changes occur in time and space. So the thing remembered, being changeless, must be beyond time and space. This means it is eternal and infinite. Only the Ultimate is such. So you remember only the Ultimate.

You can understand memory only if you withdraw into your own being.

6th October 1954

1050. WHY SHOULD ONE TRY TO ESTABLISH ONESELF IN TRUTH, AFTER VISUALIZING IT?

On listening to the Truth from the Guru, you were thrown into a particular state where you visualized the Truth; even then you have to be reassured by your Guru and proved through logic that you were there. Left to yourself, you slip down and find it difficult to visualize the Truth once again.

By trying to get established in the Truth, you are only trying to create the same state as the one in which you realized yourself in the presence of the Guru. You have to do this till you are able to visualize the Truth without any effort. This is what is called the *sahaja state*, where you feel without feeling that you are there always. The habit channels of thought have to be counteracted by new channels in the direction of the Absolute.

The first visualization was time limited. That time limitation must go. That means āvaraṇa [the obscuring of Truth behind appearances] must go. Thus you get established in the Truth.

1051. *RĀDHĀ-MĀDHAVAM* (LIKE THE DRAMA OF LIFE) IS A DRAMA IN THE PRESENCE OF CONSCIOUSNESS (RŪPAKAM CIT-SAMAKṢHAM). WHAT DOES IT SIGNIFY?

All the world is a stage and all the men and women are only actors. The audience is that *cit* alone. The purpose of acting is not to please the actors, but to obtain the approval and recognition of the audience.

10th October 1954

1052. WHAT HAPPENS TO THOSE WHO ARE SAMĀDHI-MINDED?

When you remain samādhi-minded, you try to fit the unconditioned into the compass of the mind, and you fail to reach the Ultimate.

1053. THE HIGHER REASON

It is a supra-rational instrument of thought, and its function cannot rightly be called thinking.

1054. THE ABSENCE

The absence of anything is not directly perceived. It is only the background that is really perceived, and the absence of a thing is superimposed on that background.

3rd January 1955

1055. WHAT ARE THE TESTS OF REALITY?

1. Continuity of existence.
2. Existing in one's own right (self-luminosity).

nā 'satō vidyatē bhāvō nā 'bhāvō vidyatē sataḥ …

Bhagavad-gītā, 2.16

The quotation means that which is non-existent can never *be* and that which is existent can never cease to *be*.

1056. WHAT IS IT THAT HAPPENS WHEN WE ARE LISTENING TO THE TALK OF THE GURU?

Gurunāthan replied: 'I am realizing myself in all of you, when I am talking to you about the Truth; and you are realizing yourself in me, when you are understanding what I say.'

dṛṣṭīṁ jñāna-mayīṁ kṛtvā paśyan brahma-mayaṁ jagat

Shrī Shankara, Aparokṣhānubhūti, 116

The quotation means: Convert the ordinary vision into the vision of knowledge, and then you will see that everything is in you and that you are everything.

1057. PERCEPTION OF AN OBJECT AND THE KNOWLEDGE OF THE PERCEPTION – ARE THEY SIMULTANEOUS?

From the standpoint of perception they must be said to be simultaneous. But from the standpoint of the witness itself, it cannot be said to be simultaneous. Because the witness transcends time.

5th January 1955

1058. IN AN EXPERIENCE OF TOTAL LOVE, I FEEL INCAPABLE OF BEING GRATEFUL. WHY?

Total love is objectless. In such love you (the ego) die, and so also in knowledge you die. By dying I mean that the ego disappears completely.

Gratitude is only the prelude to love. When love is objectless, it transcends all gratitude. It is said: 'When the heart is full, the tongue refuses to speak.' Because, in speech, the fullness of the heart is limited.

Beyond the subject-object relationship, *to know is to be.*

1059. WHAT IS THE REAL SĀDHANA?

That which removes the ills of the waking state alone, is not the complete sādhana. That alone is the real sādhana which removes the ills of all the three states.

1060. WHAT IS THE EGO?

The ego is the father of duality, he himself being one of the many, and his experience is always the apparent combination of himself with another object.

10th January 1955

1061. WHAT PRINCIPLE IN THE DISCIPLE IS THE GURU ADDRESSING?

The Guru is addressing the Guru in the disciple. But you should never contemplate oneness with your Guru, in any manner. The Guru teaches you to be one with everything. Attain that first, by bringing it into your experience. Then the question will not arise; because then you will see that the Guru still stands beyond even that knowledge of oneness with everything.

Truth, feeling that it is not the Truth (the disciple), is taught by the Truth which knows that it is the Truth (the Guru).

13th February 1955

1062. WHAT IS THE PLACE OF *BHAGAVAD-GĪTĀ* IN THE *PRASTHĀNATRAYA* – THE TRIPOD OF INDIAN PHILOSOPHY?

The *Bhagavad-gītā* expounds karma-yōga, which is nothing but the exterior of a Jnyānin. Apparently it is just the opposite of karma-sannyāsa. Karma-sannyāsa is all mental.

But karma-yōga is clearly beyond the mind. So it is not a means, but the end in itself. The Truth appears in the guise of a means to the end, just as the Sage (Truth) appears as a man to others and is so addressed.

25th February 1955

1063. WHAT IS THE 'IT'?

The 'it' that is thought of is not the 'it' that is perceived. The 'it' that is thought of is not the 'it' that is known. The one vanishes, the moment you change your stand. This last alone is permanent.

28th February 1955

1064. EVEN AFTER ONE IS ESTABLISHED IN THE ABSOLUTE, HE APPEARS TO CONTINUE HIS ACTIVITIES. WHY?

For him, the personal has changed into the impersonal. But all the activities of the personal, which you appear to see, depend upon his way of life before liberation. His samskāras or tendencies which have not been destroyed, continue to guide his subsequent actions.

But he stands separate from all that, as the impersonal. The mind takes the place of the personal and directs his actions. If his samskāras have been destroyed by his former sādhana (which happens only if he is a yōgin), he remains quite passive in life.

The Jnyānins may appear dominated by apparent activity of life, or dispassion, or discrimination (vyavahāra-pradhāni, or vairāgya-pradhāni, or vivēka-pradhāni) – all depending upon the approach each had adopted to reach the Ultimate.

3rd March 1955

1065. WHY SHOULD I TRY TO VISUALIZE MY REAL NATURE AGAIN AND AGAIN?

In order to add momentum to the knowledge you have already obtained about your real nature. It is not to obtain liberation. Liberation was obtained even at the first listening to the Truth from the Guru. The light of knowledge dawned that day and ever since it is at your disposal. You have only to sense the Absolute through that eye of knowledge as often as possible until you are securely established in the Ultimate.

7th March 1955

1066. RENUNCIATION AND SPIRITUAL LIFE OF INDIA

How did renunciation begin to dominate the spiritual life of India, where once there were so many Sages who were ruling kings and house-holders, advocating true vicāra-mārga?

The change was brought about by the ingrained samskāras of the disciples. If one is engrossed with the outside world and sense-pleasures and incapable of directing attention to the Ultimate, the only alternative is to divert the attention from the world and the pleasures of the senses by advocating renunciation. This was meant only as a preliminary step to prepare one to listen to the Truth. But unfortunately, the means became an end in itself in course of time, and the real goal came to be forgotten.

8th March 1955

1067. IS NOT THE WITNESS ONLY ONE?

No. It is neither one nor many, but beyond both. When you say that it is only one, you stand in the mental realm as an expanded ego and unconsciously refer to the many.

1068. SUPPOSE I TAKE THE THOUGHT: 'I AM PURE CONSCIOUSNESS.' WILL IT TAKE ME TO SAMĀDHI?

No. Not always. If you take it only as a thought it will lead you to samādhi. But if you know that Consciousness can never be made an object of thought, you will be thrown into a state where the mind expires, and you will be left in your real nature as in deep sleep. It is no samādhi at all, but far beyond.

1069. WHAT IS KNOWING THE TRUTH WITH ONE'S WHOLE BEING?

To forget oneself completely in knowing the Truth is to know it with one's whole being. Or in other words, it is knowing with the head and the heart combined in complete unison. When the heart is full, the tongue refuses to speak.

5th April 1955

1070. HOW TO DISPOSE OF PHENOMENAL QUESTIONS?

Dispose of questions relating to gross objects by referring to dream experiences, and dispose of questions relating to the subtle world (thoughts and feelings) by making reference to the deep sleep state. This is the phenomenal way and is not final.

27th July 1955

1071. HOW AM I DEATHLESS?

Sat is existence Absolute.

Life: You are 'life'. Life knows no death. So you are, deathless. You can have death only if you have life. But when you are *life itself*, how can you die, unless life dies; and life can never die.

Childhood, boyhood, youth etc., take birth and die, or come and go in the changeless 'I'-principle. That 'I' is birthless and deathless.

You talk of your past and future lives. Unless you are equally present in the past, present and future, you can never connect these three, which come and go in you. That 'You' is deathless.

Any knowledge apparently limited, if understood without reference to the object, is knowledge Absolute (Truth itself).

1072. ANALOGY OF THE SELF TO THE CINEMA SCREEN

A changeless screen is needed for the manifestation of forms and their movements upon it. Likewise, a changeless background is needed for the manifestation of the changing universe upon it. This background is the real 'I'-principle. If you attempt to seize a person on the screen, it is really the screen alone that is seized and not the person. Likewise when any part of the universe is seized (perceived), it is the background Reality that is seized (i.e. it is Reality that shines).

A thought-form (or a subtle object) can never be of a gross object, and knowledge can never be of a thought-form; because they are all in three distinct and separate planes, where one plane can never transgress into another without losing its identity. Perception is always in terms of the instrument used and the object of perception is always in the perception itself. Similarly the object of knowledge is always in knowledge, and knowledge is not affected by the thing known. So there is knowledge and knowledge alone, without reference to the thing known. This is the ultimate Truth or *Ātmā*, your real nature.

Objects cannot exist independently of the senses, nor the sense perceptions independently of the mind, nor mentations independently of Consciousness. Therefore all is Consciousness or *Ātmā*. When a perception vanishes, the object perceived also vanishes and ceases to exist in any form whatsoever: like the objects of the dream that has passed. Therefore that object can never be connected with any subsequent thought-form.

A gross object is limited by both space and time.
A subtle object is limited by time alone.

Whenever you take a thought, the corresponding gross object can never come in, because of its space limitation. If it gives up its space limitation, it ceases to be a gross object and vice-versa. Therefore a gross object can never be thought of, and a thought-form can never become gross.

Strictly speaking, you cannot say that an object exists in space, nor can you say that a thought-form exists in time. Because space is itself an object and time is itself a thought-form. You can never perceive two objects or two thought-forms simultaneously, and unless two or more objects are simultaneously perceived, you can never say one thing exists in another.

1073. The activities of the ignorant man, the sādhaka and the jīvan-mukta

An activity has two parts, the material part and the knowledge part. No activity is possible unless it is recorded in knowledge.

The ignorant man, in his perceptions, ignores the knowledge part and emphasizes only the material object part.

The sādhaka tries in the beginning to emphasize at least equally the knowledge part and the material part, and towards the end of his sādhana gives more emphasis to the knowledge part than to the material.

The jīvan-mukta, at heart, ignores the material part completely and recognizes or emphasizes only the knowledge part; but knowingly, he appears to emphasize the material part as well.

1074. Progress from objects to Consciousness pure

1. *Objects:* Not objects in the technical sense, but merely things. Here the Consciousness part is not referred to at all. This is an ignorant man's stand.
2. *Consciousness of objects:* This is also an ignorant man's stand, but a little higher than the first.

3. *Objects of Consciousness:* This is the sādhaka's stand at the beginning.

   Proceeding further, he sees –

4. *Objects in Consciousness:* This is also the sādhaka's stand, a little later.

5. *Objects As Consciousness:* This is a jīvan-mukta's stand – compare the dream state.

   Higher still –

6. *Objects vanish and Consciousness reigns.*

Gross forms appear when you perceive with gross sense-instruments. Thought-forms appear when you think (i.e. when you perceive with subtle senses).

> Knowledge-form alone shines when you know.
> But knowledge cannot be limited by any form.
> So the world is pure knowledge alone.

It is this one pure knowledge that appears as gross-form, thought-form and knowledge-form. Thus objects appear in terms of the instrument used.

30th July 1955

1075. WHY IS IT THAT EVEN AFTER VISUALIZING THE TRUTH ABOUT MY REAL NATURE I DO NOT FEEL FULL CONFIDENCE OR CERTITUDE?

It can be answered in many ways:

1. Who asks the question? Certainly, the mind. Because Ātmā cannot complain. The mind that is complaining never visualized the Truth. It died in that sacred attempt. Then how can it raise any question regarding an experience which occurred when the mind was dead? Both visualizing Truth and the certitude thereafter are in the non-dual realm, beyond the mind. The mind is no part to it and not competent to put forward any question relating to that matter.

2. The first part of the question asserts the visualization of Truth. By 'visualization' is meant knowing and being. Strictly speaking

there is no object to knowing, because knowing and being are one in realization. If it had been visualized it cannot leave room for any further question. If any question sprouts in the realm of the mind, one has only to refer to one's own stand during the visualization and the question vanishes at once.

3. The answer is in the question itself. The mind has to cease to be mind for visualization (i.e. realization of Truth). It is the mind that wants 'feelings' (confidence and certitude). The mind expects the Truth to shine in the realm of the mind. That is impossible.

1076. SPIRITUAL STRIVING AND ENLIGHTENMENT

The ignorant man feels that he is a sufferer. He finds that suitable objects give him momentary relief, and so he seeks to hoard such objects.

But the earnest man soon discovers that nothing on earth can give him permanent relief, and so he turns to something beyond the world. This is the beginning of spirituality. Of such few, the fortunate one obtains a Kāraṇa-guru.

The Guru tells him first to analyse the 'seeker' in him. According to the aspirant, the seeker is only a vicious group consisting of body, senses and mind. He is shown that each of this triad is impermanent and that, as any one of them, the seeker can never attain permanent happiness. But still the urge to obtain permanent happiness does not leave him. Then he is shown that there is a permanent, changeless principle behind this group (the seeker), and that the source of the desire for permanent happiness is the presence and nature of that background.

Next he is shown that he is himself that permanent principle. He is then told its real characteristics, and he ultimately visualizes it (*Ātmā*) beyond the shadow of a doubt. This is enlightenment. The attempt is not to remove suffering from the sufferer, but only to make the seeker visualize his real nature of permanent Peace, and thereby to make him understand that he is not the sufferer even when the suffering seems to last. When he realizes that he had all along been the *Peace*, all questions disappear.

If you want to remove the suffering alone and retain the sufferer, it is never possible. Because the suffering and the sufferer always appear and disappear simultaneously.

9th August 1955

1077. VICĀRA AND DHYĀNA

Vicāra is a term used exclusively in the jnyāna path. It means the removal of all obstacles that stand in the way of one's realization of Truth.

The term 'viçāra' is used in entirely different senses by yōgins and by devotees. It is not used in their sense in the path of knowledge. *Dhyāna* [meditation], as it is understood by 'upāsakas' [worshippers], is of three kinds or stages:

1. The lowest is '*pratīka-dhyāna*', exactly in the form of a gross model set before him, which allows him no deviation from the stiff model. The process is more physical or sensuous than anything else.
2. *Dhyēyānusṛita-dhyāna,* in accordance with an ideal, the fundamentals of which are set in a 'dhyāna-shlōka' or verse given to the aspirant. Here he has the freedom to adorn the fundamental form according to his taste and fancy. The process is mental. You attribute sublime qualities to your 'iṣhṭa-dēva' at this stage and conceive him as the embodiment of all that is good. Thus the aspirant's mind becomes pure and sāttvic.
3. *Aham-gṛiha-dhyāna:* Here the aspirant draws his iṣhṭa-dēva still further inward into the inmost core of his heart, and soon he recognizes his own identity with the iṣhṭa-dēva.

But with all this, the aspirant has only become eligible, so as to feel the necessity of approaching a Kāraṇa-guru to attain his goal. Therefore he seeks a Sage and fortunately meets one. Through his instructions the aspirant visualizes his own real nature and is gradually established in it.

1078. WHAT DOES 'LŌKA-SANGRAHA' MEAN?

Lōka-sangraha [concern for universal welfare] produces subjective results as well as objective. The subjective course, according to Hindu tradition, is only a means of attenuating the personal ego, by diverting the goal of your actions from your narrow, cabined and cribbed personal self to the world at large. This practice slowly makes you a universal being. To follow this sādhana, unaided, is a laborious task. Even if you succeed there, you have not reached the goal, and then you seek a Kāraṇa-guru who takes you beyond it and establishes you in the ultimate Truth. If on the other hand you have the instructions of a Kāraṇa-guru, from the very beginning, you succeed in establishing yourself in the ultimate Reality by the sādhana of service itself.

The objective side is manifest in this sādhana inasmuch as you engage in actions. They produce the result of raising the humanity from level to level and making them contented and happy by degrees. Even after standing established in the ultimate Reality, you may continue to perform actions of this nature, knowing full well that your real character is not affected, one way or the other, by such actions.

The course of *lōka-sangraha*, when rightly understood and followed as a sādhana under instructions from a Kāraṇa-guru, is not intended to improve the world (or parts of it), as is professed by some faiths. When service of the world becomes your goal, you conceive the world not in the particular but in the generic sense. The generic, in all cases, is nothing but the absolute background, since all agencies of discrimination have been eliminated.

Therefore your service is directed to *Ātmā*, the real background. You are also told that the background of your personal being is the same Ātmā. This means you are serving yourself and you stand visualized as that Ātmā itself. Every action of yours in the light of this ideal of service brings you into contact with that common background Ātmā, and slowly you get established there. This is how lōka-sangraha takes you to the ultimate Truth.

1079. WHAT IS MEANT BY 'SELFISH'?

It is selfish to do, think or feel anything in the interests of the apparent 'I'.

13th August 1955

1080. THE 'THEORETICAL' AND THE 'PRACTICAL', COMPARED TO EXPERIENCE

The ignorant man considers the body as being more real than the mind. In ordinary parlance, what is retained in the mental sphere is called 'theoretical', and what is translated into action in the physical sphere is called 'practical'. The advocates of the 'practical' assume that what they believe to be 'practical' has greater reality than the 'theoretical'.

But a close and impartial enquiry proves that body, senses and mind are all changing in the three states, and that the only principle that remains changeless, all through, is the 'I'-principle. This 'I' is neither gross nor subtle, but beyond both. In other words, the 'I' is neither 'practical' nor 'theoretical' in the ordinary sense, but beyond both. It is the only one that does not need any proof of its existence. It is the only absolute Truth or Reality.

If by 'practical' you mean 'real', the 'I' is more real than the changing body, senses or mind. These can exist only in the presence of the 'I', while the 'I' can exist all alone without anything else. Therefore the 'I' is more practical or real than the rest. The 'I' is the innermost principle in man and is the ultimate Truth.

The degrees of reality of a thing, if any, can be measured only in proportion to the proximity of the thing to the 'I'-principle. According to this standard, gross objects (including the body) are the farthest from the 'I' and are therefore the least practical or real. The senses are nearer to the 'I' and so the sensations are more practical or real. The mind is still nearer to the 'I' and so mentations are still more practical or real than the rest.

Strictly speaking, Reality can have no degrees, there being only one Reality – the *Ātmā* – and that alone can be called experience. Experiences of the body, senses and mind are no experiences at all.

14th August 1955

1081. WHAT IS THE NATURE OF VICĀRA?

Vicāra begins with a course of uncompromising arguments within yourself to prove and affirm that you are not the body, senses or the mind, and that even when all these are changing in the course of the three states, you alone stand changeless as the background, knowing the apparent changes. When the argument goes home, the objects drop away, one by one, until at last you stand alone in your own glory as the background. Then you cannot even say 'I know', because there is nothing else to be known and you stand as that knowledge, pure. This is, in short, the course of Ātma-vicāra.

> mādhuryyattāl anya vastu madhurī kṛtam ākayāṁ,
> vastvantarattāl māduryyaṁ madhurī kṛtamāyiṭā .
>
> [It is from sweetness that some other
> thing can get to be made sweet.
> But sweetness in itself is not
> made sweet, by any other thing.]

Bhāṣha Pancadashi, Pancakōsha-vivēka, 15
(Malayalam translation)

This is a significant verse to show the self-luminosity of Ātmā.

By association with sweetness, another thing becomes sweet. But sweetness by itself does not need the association of anything else in order to be sweet.

Similarly, all objects become known when they come into contact with the 'I'. But the 'I' does not need the help of anything else in order to be known. It shines, by itself, even in deep sleep where no object exists. Therefore the 'I' is self-luminous.

1082. HOW AM I PEACE AND CONSCIOUSNESS?

Gurunāthan: Well, let me ask you another simple question in return. Have you the faculty of sight?

Disciple: Yes.

G: How can you prove it? Is it as a result of looking at your fleshy eyes that you assert that you have eyesight?

D: No.

G: Then what is your evidence?

D: I see objects and so I am convinced that I have eyesight, without which I know objects would never be seen.

G: So you admit that objective perception of a faculty is not necessary in order to prove its existence?

D: Yes.

G: Here you must remember that when you see objects you are not possessing eyesight, but that you are actually standing as the faculty of eyesight. Do you admit that?

D: Yes.

G: Now apply the same argument to your own self. Don't you know your perceptions, thoughts and feelings?

D: Yes, of course.

G: What is your position when you know them? Examine it carefully and tell me.

D: I stand as that faculty of knowledge, or objectless knowledge, when I know anything.

G: Then, is there any moment in all the three states when you do not stand as that pure Knowledge?

D: No, I am there always.

G: Well, what may be the relationship between that knowledge and yourself?

D: (After a pause.) That knowledge can only be myself or my real nature.

G: Now, do you see how you are Consciousness?

D: Yes. Perfectly.

G: Be there always.

15th August 1955

1083. KNOWLEDGE IS ALWAYS APARŌKṢHA OR EXPERIENCE PURE.

I am not one who knows, but Knowledge itself.
I am not one who exists, but Existence itself.
I am not in peace, but Peace itself.

With my contact even the unknown becomes known.
With my contact even the non-existent appears existent.

Non-existent body + Existence = Existent body

Objects of knowledge may be *parōkṣha* (indirect) or *aparōkṣha* (direct), as the case may be. But knowledge is always *aparōkṣha* or experience pure.

16th August 1955

1084. WHY DO I SEE DIVERSITY?

Because you stand as diversity yourself (you stand as body, senses and mind).

1085. AS LONG AS I AM A HUMAN BEING, IS IT POSSIBLE FOR ME TO KNOW THE TRUTH BEYOND?

The question presupposes that you are a human being. I question that statement first. Are you a human being? Define a human being. A human being is an incongruous mixture of body, senses and mind with the 'I'-principle. All except the 'I'-principle are changing every moment.

But you will admit that you are that 'I'-principle. You, as that 'I'-principle, stand as the permanent background connecting all these changes that come and go. That 'I'-principle is distinct and separate from the changing body, senses and mind. Where is the human being in your deep sleep, when you have no body, senses or mind? Certainly nowhere.

Still 'you' are there, as that 'I'-principle. Therefore you are not a human being but a changeless, permanent principle. As such, you can very well understand that Truth, beyond.

17th August 1955

1086. PROLONGING INTERVAL BETWEEN MENTATIONS

Question: Since I am myself alone between two mentations, and that only for an infinitesimal part of a second, am I to try to prolong that period?

Answer: No. You are mistaken about your position between two mentations during the so called interval. It is true that it appears as an interval to you, when you stand in time and look at it from there.

But when you reach that interval, you find yourself divested of body, senses, mind, space and time; and then the so called interval appears no longer an interval but 'timeless'. The idea of prolonging the timeless is absurd. The mistake arises because you stand as an embodied being and look at it from a distance, in the waking state.

All you have to do is to get into that so called interval, discarding all that you possess – namely, body, senses, mind, space and time. In that state, everything is perfect.

The idea of prolongation is a 'vicious samskāra' of time, which arises only after the inception of the mind. If you dance to the tune of this samskāra, you will never reach the ultimate goal. Even great yōgins have often been stranded for years in nothingness, as a result of this subtle miscalculation.

Another answer: You say you are all alone in that interval. You do not take in the full significance of that statement; instead you give it a limited interpretation. You take time along with you and think of prolongation.

But really, you are absolutely alone and there is no sense of time in it to disturb you. Hence the idea of prolongation is quite irrelevant and contrary to the idea of your being all alone.

1087. THE DIFFERENCE BETWEEN THE APPROACHES OF MODERN SCIENCE AND VĒDĀNTA

Science ignores the ultimate subject altogether; and its approach is an objective one, taking for granted that the apparent universe is real. It takes into consideration only the relationship between object and object, utilizes the lower reason or intellect as its instrument, and in coming to a decision it relies upon the stored-up experiences of the mind, which are as varied as the universe itself. Therefore, we cannot expect any finality in its conclusion. This is why science, after all its somersaults, is bewildered and knocks against the blank wall of ignorance.

But Vēdānta recognizes the ultimate subject alone; and its approach is a subjective one, taking the universe only as an appearance. It examines only the relationship of any one object with the subject 'I'. This object is considered as a symbol. Its solution applies equally to all objects, and the conclusion arrived at applies to the whole universe.

Vēdānta proves that every object depends upon the subject 'I' for its very existence. It utilizes the higher reason (vidyā vṛitti) and not the intellect as its instrument, and in order to come to a conclusion, its reference is only to the real changeless being within and to nothing else. This 'Being' or the 'I' being one, and the reference being always to that, the conclusion can be only one and the same, always the ultimate Truth.

18th August 1955

1088. REALMS OF HUMAN EXISTENCE AND ACTIVITY

Man has three distinct and separate realms of existence and activity.

1. As a physical being possessed of senses, man has the world of sense objects.
2. As a mental being, man has the world of ideas.
3. As a spiritual being, man has Consciousness alone.

Of these, the first two realms and their objects are changing and ephemeral, while the third one alone is changeless and permanent, supporting the other two realms as well. Man's endeavour should be to reach the third realm somehow, and to be a spiritual being. For this, he must give up the other two realms, at least for the time being.

When he reaches the third realm of Peace and Consciousness and looks back, he will find that it lights up the other two realms as well and proves them to be nothing but Peace and Consciousness. When he understands that to be his own real nature, he is free.

You cannot have a negative experience of any kind. If you should ever experience the absence of any object, you can never do it deliberately. If you try to forget anything, the thing actually becomes more strongly manifest.

But there is one way of accomplishing the desired end. You have only to turn your attention to the background, or that which supports the object. For example; if you want to experience the absence of the chair, you need only turn your attention to the ground that supports the chair. Immediately, the chair idea vanishes.

Man is swayed to and fro by the varied experiences of the world in the waking state. He badly wants relief from this strain. In other words, he wants to forget the world, for a short time at least. So his attention is spontaneously drawn to the background. Immediately the world disappears; and Peace and pure Consciousness alone are experienced in deep sleep.

19th August 1955

1089. RESULT OF ELIMINATING FROM ME ALL THAT I AM NOT

Question: Would the process of eliminating from me all that I am not, take me to my real nature and establish me there?

Answer: Certainly it will do both, provided you have heard the ultimate Truth about your real nature from the lips of a Kāraṇa-guru. Otherwise you will get stranded in nothingness, mistaking it for the Ultimate; because the experience of nothingness also gives you a reflected and limited peace or happiness.

After listening to the Truth from the Guru, if you take to any thought – and more so a spiritual thought – it expires not in nothingness but in Consciousness alone. Therefore, when all that you are not – namely the body, senses and mind – have been eliminated from you, you alone remain over as the background – Consciousness and Peace. This is nothing short of Self-realization. Repeat the same vicāra for some time. This will help you to stand established in your Real nature.

Regarding one's own real nature: '*To know is to be.*'

If you enquire into the ultimate goal or meaning (purport) of the term 'I' used by everybody alike, and if you succeed in reaching that goal, there is nothing else to be attained. I am that principle in man permeating all men alike, but at the same time distinct and separate from the body, senses and mind of all. That am I. That is *Ātmā*.

If you watch the activities of a Sage, an apparent indifference or hesitancy might often be noticed. Because with him the 'I' is never helplessly mixed up with objects and perceptions, as is the case with the ignorant man.

20th August 1955

1090. 'SURRENDER' AND HOW TO ACHIEVE IT?

'Surrender' has something of a negative implication. You can never achieve surrender by deliberation. What you want is to surrender your attachment to objects. In other words, you want to forget objects (body, senses and mind).

If you start deliberately to forget them, they become more strongly manifest. Therefore the only means to achieve surrender is to turn your attention to the support or the background.

If the devotee gets more and more attached to his *iṣhṭa-dēva*, surrender of all else will follow as a matter of course. You need not do anything special to attain it. An open and empty heart is the first requisite.

Surrender is an end in itself, and never a means. Surrender is something that has to come spontaneously, as a corollary to Self-realization. Surrender is no surrender, in the strict sense of the term, if you happen even to remember the fact that you have surrendered.

Surrender can never be accomplished objectively. It is only by establishing oneself in one's own Real nature, Ātmā, that real surrender obtains. Because you see that there is nothing else to be surrendered; and then, even the word 'surrender' becomes meaningless.

22nd August 1955

1091. FALLACY OF THE DESIRE TO KNOW OR FEEL THE TRUTH

It is admitted that on listening to the Truth from the lips of the Guru, you realize your real nature at once. But you will not know it or feel it.

The desire to know that you have so realized, or the desire to feel it, is the highest imaginable illusion. Because, in order to know anything, the knower has to stand higher than the known. Therefore, if you presume that you know or feel that you have realized the 'Truth' you are still in duality, and what you presume to know is imperfect. As such, it can never be the Truth.

You are ever that Truth – before, during and after the realization claimed. As far as the Truth – which is your real nature – is concerned, there had been no change whatsoever, in all time. It may be said that a Jnyānin knows that he has visualized the Truth. Yes of course. But not in the sense of knowing at the mental level, as you might desire. He knows that it is unknowable by the mind; but he knows it in an intenser light where there is no subject-object relationship. To know in that light is to be.

The ego in the mental realm is innocent and ignorant of all that has happened above his head. But he too feels that something sublime has happened, and naturally he wishes to have a taste of it in his own realm. Hence the ego's desire to know that experience, and his subsequent, unwarranted claim to have had that experience in his own limited terms. That has to be guarded against.

In *one* sense, it may be said that a Jnyānin alone knows a Jnyānin. This does not mean any recognition on the mental level as understood by the ordinary man. From *another* point of view, it is also true to say that even a Jnyānin can never know another Jnyānin. Because Jnyānin is Jnyāna itself; and Jnyāna, which is indivisible, can never be divided into subject and object, as knower and the known.

25th August 1955

1092. 'SHIVŌHAM'

It is an aphorism usually utilized by jnyāna sādhakas, after visualization of the Truth, to be established in that background. Its purpose is only to turn your attention to the inner Self. Its meaning should not be taken literally. If you do so, you objectify it, and then it does not represent the Self, which is always the ultimate subject.

The goal of all spiritual exercise is to change your identification from the personal, (body, senses and mind) to the impersonal (Self). The impersonal Self or Ātmā is ever-present and Self-luminous.

Nothing has to be done to manifest it. All you have to do is to turn your attention to it whole-heartedly, by withdrawing your attention from the body, senses and mind. This withdrawal is possible only with the help of Consciousness, which is your real nature. When the body, senses and mind are thus completely eliminated, the consciousness – which is the background – remains over, shining in all its glory.

The word 'Shivōham' does not represent anything objective. It just reminds you of your real nature. Therefore, the word 'Shivōham' helps you considerably to get away from everything objective, and you are thrown into that state when you had the first visualization of the Truth in the presence of the Guru. This is only a means to throw you into that state again and again, till at last you are established in it, the 'Ātmā', rising above all obstacles.

1093. SPIRITUAL GOAL AND ITS ATTAINMENT

The realization of one's own real nature is undoubtedly the ultimate goal of all spiritual quest. The only impediment to it is the illusion that you are body, senses or mind. For Self-realization, it is the removal of this illusion that is sought.

The methods adopted to attain this end differ with the different paths. The paths of yōga and devotion adopt the method of removing the infinite variety of illusions, by accepting a generic form called 'samādhi'. Here the diversity vanishes, no doubt. But still you remain in the realm of illusion, and in the subject-object relationship. The Truth is still as remote as before, and the happiness experienced in samādhi is not a permanent one.

The state of complete identity with non-dual Ātmā, as a result of discrimination and negation of phenomena, is the vēdāntic concept of samādhi. This is distinct from the so called samādhi of yōgins. The Ātmā is denoted by the word 'samādhi'. The illusion should not reappear ever after, in any other form. This is possible only if you realize the background on which all illusions appear and disappear. This is nothing short of Self-realization.

Therefore, removing the illusion is not a means to attain Self-realization. It is only a natural corollary to it. Taking for example the illusion of the 'serpent in the rope', we find that the illusion can be completely and successfully removed only by seeing clearly, by the help of a bright light, that it is rope and rope alone. Therefore, Self-realization is both the means and the end in itself.

The only means to attain this end is to listen to the Truth (it may be about the truth of illusion itself) from the lips of a Kāraṇa-guru. Then you may yourself examine any illusion in the light of that instruction, and certainly it will take you to the real background. All possibility of illusion taking possession of you is removed by that means.

28th August 1955

1094. PROGRESS THROUGH MANTRA AND DHYĀNA

This path is divided into four distinct stages, namely *vaikharī*, *madhyamā*, *pashyantī* and *parā*.

Instructions from a kārya-guru (one whose instructions take you to anything below the Ultimate) may suffice for the first two stages. But for the last two, the help of a Kāraṇa-guru is absolutely necessary.

Vaikharī is chanting of a mantra in audible tone and effecting concentration of the mind there.

Madhyamā is doing the same thing mentally and effecting concentration. This is still in the realm of the mind and concentration is on an idea.

Pashyantī: Here ideation is transcended. It may be said that here one gets to the languageless idea. Unless one understands its nature from a Kāraṇa-guru, one will be in an unconscious state. I may say something about this languageless idea.

I may convey an idea to you by means of one particular language. The same idea may be conveyed to another by means of a different language. One is certainly not a translation of the other. What is the language of that idea? It has no language, because it has gone beyond expression. If that is correctly understood, it is itself the background of the expressed idea of the first two stages. He, who gets into that state, touches the background and is not in an unconscious state. He understands, further, that the languageless idea can only be one and cannot be many. This is the experience in pashyantī.

Parā: Even the notion of a background is transcended here, and self-luminosity of the Reality takes possession of the sādhaka; and here he is in deep Peace, which is changeless.

1095. VIKṢHĒPA AND ĀVARAṆA

Vikṣhēpa [distraction] and āvaraṇa [obscuring] are the obverse and the reverse of the same coin (mind). They appear and disappear simultaneously. Therefore after having heard the Truth from the Guru, whenever you transcend 'vikṣhēpa', 'āvaraṇa' also disappears and you stand as the Ultimate.

31st August 1955

1096. SPONTANEITY AND CONTEMPLATION

All experience is spontaneous. You should not colour it or disfigure it.

By 'spontaneous' I mean that which cannot be related to any cause or effect, or which does not make any reference to its opposite. Every percept is spontaneous. Let us concede that it is related to its particular sense organ alone. As a percept it makes no reference to its opposite. If you dismiss it immediately at this stage, it does not bind you.

But you do not dismiss it immediately. Instead, the very next moment, you mix it up with innumerable other concepts and with samskāras stored up in the mind, and then you project them all together as what you call the object. The object you so conceive does not exist anywhere. It is only a bundle of sensations. The percept was nearer the real, when it occurred. But when you mixed it up with other concepts, the percept was transformed into a concept and became unreal.

Suppose you perceive form. The perception is spontaneous and makes no reference to anything else. It would be wrong even to say '*a* form' because the '*a*' makes an unconscious reference to other forms. Form, as a generic concept, can leave no samskāra or trace behind. It rises in Ātmā and dissolves into Ātmā. The experience of the Sage is always at this level. But knowingly he comes down and moves among the ignorant as one of them, but never forgetting the sublime Truth about it all.

Suppose you see what you call a note book. Eliminate all associated concepts and samskāras from it, and note what remains over, without reference to anything else. The note book, the book, paper, form, colour, all these vanish in succession, leaving the 'seeing' and the indefinite 'it'. Next the 'seeing' merges in the knowledge, leaving the 'Knowledge' and the 'it' as the one indivisible Truth.

'It occurred to me' is the typical language of spontaneity. The sense organ by itself can never create an object. Leave each sense organ to itself and you will be free. Contemplation depends upon the imaginary permanence of the object.

1097. WHAT IS AN OBJECT AND WHAT IS ITS ESSENCE?

That which could be said to exist or to shine is alone called an object. To what do the existence and luminosity found in the object belong? Do they belong to the object itself? Or are they derived from elsewhere? They do not belong to the so called object. Because the object appears and disappears in Consciousness, and existence and luminosity can never cease to exist or shine. So the object derives these qualities from Consciousness.

'I' am the only Principle that never ceases to exist and that never ceases to shine. Therefore, existence and luminosity belong to me. They are my real nature – one and indivisible. Existence and knowledge are one – being intrinsic in oneself, and there being no subject-object relationship with respect to knowledge and existence. My presence as that knowledge – pure – is essential for the manifestation of any object, and it cannot be assumed that an object exists when not known. Therefore the object which appears and disappears is nothing but Consciousness.

But in our traffic with the world, we put the dead and inert cart (object) before the living horse (Consciousness). In this way, we make of life a blind show. The object has been brought into existence only by the grace of Consciousness, lending its liberal presence. Immediately, this object, which is dead and inert, usurps all the living qualities of Consciousness.

If only you succeed in seeing the world as the world of objects alone and yourself as the only subject, you are free. In other words, you have only to reinstate the independent horse of Consciousness in its rightful place in front and place the cart of dependent objects in its legitimate place in the rear, ready to be discarded at any moment without notice.

The first phenomenal experience is the percept. The next moment the percept disappears and a concept takes its place.

1st September 1955

1098. PROGRESSION OF KNOWLEDGE FROM OBJECT TO THE ULTIMATE.

1. Consciousness of object.
2. Consciousness of Self.
3. Consciousness as Self.
4. Self all alone.

1099. SHĀSTRAS AND THEIR SIGNIFICANCE

It is a common illusion that one can understand the ultimate Truth from the shāstras. But the shāstras themselves proclaim from their heights that they are helpless in this matter, and that a Kāraṇa-guru alone can take you to the Truth. The Kāraṇa-guru depends entirely upon himself, the Truth, and not upon the shāstras for the purpose; though he might adopt any of the numerous methods of approach described in the shāstras. Even that is not essential. Sometimes he might adopt an entirely new approach to suit the radical change in the outlook of the world, and the peculiar aptitude and temperament of the aspirant.

The shāstras utilize only dead language as their medium. To expect light to come out of dead language is to expect the impossible. Language functions only in the realm of the mind. Beyond the mind it cannot even peep. Truth is decidedly beyond the mind, and beyond the reach of all shāstras. Even the Upaniṣhads go only so far, and take you only to the tether end of the mind. There they proclaim unequivocally that a Kāraṇa-guru alone can take you beyond, to the ultimate Truth.

This does not mean that the shāstras are of no use. To the particular aspirant who had the rare good fortune to attain a Kāraṇa-guru, the shāstras are no longer of any use. But till such a time, they can be of immense service to an aspirant. The purpose of the shāstras, in general, is to prove to you, in the light of the lower reason or intellect, the impermanence of the apparent world including body, senses and mind, and the irrefutability of the existence of a permanent principle behind the world. When the aspirant is convinced of this, the shāstras din into his mind the supreme need of a Kāraṇa-guru to show him the Truth behind all these changes.

Therefore, the real service of the shāstras is to impress upon one the need of the Guru, and to put one on the track. The moment the aspirant begins to seek a Kāraṇa-guru, *vidyā-vṛitti* (higher reason) begins to flash its light in him and the rest is safe in the light of this divine torch. He has only to cling on to it till it leads him to a Kāraṇa-guru in flesh and blood. *Vidyā-vṛitti* is the fire that burns the forest of illusions. It is only from a Kāraṇa-guru that he can get it in full. This is why all shāstras enjoin that you should study them only at the feet of the Guru.

tattvam ātmastham ajñātvā mūḍhaś śāstrēṣu paśyati
gōpaḥ kakṣa gataṁ chāgaṁ yathā kūpēṣu durmatiḥ

[When someone foolish does not know
that truth which stands as one's own self,
it's only then that one may look
into the shāstras – like a herdsman
looking hard, in some distress
through many caves, to find a goat
that has gone into one of them.]

Shrī Shankara, Sarva-vēdānta-siddhānta-sāra-sangraha, 291

1100. SACRIFICE

Sacrifice is essential for the attainment of happiness, whether phenomenal or ultimate.

To attain phenomenal happiness you have to concentrate, for the time being, upon the object you desire. This means that you have, for some time, deliberately to sacrifice all except that object. But at the moment of enjoying the desired happiness, the object attained after so much effort also disappears. Thus everything objective is sacrificed before the enjoyment of even phenomenal happiness.

So also in the quest of that ultimate Peace or Happiness, everything objective falls away when you reach the goal.

In the one case it is temporary, and in the other it is permanent.

1101. CONSCIOUSNESS AND PEACE ARE ONE AND THE SAME.

You hope to achieve happiness by the attainment of a particular object. Suppose somebody drops that object into your room when you are asleep. You do not get the desired happiness. But you get it immediately you know that you have attained the object desired. So it is the knowledge – though apparently limited by the object – that gives you limited happiness.

In the knowledge, the object known is absent. Therefore, the known must disappear, even before limited peace can be attained.

It is only the reference to the object that limits the experience of Peace. The same result arrived at without a reference to any object (that is by rising above body, senses and mind) is the ultimate Peace. The known, as known, must disappear for the ultimate Peace to dawn. When the known – as known – disappears, it is knowledge pure or Consciousness that remains over. Thus Consciousness and Peace are one and the same, being intrinsic in you.

1102. YOU ARE ALWAYS IN DEEP SLEEP. HOW?

Just think what you are in deep sleep. You will find that you are the 'I'-principle alone, divested of body, senses and mind. You see you can live quite well without any of these.

Now just see if you ever get out of that 'I'-principle in your dream or waking states. No, never. Thus you see how you are always in deep sleep. That is the real Self.

5th September 1955

1103. BEAUTY, POETRY AND LOVE ARE THE SAME REALITY.

They are all, strictly speaking, synonyms of the Ultimate. If you perceive any of these without reference to the limited clothing in which they appear, you are perceiving the Reality itself. Such expressions of the Absolute are all spontaneous. Let us examine any one of them – e.g. beauty.

Beauty: It is often perceived in objects, such as the mountain, the sea, the sky, the river, the child, etc. But it has to be examined whether beauty is inherent in them. If so, everybody should perceive beauty in each of them, at all times. This is not so. I do not see beauty exactly where another sees it. Therefore beauty does not rest in the object perceived.

The only other party to the perception is one's own Self, divested of body, senses and mind which are also objects. So beauty must necessarily be somewhere in the Self – the real subject. The objects serve only as mere symbols of or pointers to the subject.

The Self is the centre of beauty and changeless. The symbols are numerous, but the centre is only one, the inmost core of one's being. Beauty is the real nature of the Self and is unlimited. Beauty anoints with its own guild everything with which it comes into contact. When beauty is superimposed upon any object, it appears limited and unreal.

In the world, you see only the beautiful. The beautiful is an incongruous mixture of dead, inert matter and living beauty by its very nature unlimited. On seeing the beautiful, your effort should be to eliminate the material accretion from the beauty part. For this purpose, you may first conceive beauty to be resting inside yourself, and matter outside. Thus, when you discard gross matter along with the sense of the 'outside' and reach the so called 'inside', you find that the inside – being relative and the opposite of outside – has also vanished with the outside, leaving you alone as beauty – the Ultimate – beyond both outside and inside.

Poetry: When you come to real poetry, it transcends imagination and all ideation. That is the Reality.

Love: Love for a desired object is pleasure-giving. When you understand that it is not the object itself that is loved, but the happiness you suppose you derived from it, the love itself is the happiness, both being intrinsic in you. That is the Reality.

The 'Reality' is the 'Absolute', or what is 'expressed' and beyond all opposites.

Sat, *cit* and *ānanda* are the characteristics of the ultimate Reality. They are positive in form, but negative in sense. Life, thoughts and feelings are the first expressions of *sat*, *cit* and *ānanda* in the relative level. When you expand life you come to *sat*, when you expand thoughts you come to *cit*, and when you expand feelings you come to *ānanda*.

After listening to the Truth from the Guru, if you get beyond the body, senses and mind, you reach the background as *sat*, *cit* or *ānanda*. But you do not rest there. You are then taken on to the ultimate Truth still beyond, which is Ātmā, the real 'I'.

6th September 1955

1104. DEVOTEES, MYSTICS AND JNYĀNINS

These are the three distinct types of spiritual personalities recognized by the world. They have also three distinct kinds of exercises, which are usually called spiritual exercises. They have so called experiences particular to each path, which are supposed to lead them to their respective goals.

The first two follow the paths of devotion and yōga. These paths confine their practitioners to the phenomenal, and are governed by the physical and mental elements in varying degrees.

The devotee, identifying himself with his physical body, conceives his *iṣhṭa-dēva* also as a physical being, of course with infinite powers and attributes, and meditates upon him. The yōgin tries to concentrate his mind upon a set ideal, which is a thought-form, with the definite object of attaining powers and enjoying happiness. In course of time, both these sādhakas get reasonably well concentrated upon their goal, and this bears visible fruits.

The devotee enjoys sensuous visions of his iṣhṭa-dēva, which give him ecstatic joy and a limited peace. If the devotee does not rest satisfied with these and does not consider that he has gained his goal, it may be said that the ground has been prepared to enable him to receive the teachings of a *Kāraṇa-guru.*

The yōgin's mind is expanded by concentration alone, and he attains wonderful powers in the phenomenal world. He is now called a 'mystic'. His experiences are of a complex nature. If he is not influenced by the powers that he possesses and his ego is not inflated by them, it may be said that the ground has been prepared to enable him to receive instructions from a *Kāraṇa-guru.*

Those devotees and mystics who refuse to go beyond, sell their birthright for a pittance.

The third type of sādhaka is the jnyāna sādhaka. The jnyāna sādhaka questions the world including himself. He is not satisfied with names and forms. He wants to get to the Truth of everything and lives on until a *Kāraṇa-guru* takes him to the ultimate Truth.

11th September 1955

1105. A LISTENER ASKED, 'WHEN I KNOW THAT I DO NOT KNOW, IS NOT MY STAND THEN IN THE REALITY'?

First answer: No. In your statement you make a difference between your knowing and not knowing. This is possible only in duality. Therefore, your position is not in the Reality. But there is a luminous and changeless principle behind that statement, the mere presence of which has made it possible for you to make that statement. That principle alone is the Reality. Therefore Reality can be defined as 'the Principle which by its mere presence makes it possible for you to make any statement, irrespective of the merits or the subject of the statement'.

Second answer:

'I know that when I know, I do not know.'

In this statement, the second and third 'knowledge' are both objective and time-limited. If the first 'knowledge' is taken to represent that principle that knows the other two knowledges, then it is the Reality. It is as a result of the presence of that pure knowledge that you are able to make any statement. But as long as you do not knowingly identify yourself with that pure knowledge, your stand is not in the Reality.

If you have listened to the Truth from the Guru, any question logically analysed and steadfastly followed takes you to the Real background. The world is created out of the triad of time, space and causality and rests upon it. Therefore, it is but human to view the objects of its perception in terms of this triad. Causality prompts the enquiry into the cause or the source of all you perceive. Thus prompted, you seek the source of your thoughts and feelings. Following this search earnestly, you reach a state beyond, where thoughts and feelings do not appear as such, nor does anything else exist there except yourself as Consciousness.

This Consciousness cannot be taken to be the cause of a non-existent effect. In the so called cause, the effect is not present; and without the cause and effect being simultaneously present, their relationship cannot be established. Therefore, though you started to seek the cause, and though you could not find any, yet the earnestness and sincerity of your search lead you to the background, Consciousness, destroying the shackles of causality once and for all.

15th September 1955

1106. SUSPECT KNOWLEDGE AND PERMANENT KNOWLEDGE

The knowledge, 'I know I am', is the one indubitable Reality that requires no proof to establish its existence.

The knowledge of a thing which stands in need of any proof for its existence is called 'suspect'. Such suspect knowledge is neither deep nor permanent. It may be sometimes right and sometimes wrong. All knowledge within the triad (of tripuṭī) is suspect knowledge. [Tripūṭī is the triad of knower, knowing and known; or doer, doing and deed.]

But the knowledge beyond the triad is deep and permanent. No proof is needed to establish it, and nothing can refute it.

Even the knowledge obtained in the relative level, when it is eliminated from the object known, is the Reality itself.

17th September 1955

1107. HIGHER REASON OR VIDYĀ-VṚITTI

This is a supra-intellectual organon to be found in everyone. In the presence of the Guru, this organon is aroused, and is made use of, in order to understand the Truth. It corrects and supplements the findings of the lower reason. It destroys all that is objective and unreal, created by the mind; and when nothing else remains to be destroyed, it stands revealed in its own glory as the Reality – just as the fire that consumes the forest extinguishes itself when nothing else remains to be consumed, and Peace prevails.

20th September 1955

1108. PLEASURES AND SPIRITUALITY

A life of placid enjoyment is inimical to you if you are given to serious thinking on any serious subject, and much more so when that thinking is spiritual.

An ordinary man believes that if he can provide for a constant stream of pleasures, he can be happy. He does not know that pleasures can never be constant.

24th September 1955

1109. VĒDĀNTIC CONCEPTION OF SAMĀDHI

Samādhi, as a result of the process of absorption, does not by itself take you to the Reality. Shrī Gauḍapāda says: 'Take away the mind from its tendency to go to samādhi to enjoy happiness and also from its tendency to enjoy the so called happiness supposed to be derived from sense objects, and it leads you to the goal.'

But how can this be done by the mind itself? It is never possible to reach the goal by any amount of effort on the part of the mind itself. By effort, you can prolong the duration of the samādhi to a certain extent and do nothing more. The complete elimination of the mind is what you have to obtain, somehow.

For this, some principle higher than the mind itself has to be depended upon, namely the higher reason. Its function is discrimination. The higher reason proves to you that it is not from the mind itself that happiness is experienced in samādhi, and that there is no enjoyer there. It is your own real nature of Peace, standing in its own glory, when the mind is temporarily stilled. It proves that the mind in any form only obscures the Reality. When you understand this correctly, your dependence upon the capacity of the mind to take you to that sublime Reality crumbles. This is how the mind is to be eliminated from the scene.

Samādhi is all right if the mind understands that samādhi is complete identity with non-dual Ātmā, where there is neither the enjoyer nor enjoyment. And when the mind knows that, it is itself changed.

28th September 1955

1110. HOW TO DESTROY SAMSKĀRAS?

Shrī Gauḍapāda in *Māṇḍūkya-kārikā* says: 'Exercise of discrimination and reason alone can destroy your samskāras and take you to the ultimate Truth. But the method of using them has to be obtained from a Kāraṇa-guru.'

The exercise of the higher reason alone can destroy one's innate tendencies and lead one to the goal.

3rd October 1955

1111. SĀKṢHĀT-KĀRAṆA

The ultimate cause (if any) of Self-realization is the fact of your having been accepted by a Sage as his disciple. This fact guarantees the disciple's realizing the corresponding fact that he had never been bound.

The moment the relationship between the Sage and the disciple is so established, the attention of the disciple is irrevocably directed to *Ātmā*, and the only thing that remains to be done is the removal of the 'mind', the one obstacle in the scene. All the attendant formalities of initiation, listening to spiritual discourses etc., are calculated only to give the mind a dignified and decent burial.

The life-story of Sages like Vaṭivīshvarattamma proves this beyond doubt.

1112. SOCIAL UPLIFT WORK AS A MEANS TO GET TO THE TRUTH

The work of social uplift is usually accepted by the world as a spiritual path. Every worker should be qualified for the particular task he undertakes, in order that the work may be orderly and fruitful. The social worker is no exception to this rule. The essential qualifications of a social worker are a clear knowledge of his own self, of the world, and of the thing common to the two. Next he should know the purpose of his work, and lastly the method of its implementation.

The very idea of social work rests on the fundamental misunderstanding that the world as it appears is real. The purpose of the work is the permanent happiness of the worker and of the world alike. When the worker happens to know the Truth that himself and the world are *Ātmā*, the ultimate Reality whose real nature is the Happiness which he has been seeking so long, his search ceases and he chooses to remain self-contented. But the ordinary social worker continues in the field, and often reaches the goal of his desire, though ephemeral. If he is sincere and earnest, his ego may get attenuated and he may become ripe, as a result of his preparation of the ground, to imbibe the teachings of a Kāraṇa-guru, which will take him to the goal.

(Shrī Ātmānanda was a strong social enthusiast and he contributed liberally for the cause. But he only held that it was wrong to attribute any spirituality to it.)

1113. FUTILITY OF SOCIAL SERVICE, BY ITSELF TO TAKE ONE TO THE TRUTH

Work for the enjoyment of satisfaction of any kind is opposed to jnyāna. Jnyāna alone can take one to the goal of Truth.

Work emphasizing the world brings in diversity. Jnyāna destroys it. It is the destruction of variety that can take one to Truth – one's real nature. Work with right discrimination may prepare the ground for spiritual enquiry. It cannot do anything more.

9th October 1955

1114. EVERYTHING IS BRAHMAN.

sarvaṁ khalv idaṁ brahma

Chāndōgya Upaniṣhad, 3.14.1

The Truth about this world is that the Reality, which is imperceptible to the senses, appears as this world when looked at through the senses. The ordinary man sees only the appearance and attributes complete reality to it. At the same time, he sees also the change-ability of the appearance, but he shuts his eyes to it. All spiritual paths attempt first to show the Reality behind the appearance. When looked at from the Reality itself, there is no appearance either.

To take the disciples to the Truth, phenomenal illustrations are often made use of. For example take the gold and the ornament. The ordinary man, at the first glance, sees only the ornament. But on second thought, he admits that it is made of gold. He still lays greater emphasis on the form rather than on the gold, because he relies on his sensual perceptions. After some more thought, he admits that between the form and the gold of the ornament, the form frequently changes, while the gold remains constant. Since gold is the essential constituent of all gold ornaments and since the form is only a temporary appearance leaving nothing behind, he is forced to admit that the gold alone is permanent and that the form is merely an illusion. Thus, having been shown gold in its pure formless nature, he is asked to look at the ornaments from the standpoint of gold. Then he sees nothing but gold in the ornaments (just as a banker would). Even in the appearance it is the gold that appears and not the ornament. An 'ornament' is an 'ornament' only by convention, but actually it is only gold.

Now applying the illustration to the Self and the world, having separated the world including your own body, senses and mind from the Self, you are shown the Self in its pure nature. Taking your stand in that pure Self, if you look at the world, you see the whole world as nothing but your own real Self. This is how you are helped to experience the Truth of the aphorism: 'All is brahman'. The object of Vēdānta is not to help you not to perceive the appearance; but to help you to see the essence, even when perceiving the appearance through the senses.

> There is no superimposition
> at any time.
>
> Even the thought that there is superimposition,
> is a superimposition.
>
> There is no serpent in the rope
> at any time.
>
> There is no world in the Reality
> at any time.
>
> The Earth is not pot.
> But the pot is Earth.
>
> Consciousness is not the object.
> But the object is Consciousness.
>
> The wave and the ocean are both objects as such.
> But in essence both are water, one and the same.

If you try to take away your mind from the ornament (as yōgins do), the ornament disappears not by itself alone, but along with the gold; and you are left helpless, in the dark. But if you succeed in seeing the gold in the ornament and understand that the gold is the only part which is permanent, then in every subsequent perception of the ornament, you will emphasize only the gold in it.

Similarly, when you see you are not the body, senses or mind – which are but ornaments of the real 'I' – you have only to emphasize the 'I' in each. It is only a shifting of your interest, from the appearance to the essence, that is needed. Then, everything appears as gold or the real 'I'.

Pure gold comprehends all ornaments. It is formless, imperceptible and is by itself no ornament. The ornament is gold in some form, and is perceptible. When you put an ornament in a crucible and apply heat to it, it melts. Then the ornament part disappears and the gold alone remains over. Of course, this gold also appears in the form of the crucible. You cannot help this as long as you look through your eyes. Pure gold is formless and imperceptible. Having transcended objectivity, it is the Reality itself.

But there is, in daily practice, a temporary and artificial reality posited between the ornament and the gold. This is what we call the bullion. It is supposed to be more permanent than the ornaments and is therefore used as a standard to measure all ornaments. The bullion has also a form and is an ornament when coined. This fact is conveniently ignored when you consider the bullion as standard gold.

Similarly, the state of samādhi, considered by the yōgins as the Ultimate, is only a state, limited by time. The absolute Reality is beyond all samādhi.

10th October 1955

1115. THE INCOMPETENCE OF SAMĀDHI TO ENLIGHTEN ONE.

Yōga or mental effort is the cause, and samādhi is the natural effect. But the Absolute is uncaused. Therefore, samādhi can never be the Absolute, but only a state; and as such it can never enlighten you.

1116. A MUKTA AND AN ĀCĀRYA

Liberation consists in realizing one's own real nature, and it makes one a *mukta*. But an *Ācārya* is one who has realized the Truth, is established in it, and who is living the Truth himself in all his apparent life.

1117. THE BEST MEANS TO REALIZATION

1. Allow Consciousness to come in at every stage of your perceptions. Recognize Consciousness in all your perceptions, and see that it is the only real part of the perceptions. Gradually, you realize that the whole world – including your own body, senses and mind – is nothing but Consciousness, and you are free.
2. Examine your statements regarding your own experience. A changeless 'I' is found underlying every such statement. It is the ultimate Reality itself.

13th October 1955

1118. INDEPENDENCE

Man is born and brought up in a state and spirit of dependence. He has to depend upon his mother in his babyhood and childhood; upon his parents, teachers and friends in his boyhood; upon his wife, family and society when he becomes a householder; upon the whole world when he becomes a man; and upon God and nature all along – until he is temporarily relieved by death, or liberated for all time by knowledge.

But the spirit of independence, which is an urge from his real nature, sprouts up and rebels against this dependence at every stage of his life. All forces of nature, including his parents, try to restrain this spirit of independence in some form or other. Parents, teachers and society do this in the name of culture and education. What they mean by culture and education is only directing the mind of the boy from one set of objects, which they consider injurious, to another set of objects, which they consider beneficial, to the good of the boy in the phenomenal world. But all the while, the boy is pinned to the body, senses and mind.

This sort of curbing of the independence of the child cannot be justified, unless there is a better substitute to be given in its place. The boy's spirit of independence will never be satisfied until his attention is somehow directed to the permanent life principle in him, which is the seat of independence, from where his own urge of independence has sprouted.

Body, mind and senses are by their very nature dependent. Therefore, whenever you attempt to restrain your child from any of his physical or mental tendencies, you would do well not to do it by force, in the name of empty slogans like virtue and progress, but to try to impress upon his tender mind the existence of a permanent and luminous principle within him, which is the life principle. Slowly, he can be made to become aware of the real glory of his life principle, and he will learn to be attached more and more deeply to that principle.

This life principle is the first emanation of the ultimate Truth and, as such, there can be nothing more sublime and ennobling than this. Therefore the attachment of the boy to his life principle will transform his tendencies into sublimity and nobility much more quickly and with greater stability than any object lesson ever will.

Having obtained such a glorious start from very boyhood, when he grows up with these samskāras, he will undoubtedly come across a Kāraṇa-guru, receive instruction from him and be liberated. This is the law of nature and has no exception. Then he will find that in that state, the urge for independence has been fulfilled. Because, in liberation, he is alone and there is no place for dependence.

The parents are responsible for having given the boy a body, which by itself is the source of his bondage and misery. This is no doubt a sin in the phenomenal sense. The parents, if they are conscientious, must certainly atone for it, at least by bringing up the child in such a manner as to make him conscious of his bondage, and to instil in him that deep desire for liberation. There is no easier method of fulfilling this goal than the one just chalked out.

1119. VĒDĀNTA

Vēdānta is the unfoldment of one's own real nature (the Truth), from the lowest level to the highest.

Reality is positive in form, but negative in meaning. When I say, 'It is existence', I mean only that it is not non-existence.

1120. HIGHER REASON

Higher reason is that supra-intellectual organon present in all human beings, which begins to function only when the aspirant tries to understand something beyond the body, senses and mind. It may also be called functioning Consciousness. When the function ceases, it is pure Consciousness itself.

25th October 1955

1121. WORSHIP AND ITS SIGNIFICANCE

Worship is a method adopted all over the world, to show one's respect and reverence to another, and to rise thereby to the level of the worshipped. Phenomenal perfection is attained through devotion to a personal God; and spiritual perfection through devotion to the ‘impersonal’, represented by the ‘Kāraṇa-guru’. The method of worship usually adopted is generally the same, and the only difference is with regard to the goal.

The fundamental characteristic of worship and devotion is the resort to any process of incessant thinking about the object of worship. But this becomes sometimes monotonous and mechanical. To avoid this, and to give variety and ease to the exercise, certain deviations are adopted. It is but natural that one is inclined to love and revere everything related to the object of adoration. The sacred material relics, preserved and worshipped in all religions, such as the Bōdhi Tree, the chip of the Cross etc., are examples. These relics are revered not for their intrinsic worth, but only for the solemn fact of their having once been intimately connected with the goal of our devotion. Thus, in each case, these relics are mere pointers to the goal of our devotion.

This is all the more true when the aspirant is on the path to the ultimate Truth, and he has to be doubly guarded against probable pitfalls.

The devotee of the Guru should never forget that objects or persons of whatever relationship to the Guru should be utilized only to draw his attention to the Guru. Otherwise, they should be dismissed summarily.